An Interested Life

*For Louise, whose love, patience, and
support have made it all possible.*

An Interested LIFE

Earl C. Dudley, Jr.

CARLYLE CLASSICS
Charlottesville, Virginia

Library of Congress Control Number: 2009908872
ISBN 978-0-615-32604-7

Printed by Thomson Shore, Inc., Dexter, Michigan.

* CONTENTS *

I decided to write this book for two reasons. First, sometimes through no initiative of my own, I have lived through a lot of events that are in themselves of more than passing interest. On two identifiable occasions in my early childhood my life was saved by the heroic deeds of women and men in the American armed services in World War II. Many years later I was privileged to work with several giants of the American legal and political scene in the second half of the 20th century and to take part in exciting events that shaped some aspects of our political and legal culture. I have been involved as a lawyer in countless legal disputes, some of great interest and significance. I do not claim to bring a unique, or an even arguably objective, perspective to the events I have lived through. This book is not intended as a contribution to public discourse on any of the events it describes. But I concluded that a worm's-eye view of some of these events was worth writing down. I hope that some others may find *my* worm's-eye view worth reading.

Second, I have separately undertaken the project of researching and writing about the history of my family. I dearly wish that some of my ancestors had taken the time to write down their own stories. I would give a great deal to know more about what they did and what it was like to live in their times. At the risk of adding too much detail in places, I have sought to impart something of the flavor of the era in which I have lived.

So this book is mostly for my family and especially for my descendants. In particular it is aimed at someone like me in the family a hundred years from now, trying to reconstruct a little of what went on in my generation and those immediately adjacent to it. If my children and grandchildren enjoy this book, and if I have a satisfied reader or two a few generations from now, it will have been worth the effort.

Not surprisingly, however, the effort has in large measure turned out to be its own reward. Writing this book has afforded me the opportunity to review and reflect upon the first sixty-seven years of my life. I am certainly not happy with everything I have done. But I feel that, having taken a long look at my life up to this point, I understand myself and what has made me tick a lot better than I ever did before. More importantly, the project has brought home to me the debts of gratitude I owe to so many people who have supported, encouraged, inspired, and sustained me along the way. I cannot measure the good fortune that has brought me this far.

I have not been alone in the effort to produce this book. Countless conversations, especially with my wife, Louise Merrill Dudley, and my sister, Elizabeth Dudley Wilbur, have shaped many of the stories told here. Louise, who is a world-class editor, has read the manuscript more times than she would like to count. Liz, my son Will Dudley, my daughter Susan Dudley Klaff, and my colleague and friend George Rutherglen have each read large portions of the manuscript. All have made very helpful suggestions. Mary Murray has brought the project to fruition with her outstanding design and production. Of course, all errors and flaws are my own.

One note of warning to some readers. Having spent my career in the law, I have described some cases in which I was involved as a law clerk and as a lawyer. I may have done so in too much detail for the taste of non-lawyers, though I have tried in telling the stories of these cases to make them interesting for a general audience. I assure all readers that I have been selective and have included only those cases that I thought significant or of general interest. They were an important part of my life.

CHAPTER ONE

1941

I was born in January 1941 in Manila, in the Philippine Islands. 1941 was not a good year to be born in many places, but it was an especially difficult year to be born in the Philippines. World War II was raging around much of the globe. German armies had overrun most of eastern and western Europe and a good deal of North Africa, the Luftwaffe was battering Britain, and early in the year Hitler's generals were drawing up plans to invade the Soviet Union. Closer to what was home to my parents and me, Japan had invaded Manchuria, China, Indochina, and Burma in the pursuit of what its leaders euphemistically called the Greater East Asia Co-Prosperity Sphere.

By the late fall Japan was hungrily eyeing, not only British possessions in Hong Kong, Singapore, and Malaya, but the United States' principal colonial base in Asia, the Philippine Islands. Everyone, save apparently the top leadership of the War Department in Washington, seems to have known that a Japanese invasion was imminent. Certainly many people in the Philippines understood this. My father was at the time a mid-level civilian employee in the U.S. Navy's Bureau of Supplies and Accounts (known by the odd acronym BUSANDA), and thus he was not, I am sure, privy to the highest levels of intelligence. Yet by the weekend of December 6-7 he had become thoroughly convinced that the Japanese were planning an immediate aerial attack on the American naval base where he worked at Cavite, around the bay from Manila, and on the town of Cavite itself, where we lived. Thus he sent my mother and me away to what he thought was safety, to the small spa town of Baguio, in the mountains north of Manila. The cooler mountain air in Baguio attracted the Filipino elite, and it was known as the "summer capital."

There was a small U.S. Army post at Baguio, Camp John Hay, but it was largely an R & R center, and thus was not seen as a likely target for the Japanese. My father arranged for us to stay in guest quarters at the camp. Natalie Crouter, in her powerful record *Forbidden Diary*, which details the wartime experience in a Japanese internment camp in Baguio, noted our arrival:

December 7, 1941. We stopped at the caddy house at Camp John

Guest quarters at Camp John Hay in Baguio before the war. My mother and I stayed in one of these the night of December 7, 1941.

Hay for a peaceful Coca-Cola. Mrs. Dudley had come up from Cavite with another civilian wife and child, thinking Baguio was safe in case of attack.[1]

What my father did not know—but Japanese military intelligence did—was that there was a meeting scheduled at Camp John Hay at 8 a.m. on December 8 between Douglas MacArthur, the American commander in the Far East, and Manuel Quezon, president of the Commonwealth of the Philippines, the pre-independence American colonial government. The Japanese attacked the American naval base at Pearl Harbor in Hawaii first, at 2 a.m. Monday, December 8, Philippine time (because of the International Dateline, the attack took place at 8 a.m., December 7, Hawaii time). Six hours later they loosed their planes on Camp John Hay from their base in Formosa (now Taiwan) in an effort to catch MacArthur and Quezon unaware and kill the two most important men in the Philippines at the very outset of the war. But having heard about the attack on Pearl Harbor, the two men had cancelled their Monday morning meeting and were nowhere near Baguio when the attack came.[2] The Japanese found instead my mother and me.

My mother had risen early, as the mothers of eleven-month-olds are wont to do. She dressed and fed me and had breakfast in the officers' mess at the camp, where she learned of the overnight attack on Pearl Harbor. Still not fearing a Japanese assault on the obscure outpost of Camp John Hay, she put me in my stroller and went out for a walk a little before 8. She heard the planes before she saw them. She snatched me from my stroller and tried to run for cover, any cover. She did not make it. A bomb exploded to her right, and shrapnel ripped through her body below the waist. Her right leg was hopelessly mangled and had to be amputated, and she sustained additional shrapnel wounds in her left leg and other places, including metal splinters in her eyes. She must have been carrying me in her left arm, or else holding me high enough in her right that I escaped most of the shrapnel. I sustained a single wound in my left knee. The shrapnel blew out my knee-cap and destroyed a portion of the epiphiseal, the soft segment of the bone where growth takes place, at the end of my femur.

Natalie Crouter's diary provides an eyewitness account of the bombing:

December 8, 1941. After the children left for school, we turned on the radio about 8:15—and heard of the attack on Pearl Harbor. While listening, we heard planes and went out as usual to see them. Almost over the house, quite high, came seventeen big bombers in formation. We could see them plainly and thought they were American. I remarked, "Well, we probably won't be standing here looking up at planes like this much longer." As they passed almost opposite the house, we heard a long ripping sound like the tearing of a giant sheet and saw an enormous burst of smoke and earth near officers' quarters at Camp John Hay—the first bombing of the Philippines before our eyes. Huge billows of smoke and dust covered the Post as we looked. No one said a word. We turned to each other, speechless. At last Jerry said, hoarsely, "My God, those are Japanese planes." The smoke rolled up and the smell of powder reached us. We could hear screaming and men yelling orders. Suddenly we all ran into the house. The planes passed out of sight over the mines and mountain ridge.[3]

My mother and I were, I was told, the first two American casualties in the Far East in World War II.

In many ways, however, we were extremely fortunate. First, we received immediate and heroic medical care at the base hospital at Camp John Hay. My mother was in terrible shape and required an emergency amputation.

Though much less seriously injured from a long-range standpoint, I was apparently nearer death. Elizabeth Norman told the story of the saving of my life in her book *We Band of Angels*, which describes the courage and resourcefulness of the American military nurses in the Philippines through-out the war:

> ... Ruby Bradley, a thirty-four-year-old career army nurse on duty at Camp John Hay Hospital, was busy sterilizing the instruments she would need for her first case, a routine hysterectomy.
>
> All at once a soldier appeared at the door and summoned her to headquarters. No surgery that morning, she was told; the Japs had attacked Pearl Harbor, the high command was convinced the Philippine Islands would be next, and Baguio, the most important military and commercial center in northern Luzon, might be one of the enemy's first targets.
>
> Bradley stood there stunned, almost unable to move. What did it mean? Surely the Japanese would not waste their ordnance on such an up-country post. She reported to the surgeon's office for further instructions.
>
> Then the bombs began to fall.
>
> The first hit so close the explosion left their ears ringing. Nurse and doctor ran to the window. Airplanes with big red circles on their wings and fuselage were coming in low, so low Bradley was sure she could see the pilots staring down at her. By instinct, she glanced at her watch—it was 8:19 a.m., December 8, 1941. Scuttlebutt was now substance; war had come to the Philippines.
>
> A few minutes later the first casualties started to crowd the wards and hallways at John Hay Hospital. A civilian dependent named Susan [*sic*; her given name was Susie] Dudley and her year-old son had been out walking and were severely wounded in the attack. A Filipino passerby snatched up the wounded boy and rushed him into the receiving room. Bradley could see that the child was in bad shape; his face was blue—clearly something was wrong with his heart—and his kneecap seemed to be shattered. Bradley felt herself starting to flinch. She was a sturdy and experienced clinician, but even years of practice had not prepared her for something like this. Her heart raced, her stomach started to tighten.
>
> The doctor on duty tried giving the boy oxygen, then he and Bradley took turns at mouth-to-mouth resuscitation, but nothing

worked, and it was clear that the child was slipping away.

Leave him, the doctor ordered. The wounded were beginning to mount, he said, and they had no time to linger over a dying child.

Bradley balked. "How about a stimulant in the heart?" she said, imploring him.

The doctor thought for a moment; it was probably hopeless, he said, but if Bradley wanted to try it, she should do it herself.

The needle was six inches long; if she plunged it into the wrong place in the baby's heart she would instantly kill him. Meanwhile the boy was turning a deeper shade of blue, and the nurse, watching him wane, was growing angry and afraid. Then, looking around the room, she hit on an idea. In the medicine cabinet she spotted a bottle of whiskey and, remembering that liquor was sometimes effective as a heart stimulant, she took a piece of gauze, laced it with some sugar, soaked it in whiskey, and stuck it in the boy's mouth. At first the baby did nothing. Then, slowly, he started to suck, harder, and harder, until, at last, blue gave way to white, white to pink, pink to crying.

"Where's my baby? Where's my baby?" his mother yelled from her bloody gurney. Bomb fragments had shattered the woman's legs, and she faced certain amputation.

"You hear him in there yelling?" said the nurse, bending over her. "Well, he's ... he's all right now."[4]

At least equally important, my father, having heard of the attack on Baguio, left Cavite and drove up into the mountains that night to find what had happened to us. He may have been in the gravest danger of the entire war driving on the unmarked, single-lane Filipino mountain roads, with no guard rails and no headlights because of the blackout. Nonetheless, he made it and found us in the hospital. While he was with us in Baguio, the Japanese attacked the principal anticipated target, the base at Cavite. There was a direct hit on my father's office, and had he been at his desk, he certainly would have been killed.

My father returned to his duty station at Cavite on December 20, after having determined that my mother and I were safe and in good hands. Thus he was taken prisoner in January 1942, when Manila fell to the Japanese. He was sent to the campus of the University of Santo Tomás in Manila, the oldest university in East Asia, a Dominican establishment dating from 1611, which had been offered to the Japanese by the Dominican friars as an internment camp.

My mother and I remained in Baguio until June of 1942, at first under the care of the doctors and nurses at Camp John Hay Hospital. The war had just begun, and medical supplies were relatively plentiful. We received the best care possible.

Mother used to tell a story from our period of recovery at the hospital. I was well enough to be crawling around again, and appar-

Ruby Bradley, left, with my mother and Philippine Ambassador Carlos Romulo, on the occasion of an award to Col. Bradley.

ently one day I began stroking the stockinged legs of one of the nurses—I think it was Ruby Bradley—who, without batting an eyelash, said, "Butch [my childhood nickname], I have slapped many a man's face for less than that." Ruby Bradley went on through internment by the Japanese and later more heroic service in Korea to retire as one of the first female full colonels in the U.S. Army and the most decorated woman in the history of the army.[5]

My mother never told me the story of Ruby Bradley's heroic saving of my life. Mother was an inveterate story-teller, and she certainly did not spare me many other frightening details of the war, so I can only surmise that Nurse Bradley spared her the story in an effort not to add to her already difficult load of anxiety. On the other hand, I do know that my mother worshiped the ground Ruby Bradley walked on and that in later years she used whiskey and sugar as a cure for various childhood ailments, so perhaps she did know after all. In any event, it was to say the least a startling experience to read the story for the first time in Beth Norman's book when I was more than sixty years old.

On January 29, 1942, my mother and I were taken prisoner and interned at Camp Holmes in Baguio. My parents were at least in some degree of communication during this period. On March 8, 1942, my father wrote a short note to my mother, saying "I think of you and Butch continually, trusting that you are all right." He said that he had asked to be transferred from Santo Tomás to Baguio, without success, and added "Do not worry about me and

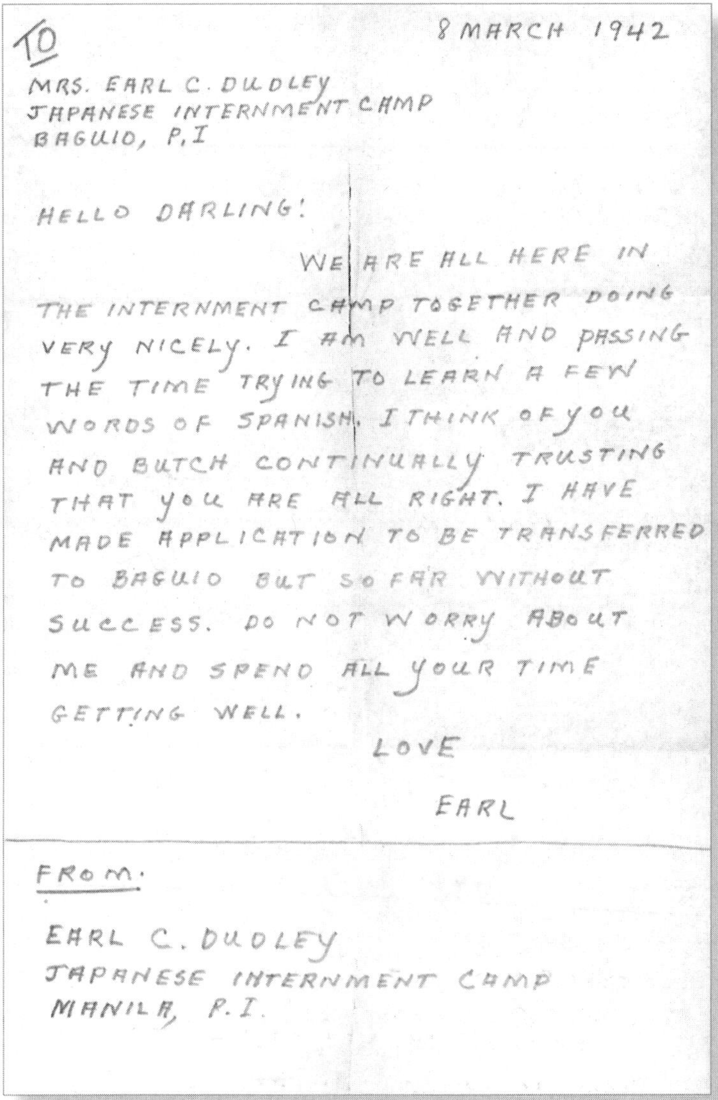

```
                                              8 MARCH 1942
TO

MRS. EARL C. DUDLEY
JAPANESE INTERNMENT CAMP
BAGUIO, P.I


HELLO DARLING!

              WE ARE ALL HERE IN
THE INTERNMENT CAMP TOGETHER DOING
VERY NICELY. I AM WELL AND PASSING
THE TIME TRYING TO LEARN A FEW
WORDS OF SPANISH. I THINK OF YOU
AND BUTCH CONTINUALLY TRUSTING
THAT YOU ARE ALL RIGHT. I HAVE
MADE APPLICATION TO BE TRANSFERRED
TO BAGUIO BUT SO FAR WITHOUT
SUCCESS. DO NOT WORRY ABOUT
ME AND SPEND ALL YOUR TIME
GETTING WELL.
                          LOVE

                            EARL


FROM:

EARL C. DUDLEY
JAPANESE INTERNMENT CAMP
MANILA, P.I.
```

Note from my father to my mother dated March 8, 1942, when he was interned in Manila and she and I were interned in Baguio.

spend all your time getting well." On May 30, 1942, my father petitioned the commandant of Santo Tomás again to be transferred to the internment camp at Baguio so that he could be with us and help my mother care for me. His petition described my mother's injuries as "the loss of her right leg, badly cut left leg, and permanent injuries to the right eye." He said that my mother "obviously needs me to help look after her and the baby, due to her physical incapacity and generally poor health because of nervous shock." He attached to the petition a "note" he had received from my mother on May 24, which, he said, "will give you some idea of the difficulties under which Mrs. Dudley is living with a baby to take care of." I do not have a copy of the note, or of any direct response to the petition from the commandant, but in June 1942, possibly as a result of the petition, my mother and I were transferred to Santo Tomás. I did not recognize my father.

❖   ❖   ❖

In the years leading up to the war, Manila, known as the Pearl of the Orient, and its environs offered a charming, even opulent, lifestyle, at least if you were American or had some money in your pockets, two conditions that generally went together. And one did not need a lot of money. I do not know what my father was paid by BUSANDA in the 1930s, but I do know that in 1947, after we had been liberated and repatriated, and after he had climbed several rungs up the ladder of government service, he was earning $5,200 a year. I would be very surprised if before the war he was earning more than $3,500 to $4,000 annually, though that was probably supplemented by some form of overseas living allowance. In any event, my parents did not have a lot of money by stateside standards, even at a time when the economy was still climbing only slowly out of the depths of the Great Depression. But in the Philippines it was enough to live in very grand style indeed.

My parents had a very large house in Cavite and could afford three full-time Filipino servants. One of them, Josefina Bautista, known as Pening, served as my amah after I came along. My mother used to tell of their houseboy, who would polish the hardwood floors every week by "skating" on freshly cut coconut halves until the wood had been burnished to a high shine by the coconut oil.

My mother talked often of the beauty of the Manila Bay region, especially the soft and spectacular tropical sunsets. Manila also sported a lively night life. Mother often reminisced happily about evenings out on the town with friends in Manila and told of my father singing "The Road to Mandalay" at the top of his lungs on the twenty-mile drive back to Cavite.

While my father never talked much about the pre-war years, it was clear that they were among the happiest times of my mother's life. They had lived through the last, shimmering sunset of colonialism. It was shattered forever by the bombs that exploded at Camp John Hay.

Notes

[1] Natalie Crouter, *Forbidden Diary* 2 (1980).

[2] I learned this many years later from a former captain in U.S. Army Intelligence, who was stationed at Camp John Hay and who told me he was the first person to reach my mother and me after we were injured. I had always wondered why the Japanese chose to strike first at a target of no intrinsic military importance.

[3] Crouter 2-3.

[4] Elizabeth M. Norman, *We Band of Angels: The Untold Story of American Nurses Trapped on Bataan by the Japanese* 7-8 (1999).

[5] Norman 250–53.

CHAPTER TWO

Guests of the Japanese

1942-1945

I have little memory of the three years my parents and I spent in two Japanese internment camps. I had just turned four when we were liberated. But the wartime experience was plainly the pivotal, the most important, chapter in their lives. I grew up listening to them talk about it. I had the opportunity to see and talk to many of their internee friends in the postwar years, and I have read something about the history of the internment and the conditions in the camps. In 2005 I returned to the Philippines with a group of ex-internees to visit the scenes of my childhood, to celebrate the 60th anniversary of the liberation of the Islands, and to listen to the stories of those who remembered. What follows is what I have been able to piece together from these sources.

❖   ❖   ❖

My parents and I were technically not prisoners of war. Under international law, we were non-combatant citizens of an enemy nation captured in an occupied country in time of war. The Japanese were legally obligated to make efforts to repatriate us, and indeed a few internees held in Santo Tomás were repatriated during the war, most of them aboard the Swedish ship the *Gripsholm* that sailed in the summer of 1942 with several hundred former Japanese prisoners. But the Japanese refused to negotiate for the large-scale repatriation of American citizens as long as the United States continued to assert the right to govern the Philippines. Thus we were stuck for the duration.

The Santo Tomás campus, where my mother and I joined my father in June 1942, has been described as well-kept and beautiful before the war. But it was entirely unsuited to housing several thousand prisoners. To begin with, it had no dormitories, as it was solely a day school, with no boarders. The buildings were old, and they were no more designed to provide around-the-clock sanitary, bathing, dining, or medical facilities for large numbers of people than they were for sleeping. Into this relatively small day-school

The Main Building at Santo Tomás University in Manila.

campus were crammed almost 4,000 prisoners, roughly three-quarters of them Americans, of all ages and widely varying states of health.[1] Nor were the Japanese geared up to feed, clothe, and care for a civilian crowd of this size. Moreover, it was the tropics, and all kinds of undesirable plants, insects (some of them huge), other animals, fungi, and bacteria flourished out of control, nourished beyond even their ordinary luxuriant levels of growth and proliferation by the seriously unsanitary conditions that soon came to prevail.[2]

Things were extremely crowded and primitive, but at the beginning, at least, the Japanese officials seem to have tried to alleviate these conditions to some degree. In the early months passes were given to internees to leave the camp for medical treatment that was beyond the capacity of the few doctors who had been interned. As I learned only upon my return in 2005, my parents and I lived for a time outside the camp while my mother received hospital care—eye surgery, I believe.

People with friends on the outside could receive food and clothes from them, and those with money could purchase food and other items from those merchants who still had things to sell. Some merchants and bankers on the outside ran real risks to lend money to prisoners to purchase necessities, which was against the Japanese rules, and sympathetic Filipinos and others donated what little they themselves could spare. The Red Cross provided what it could and underwrote loans and the purchase of supplies. Accounts of life in Santo Tomás make it clear that money was important, at least at the beginning. People with money could purchase items for their own use, or often for resale to other internees in what developed as something of a black market. In addition, money allowed some internees to erect small shanties outside the buildings of the campus, where they could pass the days in some greater comfort. These shanties were small and incommodious affairs, which had to be open on two sides, so the Japanese guards could see that no sex was going on. (The Japanese had no desire to increase the

A mock-up of a shanty like those some of the prisoners built in Santo Tomás Internment Camp.

number of mouths to feed in the camp.) But they offered some escape from the crowded conditions and the heat, and they cost money to put up.

My parents never talked about money as an issue in the camp, but I strongly suspect they had little or none. We never had a shanty. And I found in my mother's papers a letter written to her after the war by a woman from San Francisco seeking repayment of a loan she and her husband had made to my parents in the camp. It was a kind letter, and the woman said that she and her husband had never intended to collect on the loan, but that they had now fallen on hard times and needed the money.

There was relatively little overt brutality from our captors, at least in comparison to the way military prisoners were treated by the Japanese, but that is not to say there was none. The Japanese army, like all armies, had its share of sadists, and the possession of absolute power over the helpless often brings out the worst in people. I heard my parents and others talk, and I have read, of unnecessary beatings, of constant demands for servility—one had to bow to each Japanese soldier, and the bow had to be satisfactorily low—enforced by slaps to the face, and of mindless rigidity in the face of real human privation. One of my earliest memories is of going with my father to take a shower and hearing a gunshot. We later learned that an American prisoner had been shot and killed for crossing a forbidden barricade in an effort to get the Japanese officials to afford his very ill wife some medical attention.

As the war went on, food, clothing, and other goods became much scarcer. Local merchants had little to sell, and the internees had no money left in any event. The only things to be had were what the Japanese were willing, or able, to supply and occasional packages from the Red Cross. Our welfare was not a high priority budget item for the Japanese government, and not surprisingly, as the tide of war in the Pacific turned in the Allies' favor, the Japanese had less and less to give us in the way of food and other necessities. The principal food I can remember from my early childhood is rice, which was often served up in a semi-inedible mush called lugau, whose actual rice content lessened severely as the war dragged on. We also on rare occasions had bananas, coconuts, mangoes, and papayas. The food we were given was often infested with bugs and worms, but after a while the internees adopted the philosophical view that at least they provided a source of otherwise scarce protein. The internees, my parents included, became gaunt and emaciated. My father, who stood six feet tall and normally weighed roughly 180 pounds, weighed around 125 when we were liberated. My mother, like many others, was ill much of the time. The malnutrition made the internees vulnerable to diseases, including such tropical maladies as malaria, dengue fever, and beri-beri.

Morale was obviously a problem among the internees. No one knew how long they would have to endure imprisonment at the hands of the enemy. Despite lofty promises from Washington of swift retaliation for the sneak attack on Pearl Harbor and the Philippines, America at first lacked the resources to fight a two-front war, and industrial production was not on a wartime footing. There was little or no news from the outside world. What information we did receive was heavily censored by the Japanese, except for occasional broadcasts picked up by a jerry-rigged (and carefully hidden) radio set put together by a few of the internees. Even this information was not widely shared for obvious security reasons.[3] Many internees had loved ones, in and out of the military, scattered throughout East Asia, about whose welfare they were desperately worried.

There was a camp "governmental" structure, with committees staffed by internees to help maintain order, resolve disputes, and see to it that the work of daily life in the camp—cooking, washing dishes, cleaning up, waste disposal—was done. There were even schools for the children, organized and staffed by internees. But all reported to the Japanese, who controlled everything.

The internees mostly made the best of things, and they retained a robust sense of humor. Indeed, my mother often said that the Japanese could not understand the crazy Americans who kept on laughing under the conditions of internment. She added that what they really didn't understand was that this was the way the prisoners kept their sanity.[4]

The pre-war occupations of the internees ranged from priest to prostitute, with many businessmen, government employees, and housewives inbetween. Crammed together in extremely close quarters under conditions of major privation, reminded constantly of their status as prisoners, bereft of any hope of immediate release, they reacted in widely varying ways. Some were saints, sacrificing their own welfare and constantly tending to the needs of others. Others were whiners, shirkers, even thieves. Most were somewhere inbetween. There was a significant amount of distrust among the internees, and some were accused of being spies or of feathering their own nests by cozying up to the Japanese. It was, I think, a major revelation to my parents that neither social class, ethnicity, education, occupation, or any of the other things they had been brought up to respect seemed to predict with any accuracy how people behaved under the stress of internment. I know that they both came through the experience convinced that the hooker with the heart of gold was for real, and they were often disillusioned by the behavior of those they thought of as "betters."

What was life in the internment camp like for a small child? Perhaps curiously, I have no sense of having had a deprived or unhappy childhood. True, I lacked what we often think of as the accoutrements of childhood happiness—toys, books, nice clothes, furniture, good food—but then, I didn't know that I didn't have them. And I did have the full attention of my mother, when she was well enough to care for me, and of my father, when he was not performing the work details demanded of all able-bodied men in the camp. I felt loved and cared for, and that was what mattered.

When my mother was seriously ill, I was cared for by a wonderful woman, then in her mid-twenties, named Bessie Brazee. "Auntie Bessie" was part of a large Spanish-American family with roots in the Philippines and in California. Her mother, Consuelo, known universally as Grandma Brazee, had been born in the Islands and had met and married an American naval officer who came to Manila during the Spanish-American War. (Many years later, when she was in her 90s, I spent a wonderful evening with Grandma Brazee, Bessie, and Bessie's sister Florence at their home in Montebello, California, during which Grandma proudly showed me photographs of her husband in his naval uniform and of their wedding in Manila.) She moved with him to California, but they had maintained a close connection with her relatives in the Philippines. Grandma, Bessie, and several other members of their family were in Manila when the war broke out and were interned in Santo Tomás. Bessie was a huge, and wonderful, part of my childhood.

The sign my parents placed on my high chair in Santo Tomás to keep me from chattering with all passersby.

My parents sacrificed their own health and welfare to make sure that I had enough to eat. And my father played poker—successfully, for the most part—for food rations, adding a little extra to the family pot. Pictures of the three of us taken shortly after we were liberated show two extremely thin and very unhealthy-looking adults and one entirely normal-looking four-year-old (see page 24). My life-long robust health is in my view a testament both to my parents' sacrifices and to the degree to which some aspects of standard childhood nutrition theory—for example, the vital need for milk to promote the growth of bones—are simply overrated.

I had begun walking before the bombing at Baguio, and I had to learn to walk all over again after I was injured. By the time I was an adult, the partial destruction of the epiphiseal on the end of my left femur had created a six-inch difference in the length of my legs. But while we were interned, the difference was minimal, though gradually increasing, and my weight was low enough that I had no real trouble walking, albeit with a noticeable limp.

Apparently I was quite talkative and something of a camp pet. My mother put a sign on my high chair to keep people from talking to me while I was eating, but she claimed I played favorites. If someone came along that I wanted to talk to, I would chatter away, but if I was approached by someone I did not wish to engage in conversation, I would simply point to the sign. There is a picture of me taken in Santo Tomás when I was between two and three years old by an official Japanese photographer. I was dressed in a clean white suit with short pants and was wearing a baseball cap that

The propaganda picture taken of me by an official Japanese photographer in Santo Tomás when I was about two years old.

someone had given me. I looked quite healthy and happy, and I am sure the picture was taken for propaganda purposes.

The only sign of which I am aware that at some level I was afraid and knew that things were not right was a recurring nightmare that I had. The nightmare was particularly frightening because in the dream I was in my bed, from which I could look out into the hallway of the building where my mother and I were staying. I saw a Japanese soldier coming up the stairs of the building on a blue horse to get me. I had this dream often, and I would wake up screaming. It was hard to calm me down because, since I was in my bed in the dream, I couldn't tell the difference between sleeping and waking.

❖　　❖　　❖

One of the worst features of life in Santo Tomás for my parents was the segregation of men and women into different buildings. The separation at night increased for my parents the sense of isolation and privation. In 1943 the Japanese, using internee labor, converted a former agricultural research station some thirty miles south of Manila at a place called Los Baños into another internment camp. In 1944 they offered to allow internees at Santo Tomás to move to Los Baños. The move was especially attractive to married couples, who could live together in small cubicles. My parents decided to make the move and left Santo Tomás on April 7, 1944. It was almost a fatal decision.

Interestingly, my mother apparently became pregnant after the move. Many years later she told my sister— but never me—that she had asked the American internee doctor at Los Baños to perform an abortion.

Life in Los Baños was at the outset, for a family at least, an improvement over Santo Tomás.[5] The three of

Farewell card drawn for my parents and me by Teedie Cowie when we moved from Santo Tomás to Los Baños on April 7, 1944. Teedie Cowie Woodcock later published a book of her drawings from the camp, Behind the Sawali.

us shared a tiny little cubicle in a hastily constructed wood and bamboo barracks, but at least it afforded a place to be together and some small measure of privacy. And not long after the move, the hopes of the internees for release began to rise dramatically. American military planes began to dot the sky, signaling the air superiority that was so important to the retaking of the Philippines. I have a vague memory of watching my father and one or two other internees dig an air-raid shelter under the orders of the Japanese. The latter apparently showed great consternation whenever the American planes flew overhead. According to my mother, one day I went over to a group of Japanese guards, who were gesticulating and talking excitedly as they looked at the aircraft overhead, and told them not to worry, that they were American planes and they would not hurt us!

Wartime has its quirky moments of tenderness between enemies. On our last Christmas in the camp, one of the Japanese guards, apparently a Christian and perhaps missing his own children, asked my parents' permission to take me down to the guardhouse for a while to play with me. My mother was strongly opposed to his request, but my father intervened and gave his permission. I was gone for a couple of hours, and when the guard brought me back to my parents, my small hands were loaded with as much brown sugar as they could hold, the only gift the guard had to give.

❖   ❖   ❖

The war was a time of great anxiety for people in this country with loved ones trapped abroad in unknown situations. Correspondence with internees was essentially impossible, especially since family members often had no idea if their loved ones were alive or where they were. There was little or no information, and much of what there was was wrong, or at least out of date. And efforts at communication often went undelivered or were received only months, sometimes years, after they were sent.

I have an undated clipping, evidently from a Norfolk, Virginia, newspaper, which contains a pre-war picture of my father. The brief, four-paragraph story states that an amateur short-wave radio operator in California named Dreyfus had reported receiving a broadcast that my father was being held prisoner in Tokyo. The story went on to say that my mother and I were interned at Baguio. On February 19, 1943, Mr. Dreyfus sent a postcard, addressed only to "Dudley Family, Arlington, Virginia," which was delivered, partly I suspect because Arlington was a much smaller place then and partly because my grandmother worked at the Post Office. The post

The front of the envelope that contained the letter my grandmother wrote to my mother in January 1943. Note the two censor stamps and the date of receipt.

card apologized for the sketchiness of the information earlier conveyed, which Dreyfus attributed in part to "bad reception." Probably as a result of Dreyfus' information (which clearly was originally received well before the February 19 post card), my father's mother on January 14, 1943, wrote a letter addressed to my mother at Baguio saying, "Was so glad to hear just a few days ago that you were safe and well." (The letter, by the way, had been opened twice before my mother received it, once by an American censor and again by the Japanese. Their stamps appear where the letter had been resealed on both ends.) The fact that my grandmother addressed the letter to my mother alone and that in it she sent her "love to you and the baby" indicates that she believed my parents were separated and possibly that my father was being held in Tokyo. Of course, he was never held in Tokyo, and by the time my grandmother wrote the letter, we were all together in Santo Tomás. Finally, on the envelope in my mother's handwriting is the notation "Rec'd 6/20/44," almost a year and a half after it was sent, by which time we had moved on to the camp at Los Baños.

Another clipping, also I think from a Norfolk paper sometime in late 1944, reported that a repatriated prisoner from the *Gripsholm* had brought a message from my parents that we were "safe[,] … well and in good spirits," though it offered no details of where we were being held. Yet another undated clipping from a Durham, North Carolina, newspaper reporting on a letter received from an internee at Baguio's Camp Holmes, contains a handwritten note, "Is Susie [my mother] at this camp? This was in the Durham paper."

Finally, on January 29, 1944, the War Department wrote to my mother's father stating that my parents and I "have been officially reported internees of the Japanese Government and now are interned in Santo Tomás Camp, Manila, Philippine Islands." That was the only official word, and it too was soon out of date.

I have some messages from members of my father's family on International Red Cross forms dated at different times in 1944. The messages were evidently delivered, as they were found in my mother's purse that she carried through the internment experience, but I do not know when they were received or whether my parents were able to try to respond.

❖　　❖　　❖

The endgame of war almost proved fatal to the internees of Los Baños in two different ways. The American Sixth Army reached Manila and liberated those who had remained at Santo Tomás on February 3, 1945, though the battle for Manila would rage on for another month.[6] We were thirty miles to the south, with many thousands of Japanese troops between the Americans and us. Japanese supply lines were cut, and there was little or nothing left to feed us. In the three weeks between the freeing of Santo Tomás and our own liberation, many people in Los Baños died of malnutrition or of diseases or complications brought on by the lack of food. In addition, the last weeks in Los Baños were made much more miserable by the increasingly erratic and brutal behavior of the camp commandant, Lieutenant Konishi, on whose orders several prisoners were executed for trivial offenses.[7] Konishi was later himself executed as a war criminal.[8]

The bigger threat, however, was the Japanese policy to leave no prisoners alive when they retreated. This policy was ruthlessly executed in a number of instances in the Philippines,[9] and the Japanese commander in the Islands, General Yamashita, paid for this and other atrocities with his life after he was found guilty of war crimes by an American military court following the Japanese surrender.

As my parents told it, the Japanese had decided to pull out of Los Baños on February 23, and the plan was to kill all the internees by setting the flimsy wooden barracks afire and machine-gunning those who were able to escape the flames.[10] Somehow word of this plan leaked out to the internees. And somehow three American prisoners managed to escape from the camp. They hooked up with a group of Filipino guerrillas in the area. The escapees and guerrillas embarked on a dangerous trek through Japanese-held territory, heading for Manila. They had to travel at night to avoid detection, and they holed up wherever they could during the day. After more than a week of extremely hazardous travel and some harrowing near-misses, the men made it to Manila and told the story of the impending massacre to Sixth Army Intelligence.[11]

General MacArthur personally approved a mission to rescue the prisoners of Los Baños. The job was assigned to the 511th regiment of the 11th Airborne Division. The mission presented a tricky three-part problem. Los Baños was thirty miles away behind enemy lines. This demanded an airborne operation. Next, the Japanese guards at the camp had to be killed or neutralized, but widespread firefighting had to be avoided, for fear of killing the prisoners. This meant that complete surprise was essential. Finally, the prisoners—some 2,100 in number, many in very poor health—had to be evacuated swiftly to safety. The only way to achieve this without fighting through Japanese lines was over a substantial nearby body of water called Laguna de Bay. The mission thus required a coordinated airborne attack and amphibious rescue.

The internees of Los Baños, of course, had no idea whether the three escapees had managed to get word of their plight to the American forces, or whether, if they had, a rescue mission was in the offing. February 22 came and went with no help in sight.

Those internees who had managed to sleep at all on what they thought was their last night on earth woke on the morning of February 23 to the most beautiful sight they had ever seen—waves of American parachutes floating down from the sky at dawn. I can still remember my parents waking me and pointing to them with speechless joy. It is among my earliest memories.

The mission went off without a hitch. The attack achieved complete surprise. Based on intelligence from the escaped internees, the assault commenced precisely at 6 a.m., when the Japanese, without fail, stacked their rifles and performed their calisthenics. Paratroopers hit the ground exactly on schedule, while a small reconnaissance unit that had infiltrated the area overnight, enhanced by local Filipino guerrillas, began firing at the encircled Japanese. Within fifteen minutes virtually all the Japanese guards had been killed, with no loss of American life, soldiers or internees. While the brief firefight went on, the internees huddled in their barracks, using suitcases or anything else they could find for cover. My father almost got himself shot, as he scurried outside to build a fire and make a pot of the "coffee" that the internees brewed from charred rice hulls.

Within a few short hours, the American soldiers had organized us and loaded us aboard the amphibious vehicles that had arrived from across the water. This was not an easy task, as the prisoners, close to starvation and dazed by the events and by their own happiness, wanted to stand around, hug the soldiers, and thank them profusely. They were deaf to the soldiers' warning that a Japanese division was only a few miles away. Ironically, the soldiers finally resorted to what the Japanese had planned to do all along. They lit fire to the barracks as a means of herding the prisoners into the waiting amtracs. Again my father almost missed our amtrac as he tried desperately to salvage what personal belongings he and my mother had left. These few pitiful items were of no intrinsic value or practical use where the prisoners were going, but there are many stories of their stubborn attachment to their things and the risks they ran to collect and keep them. Somehow we all made it to safety.

The liberation of Los Baños was the largest successful hostage rescue operation in military history, and it is still taught as a case study in military colleges all over the world. The 511th were known thereafter as "the angels," and until the 11th Airborne Division was disbanded many years later, they wore angel patches on their shoulders. My mother never again saw a soldier wearing 11th Airborne insignia without going up to him as fast as her crutches would carry her and planting a big kiss on his cheek. February 23 was always a second Thanksgiving Day in our house. As fate would have it, however, the 11th Airborne never really received the public credit it deserved in the States for the rescue, for

My parents and I in February or March 1944, taken shortly after our liberation from Los Baños.

that same day saw an even more spectacular feat of military heroism in Asia—the capture of Mount Suribachi on the island of Iwo Jima, immortalized in Joe Rosenthal's photograph of the raising of the American flag on the summit.

❖   ❖   ❖

There is a dark and damning sequel to the rescue at Los Baños. The commandos of the 511th pulled out of Los Baños and accompanied the prisoners to safety across Laguna de Bay. Alerted by a couple of guards who managed to escape the raid—including the infamous Lieutenant Konishi—nearby Japanese infantry troops arrived in the next days and massacred the entire village of Los Baños, some 1,400 souls, to punish the Filipinos for their courageous assistance to the prisoners and their liberators. Several hundred were mowed down in the sanctuary of the local Catholic church.[12]

❖   ❖   ❖

After the dramatic rescue at Los Baños, my parents and I were sent to an American staging camp just outside Manila called Muntinlupa to fatten up and await transportation to the United States. Conditions in this camp were not wonderful—it was built as a prison—but to my parents and the other ex-internees it seemed like heaven. Real food, medical care, cigarettes (my parents were both heavy smokers), and the sheer joy of release combined to produce a state of euphoria not felt in three long years.

In April 1945 we boarded a merchant marine vessel for the long voyage across the Pacific Ocean to San Francisco. My mother was in sick bay for the entire trip, and my father and Bessie Brazee looked after me. I remember being fascinated with the many flying fish we saw leaping from the ocean. In later years, my parents spoke often of the wonderful, emotional moment on May 6, 1945, when we steamed beneath the Golden Gate Bridge. I, on the other hand, was a bit of a four-year-old skeptic. Reflecting the only things I had known, I told another former internee that San Francisco was "just another camp."

❖   ❖   ❖

Almost sixty years later Bessie Brazee's niece, Connie Ford, told me that a group of ex-internees was planning a trip to Manila to tour the scenes of their wartime experience and celebrate the 60th anniversary of the liberation of Santo Tomás. My wife Louise and I decided to go. I had never been back to the Islands. For many years I had no desire to go. I looked upon what had happened in the Philippines as a dark period in my life and simply wanted to put it all behind me. As I reached middle age my attitude changed, and I was eager to learn more about the wartime experience. But no occasion had ever presented itself, and the prospect of trying to do it on my own seemed quite daunting. The 2005 tour was the perfect chance. We would have tour guides, the logistics of travel in a third-world country would be taken care of, and I could listen to the stories of others who remembered much more than I did. I am so glad we went.

In the airport in San Francisco we were reunited with Connie Ford, whom I had not seen in many years, and we met most of the people who would be with us on the tour. In Manila we stayed in the Manila Hotel, which had been the *grand dame* of Western hotels in Asia before the war, where General MacArthur and his family had lived. The lobby had been meticulously restored to its pre-war glory after the building had been badly damaged in the battle for Manila in 1945.

We toured sites in Manila, including the infamous Fort Santiago, among the oldest Western settlements in Asia, which had been a place of imprisonment, torture, and death under both the Spaniards and the Japanese. The fort was situated on the Pasig River, and a favorite method of execution had been to chain prisoners to the walls in an underground dungeon at low tide and let the rising river drown them. Close to the spot of this dungeon was a simple cross commemorating the 600 bodies found buried in the near vicinity by the liberating American soldiers in 1945. I learned from others on the trip that in the waning days of the war the Japanese beheaded half a dozen Santo Tomás prisoners at Fort Santiago for some trifling alleged offense. The story had a chilling twist. One of those executed was the wrong man. There was a mix-up in the names, and the man whom the Japanese intended to execute held his tongue and knowingly let his innocent namesake go to his death. Within the fort we retraced the steps, now marked in bronze, of José Rizal, the leader of the Filipino rebellion against the Spaniards in 1896, who was marched to his execution from his prison cell in the fort.

Our group was well feted in Manila. We were received at the American Embassy and given a tour of its historic grounds and buildings, including the makeshift courtroom where Japanese war criminals, including General Yamashita, were tried after the war. We were invited to a lunch and reception at Malacañang Palace, the Filipino White House. President Gloria

Macapagal was elsewhere on business, but we were received and made much of by her chief of staff.

Our biggest and most moving reception was at Santo Tomás itself. The university has greatly expanded since the war, though it remains an urban commuter school, and the buildings where we were housed during the war are still in use, including the stately Main Building, which I recognized from the many photographs I had seen of it. Most current students had no idea that their campus had served as a prison during the war, and the university administration decided to seize the opportunity for a little education. The events began with a lunch at which we heard talks by two Filipinos closely associated with the camp and its liberation. Diosdado Guytenko, a distinguished Filipino lawyer with two daughters living in the United States, had been one of the guerillas leading the Sixth Army flying column to the campus in the heart of Manila. When his captain was killed by a Japanese hand grenade lobbed over the camp wall, Guytenko took the lead and was one of the first two men to enter the camp as part of the liberation force. The second talk was by a 90-year-old woman, Dr. Fe del Mundo, who had returned to Manila right before the war from her medical education in the United States. She had run a small facility called Holy Ghost Hospital, where she and others cared for many of the children of Santo Tomás who were sick, injured, or orphaned. She was very frail and in a wheelchair, but she had dressed herself beautifully and was very proud. Both talks were extremely moving.

Our group participated in opening two exhibits, one of photographs at the School of Architecture showing the heavy American influence on Filipino building design. It contained a photograph of some of the pre-war guest quarters at Camp John Hay in Baguio, where my mother and I stayed the night of December 7, 1941 (see page 4). The second exhibit, in the Main Building itself, consisted of memorabilia, photographs, and mock-ups of wartime scenes. The latter included a bamboo shanty of the kind that prisoners who could afford the materials were allowed to build in the courtyard of the Main Building and elsewhere (see page 14). Several of our group took part in a panel discussion in a large auditorium designed to educate current students about the events of the war on the campus. Later there was a dinner outside in the beautiful night air, under the hundreds of lanterns that decorated the campus, followed by speeches by the American Ambassador and a Filipino Senator whose father had been a major figure in the resistance to the Japanese. The evening concluded with a wonderful concert by the music conservatory's orchestra and chorus.

Planting a tree at Los Baños with three other survivors of the camp.

We took a day-trip south to Los Baños, which is now a bustling campus of the University of the Philippines and still home to its agricultural program. The four of us who had been interned at Los Baños planted a tree in honor of the liberation, and we searched for the actual site of the old internment camp. The barracks had been flimsy and had in any event been burned to the ground sixty years before, so there was no trace of the camp site. Much of the area where it may have been is now jungle, and we were never sure of the exact location of the camp. While in Los Baños, we visited the Catholic church where hundreds of Filipinos were massacred by the Japanese in retaliation for aiding with the liberation. It was still a chilling experience.

Later we struck out north and west and paid a visit to Subic Bay, where the American navy maintained a base for many years after the war, and where some in our group lost relatives on a "hell ship," the Orioko Maru. The Japanese transported military prisoners by ship from the Philippines to sites around Asia, where they were put to work at hard labor as slaves. The conditions on the transport ships were unspeakable—hence the name—and even worse, the Japanese, in direct violation of the Geneva Conventions, did not mark the ships as prisoner transport ships. Thus they were often attacked by Allied military aircraft on the mistaken assumption that they were Japanese navy or supply vessels, and many American prisoners were killed. This was the fate of the Orioko Maru, which sank just off the shore at Subic.

From Subic we headed for the Bataan peninsula and retraced some of the route of the infamous Bataan Death March. In early 1942, General MacArthur abandoned Manila, declaring it an "open city," and put all his men—more than 80,000, the large majority of them Filipinos—on Bataan, a sizable peninsula. It was a disastrous decision. The men were confined in a relatively narrow space on rugged terrain, surrounded on three sides by the sea. There was no way to supply or relieve them without naval power—destroyed at Pearl Harbor—or air cover—and MacArthur had inexcusably left virtually his entire fleet of planes on the ground at Clark Field more than ten hours after the Pearl Harbor strike, where they were wiped out by Japanese bombers. After holding out under extraordinarily brutal conditions from January to April 1942—MacArthur having been evacuated to Australia on the orders of President Roosevelt—the beleaguered Americans and Filipinos surrendered. They were then marched more than 100 kilometers over rugged terrain in brutal heat, with no food or water supplied by their captors. Filipinos who offered any form of aid were summarily shot. Many of the men were beaten or bayoneted to death. Others, already weakened by fighting for months on pitiful rations, collapsed in the heat and died. Many died of dysentery contracted from drinking polluted water from ditches along the roadside. The prisoners shared the road with a column of Japanese troops going in the opposite direction by truck. Soldiers in the trucks would hit the men with their rifle butts or cut them with their swords and bayonets for sport. As many as 10,000 men died on this hideous march.

We visited the little town of San Fernando, where the men were packed like sardines into boxcars for the semifinal train stage of their journey. The train cars were so crowded that there was no room for the dead or dying even to fall down. Many of the men were suffering from dysentery and were unable to refrain from defecating where they stood. As the men were unloaded at the end of the ride, in the little town of Capas, many simply fell dead. But the ordeal was not over. The survivors had to march several more kilometers to Camp O'Donnell, the ultimate destination of the march, a Filipino army training site turned into a military prison by the Japanese. Upwards of 55,000 men were held at Camp O'Donnell, and a plaque there marked the site where 27,000 of them were buried in a mass grave. We visited the old train station at Capas, now a memorial museum, and went on

The American military cemetery in Manila, taken in 2005.

to the eerily peaceful memorial at Camp O'Donnell.

Among our number was Bob Wolfersberger, a survivor of the Bataan Death March. He was a small man, 86 years old, and a newlywed. He survived the march and three more years in Japanese slave-labor camps, and proceeded to outlive two wives. His new wife and he had gone to elementary school together, and she had turned down his request to be his girlfriend in the fifth grade. Getting to know Bob was one of the highlights of the trip. He was trim and fit, and he was a wonderful storyteller, though without a trace of bombast or self-importance. His stories were still horrifying after sixty years. He attributed his survival to a middle-school health teacher who had told him that iodine was a powerful disinfectant. When he was issued his army kit before the war, he stocked up on extra iodine. On the march, when he was absolutely desperate for water, he was forced to drink the polluted water that he knew could give him dysentery. He would put a few drops of iodine in his canteen. He said it was the foulest-tasting thing he had ever consumed, but it saved his life. He was taken from Camp O'Donnell to Cabanatuan, another infamous prison camp, and from there on a hell ship to Japan. From there he was shipped to Manchuria and put to work in a factory making war materiel of some kind. The winter temperatures in Manchuria reached thirty degrees below zero. He said he and his fellow captives did all they could to sabotage the work of the factory. He was liberated by the Russian army.

At some level I knew that pent-up emotions were likely to catch up to me sometime on the trip. It happened when I least expected it. We visited the beautiful American military cemetery on the outskirts of Manila. Our tour bus was parked there for over an hour, as several members of the group had relatives buried there and wanted to locate and visit their graves. I knew we had a long day ahead of us, so I planned to walk around, take a few pictures, and return to the bus to rest up. I thought it was no big deal. I had visited Arlington National Cemetery many times without any strong emotional reaction. But when I saw the 17,000 neatly arrayed graves in the brilliant sunlight, and the semi-circle of walls with the names of 31,000—Americans and Filipinos—missing in action, it all seemed terribly personal. Nearly 50,000 young men and women in uniform had died so that I and others like me could live. I began crying and could not stop for quite a while.

Near the end of the trip we visited Clark Field, which has its own relatively small military cemetery. I was standing looking at the rows of graves in the beautiful twilight, when one of the ex-internees, John Hinck, whose army-officer father had died in mysterious circumstances at the outset of the war, said to me, "I have this feeling that my dad may be buried here." He knew that his father had initially been buried in a cemetery in the city of Manila and that his body had later been moved to another location, but he did not know where. Several of us encouraged him to check the records of the Clark Field cemetery in the morning. He did, and to his great joy and relief, he found his father's grave. We shared a very happy drink with him that night. John's own story was quite remarkable. He was about ten or eleven when the war broke out, and he was interned at Santo Tomás and Los Baños with his mother and siblings. After returning to the States, he reached military age just in time for the Korean conflict. He enlisted in the Marine Corps and saw combat duty in Korea and later in Vietnam.

One of the powerful highlights of the trip was the warmth with which the Filipinos received us wherever we went. The reservoir of good will toward Americans in the Islands runs broad and deep, despite the fact that the Philippines were for roughly fifty years an American colony. I gained some insight into this relationship through long conversations with our Filipino tour guides. The Japanese, they said, could never understand why the Filipinos sided overwhelmingly with the Americans in the war, during which the Japanese tried to tap into Asian resentment of Western colonialism. Two factors, the guides said, contributed to the Filipinos' attitude. First, despite their propaganda, the Japanese were in fact harsh and brutal conquerors throughout Asia, not liberators. And second, life under American rule had been a drastic improvement for the Filipinos over life under the Spaniards. The latter were harsh and rigid masters who dealt only with the feudal elite of the Islands, neglecting the welfare of the vast majority. By contrast, the Americans from the beginning worked to establish universal public education and to improve the welfare of the average person, and early on they looked to set a timetable for relinquishing power to the Filipinos. Indeed, the United States kept to this timetable and turned over full power in the Philippines to the natives on July 4, 1946, despite the terrible interruption of the war.

Interestingly in this regard, William Howard Taft, who is I think viewed by most Americans as a failed and insignificant one-term president, is quite a hero in the Philippines. After Spain ceded control of the Philippines to the United States in the Spanish-American War, and after the United States put down the rebellion against Spanish rule that had begun before the war, President William McKinley appointed a commission, headed by Taft, to study the Philippines and recommend a course of action. Taft and his group came to the Islands, toured the archipelago extensively for several months, gathered a great deal of evidence, and made a report, in which they recommended universal education and liberation within a reasonable period of time. These became the twin pillars of American policy in the Philippines. After his commission's report was accepted, Taft returned to Manila as the first American Governor General and began the implementation of the policies he had recommended.

I returned from our trip with a welcome sense of closure. I felt I had learned a lot more about what my parents and I lived through in my formative years.

❖   ❖   ❖

I should append a word about General MacArthur. To survivors of the war in the Pacific he is either an outsized hero or a despised figure. My parents had no use for him, complaining of his high-handed and self-aggrandizing ways and of the fact that he sent his family and his furniture to safety long before the Japanese attack, while making no effort to evacuate civilians and dependents. Bob Wolfersberger, a mild-mannered man, became animated and vitriolic when talking about MacArthur. "They should dig up his body, court-martial it, and then throw it in the river," he said.

There is much blame to be laid at MacArthur's feet. The Philippines were woefully unprepared for war, even though its imminent advent was well-known to most in the Islands. How he could have left his entire air force on the ground at Clark Field more than ten hours after the attack on Pearl Harbor and more than four hours after the bombing of Baguio is simply beyond comprehension. And the men and women he isolated and left defenseless on Bataan clearly have no reason to honor his name.

On the other hand, in 1944, as the Allies began planning an attack on the Japanese homeland, the leadership of the United States Navy wanted to bypass the Philippines, attack Formosa, and move more directly on Japan. General MacArthur convinced President Franklin Roosevelt that the liberation of the Philippines was an essential step in the conquest of Japan. If he had not persuaded the president, everyone interned in the Islands would certainly have been killed. From a purely selfish perspective, I am grateful to the general.

Notes

[1] J.E. McCall, *Santo Tomás Internment Camp: STIC in Verse and Reverse, STIC-toons and STIC-tistics* 64 (1945).

[2] For powerful personal accounts of life in Santo Tomás, see Angus Lorenzen, *A Lovely Little War: Life in a Japanese Prison Camp Through the Eyes of a Child* (2008); Margaret Sams, *Forbidden Family: A Wartime Memoir of the Philippines 1941-1945* 48-189 (1989), and Emily Van Sickle, *The Iron Gates of Santo Tomás: The Firsthand Account of an American Couple Interned by the Japanese in Manila, 1942-45* (1992).

[3] Sams 124-27; Lorenzen 127.

[4] McCall is filled with poetry and cartoons expressing both the frustration and longing of the internees and their mordant sense of humor. For a more personal example of the use of art to anchor one's sense of reality amidst privation, see Teedie Cowie Woodcock, *Behind the Sawali: Santo Tomás in Cartoons, 1942-1945* (2000).

[5] On life in Los Baños as the war moved to its end, see Sams 190-300; Anthony Arthur, *Deliverance at Los Baños: The Dramatic True Story of Survival and Triumph in a Japanese Internment Camp* 24-146 (1985).

[6] For a personal account of the liberation of Santo Tomás, see Robert B. Holland, *The Rescue of Santo Tomás, Manila, WWII: The Flying Column: 100 Miles to Freedom* (2003).

[7] See Arthur 105-46.

[8] See Arthur 257-61.

[9] For an account of the execution of this policy in some cases, see Hampton Sides, *Ghost Soldiers: The Forgotten Epic Story of World War II's Most Dramatic Mission* 7-24 (2001). Sides quotes from an order issues by the War Ministry in Tokyo on August 1, 1944:

> When the battle situation becomes urgent the POWs will be concentrated and confined in their location and kept under heavy guard until preparations for the final disposition will be made. Although the basic aim is to act under superior orders, individual disposition may be made in [certain] circumstances. Whether they are destroyed individually or in groups, and whether it is accomplished by means of mass bombing, poisonous smoke, poisons, drowning, or decapitation, dispose of them as the situation dictates. It is the aim not to

allow the escape of a single one, to annihilate them all, and not to leave any traces.
Id. at 24.

[10] I have been unable to corroborate the date of the planned pullout. None of the sources I have seen says that the key date was February 23. In particular, it is nowhere mentioned as the date of the planned pullout and massacre in Anthony Arthur's detailed account. But my parents consistently said that was the date according to the rumor in the camp, and that they spent the night of February 22-23 believing that we would be killed in the morning.

[11] For a dramatic account of the escape, the harrowing trip to Manila, and the subsequent rescue, see Arthur 147-256. In addition, the History Channel produced a dramatic television documentary, called *Rescue at Dawn: The Raid on Los Baños* detailing the entire operation.

[12] See Arthur 258.

CHAPTER THREE

My Parents

My father, Earl Carlyle Dudley, for whom I was named, and my mother, Susie Adelia Hall, were both born and raised in the Tidewater region of southeastern Virginia, my mother in Norfolk and my father in the adjacent low-lying farm country of Princess Anne County, which was swallowed up in the 1950s by the city of Virginia Beach.

My father was born June 1, 1900, on a farm in the Pungo section of Princess Anne County, where Dudleys had been scratching out a living since the end of the 18th century. He was the oldest of four children born to Horace Woodville Dudley and his wife, Nettie Geneva Morrisette. Nettie was only twenty years old when my father was born. He was followed by two sisters, Rosa Mae (who later collapsed her name to Rosamae), born in 1902, and Jane, called Janey, born in 1904. A second son, Horace Wesley, born after Janey, died in infancy.

Whether because the land was not very good to start with or because it had been exhausted by too much farming—or because the Dudleys were not very good farmers—the living was hard and hand-to-mouth. After Horace and Nettie were married, they rented a farm a mile or two away from the old family farm still being worked by Horace's father, Walter William Dudley, who was known among all his descendants as Grandpa Dudley. Grandpa Dudley had apparently found it necessary to supplement the farm income by running a grocery store in the Brambleton area of Norfolk, starting sometime in the late 1880s. Horace, in his turn, seems to have had a difficult time making it solely as a farmer. He ran for sheriff, and he later studied law. In 1916 he gave up the rented farm and moved into Norfolk, where he began practicing law. In about 1925, Horace, Nettie, and Janey, the only one of their children still living at home, moved to Arlington in Northern Virginia, where Horace reestablished his law practice in an office near the old Arlington County courthouse, where he worked until his death in 1938.

On Grandpa Dudley's death in 1933, the family farm descended to Horace and his siblings, who ultimately sold it to the middle brother,

Raymond. The one time I remember being taken to visit the farm, in the late 1940s or early 1950s, it seemed to me quite ramshackle, and Uncle Raymond seemed quite old. Nonetheless, my father loved farming, and I suspect he would have liked nothing better than to have inherited some or all of the family farm.

My father was very fond of Grandpa Dudley, who seems to have taken a special interest in his oldest grandson, whom he called "Judge." Grandpa Dudley was, among other things, a pillar of the Oak Grove Baptist Church in Pungo. In the late 1980s my Aunt Rosamae took my wife and me to the church, where we were met by two ladies who still remembered Grandpa Dudley. They said he sat every Sunday in a big overstuffed chair in the "amen corner," where with his deep baritone he led the chorus of many "amens" that punctuated the preacher's sermons. Grandpa Dudley was also a prominent citizen of Princess Anne County, having been elected both constable and justice of the peace. Apparently for much of his life Grandpa Dudley was a heavy drinker, consuming a bottle of whiskey or more a day. Then one day he disappeared into the woods and was not seen for several days. The family story was that he had a long, lonely talk with his God and never touched a drop of whiskey again in his life.

Horace Dudley was a man of real, if modest, intellectual attainment. Despite his humble rural beginning, he learned Latin and Greek, he studied law, and when he died he was studying Sanskrit. Though he was, according to my father, an atheist, Horace taught Sunday school throughout his adult life. In a multi-volume collection of thumbnail biographies of Virginians published in 1929, he was described as "one of the leading attorneys and counselors at law of Arlington County." He was said to write briefs that "in clearness, force and logical arrangements … are rarely surpassed."[1] Horace served a term as president of the Arlington County Bar Association. When I received my first traffic ticket in 1956 in Arlington County, the judge before whom I appeared somehow discovered that I was Horace Dudley's grandson and gave me a lecture on what a fine man and lawyer my grandfather had been and how disappointed he would be to see me haled into court at my tender age.

Horace was also, by most accounts, a stern and difficult man, though my mother was quite fond of her father-in-law. When she and my father would visit Horace and Nettie at their house at 915 North Taylor Street in Arlington in the pre-war years, Horace would always find a reason to invite them out to the garage, where he kept his bottle of whiskey secreted from Nettie, a true-believing southern Baptist who had no truck with liquor.

Despite his own lifelong struggle to better himself intellectually, Horace insisted that my father leave school after the eighth grade to work full-time on the farm. My father never really forgave him for that, as he too hungered throughout his life for learning and felt that he was severely handicapped by the abrupt termination of his formal schooling. The feelings between them were sometimes quite bitter, and my Aunt Rosamae told me that she would often try to think of creative ways to foster harmony between them at family holiday gatherings. Horace also seems to have quarreled with his brothers. One source of dissension was apparently the disposition of the farm in Princess Anne County after Grandpa Dudley's death, though I do not know the details of the dispute. A heavy smoker and clearly a "type A" personality, Horace died of heart disease at the age of 60.

Nettie, by contrast, lived to be 95. She was the only one of my grandparents I ever met, and we were throughout my childhood and teenage years very close. I recall many happy times at her house in Arlington. She had an old hand-cranked Victrola that played 78-rpm records, and I practically wore it out when I was small playing her recording of "Bell Bottom Trousers." After my parents moved to Northern Virginia in 1946, "Miss Nettie," as she was known in the family, came to dinner at our house almost every Sunday. Sunday dinner was *always* fried chicken, mashed potatoes, gravy, some vegetable, and hot rolls. Nettie worked for many years at the main Arlington County Post Office, and she encouraged my interest in stamp collecting by giving me many of the stamps that she had saved over the years. When my parents and my sister took an extended trip to Mexico and California in the summer of 1959, I stayed with Miss Nettie in the small apartment in the Westover area of Arlington to which she had moved not long before. I was in college and had a summer job, and she would watch out the window to see me get off the bus in the evening. She would then whisk the biscuits into the oven, and by the time I came in and washed my hands, a piping hot supper was waiting on the table. Nettie was devoted to her grandchildren—and later her great-grandchildren—but she was a quiet, country woman who did not express herself a great deal. Despite his difficulties with Horace, my father was very close to his mother.

❖ ❖ ❖

Most of what I know about my father's early life I learned while sitting up very late with him throughout the summer of 1960, when he was dying of cancer. He was in a good deal of pain and had trouble sleeping at night.

Though he was normally not a loquacious man, he seemed to need to talk that summer. The long nights were tough—my mother and I generally split the nights, each getting about four hours of sleep—but I treasure the memory of those quiet talks.

As a boy my father attended school in a one-room country schoolhouse at Blossom Hill, very close to the family farm. He loved sports, an enthusiasm that stayed with him throughout his life and that he communicated to me. He was especially fond of horseback riding, soccer, and baseball, where his favorite position was catcher. I don't think he minded working on the farm, but the loss of

My father as a young man.

his schooling was a wound that never healed. He grew up in a time before radio and movies, let alone television, computers, and the Internet, and he read a lot. In his twenties he was reading Nietzsche and Schopenhauer. He even made a run at *Ulysses*, though it was definitely not to his taste.

He did not neglect the development of other skills. He was a fine card player. After the war, bridge was his favorite game, but he was very good at cribbage and gin rummy. He was also at one point an excellent poker player. However, he described playing poker for food in the internment camp as the hardest work he ever did, and after the war he simply could not enjoy playing the game again. Though I never saw him play, he said he was best at pool, which he admitted was a sure sign of a wasted youth.

By his own account, there was something brooding, driven, self-searching about my father in his twenties. He was extremely intelligent, but he was also very intense, and he felt deeply inferior because of his lack of formal education. I am sure he suffered from depression during this period. He told me that he was at one point befriended by an older, wealthy man who offered to finance a college education for him, but for some reason my father felt unable to accept this largesse. It was also during these years that my father developed a problem with alcohol. He told me that he drank deliberately as a young man to obliterate his feelings. One of my mother's letters to him in the mid-1930s encouraged him in his effort to avoid "getting tight." Later in life, he would go for years without taking a drink, but if he once began, he would not stop for a long period of time.

Nonetheless, he had a robust, puckish, and often ribald, sense of humor.

He loved a good story and was a fine raconteur. He delighted in "shocking" straight-laced elderly ladies, who of course loved to be "shocked," with his slightly off-color stories. At home with the family, he could be, and often was, wonderfully goofy. My sister and I loved listening to him read to us. He would do wonderful "voices" of the characters in the stories, especially in the Joel Chandler Harris tales from *Uncle Remus*.

Singing was one of my father's greatest pleasures throughout his life. Though he had no formal musical training, he had a wonderful ear and a beautiful baritone voice. He was never a religious person, but during his twenties he attended three churches simultaneously, just to sing in their choirs. He had a large repertoire of songs, but the two that stand out most vividly in my memory are "Old Time Religion"—with which he used to sing me to sleep when I was a baby—and "Red River Valley." These songs were so much a part of my memory of him that, many years later, when I was in my late fifties, I burst into uncontrollable tears in the car with my wife, as we listened to a symphonic version of "Red River Valley."

In 1923 my father went to work as a civilian clerk at the Norfolk Navy Yard, the largest employer in the Tidewater area. He worked for the Navy Deparment until 1949, when he was hired away by the Department of Defense. Despite his lack of schooling, he carved a fine career for himself in the government, starting at the lowest level in the Civil Service and finishing at the highest. He retired in 1956 as a GS-18, then the highest rank in the federal government below the level of political appointees. His specialty for many years was naval logistics, though when he transferred to the Department of Defense he worked in military assistance planning.

His job with the Navy Department meant that my father was employed throughout the Great Depression. That, however, did not mean that times were easy. My father was used to poverty, but the Depression reduced people like him to scrambling for nickels. Moreover, he was not a good manager of money under the best of circumstances. As my mother was fond of saying—and as my own observation confirmed—he was a man with "champagne tastes and a beer pocketbook." One of my mother's letters to him revealed that he had filed for personal bankruptcy sometime in the 1930s, though this was not something he ever talked about. Indeed, her letters—the few that survived the war—were full of references to unpaid bills, pawned jewelry, and small borrowings to cover necessities. Though things were better after the war, when he had been promoted to higher-paying positions and when the country was entering a long period of prosperity, money was always a source of tension between my parents.

My father in his late twenties or early thirties, not long before he met my mother.

Evidently, my father on occasion simply trusted to Providence to see him through, and sometimes the results were amusing. He told me of an occasion when he took a date to old Griffith Stadium in Washington to see a Senators' baseball game. He said that as he went through the ticket line he was sweating bullets because he had in his pocket only the price of a single seat—twenty-five cents at the time, as I recall. He had no idea what he was going to do. But as he approached the window, the ticket seller asked if the young lady standing nearby was with him. My father acknowledged that she was, and the seller said, "Great. She gets in free. It's Ladies' Day." On more than one occasion growing up, I can recall my father getting into serious trouble with my mother over some purchase that she deemed extravagant. His unvarying response was to go out and buy her an equally extravagant present—a "peace offering," he would call it. She would laugh and take him back in her good graces.

My father was very close to his Uncle Rowland, Horace's youngest brother. Though Rowland was sixteen years older than my father, the two of them were close friends throughout their adult lives. Indeed, in 1920 my father and Rowland were rooming together in Washington, though I do not know how long this arrangement lasted or what my father was doing in Washington. Rowland was quite a dandy, and he was married three times— though his third wife never learned of the existence of wife number two. My father and his long-time girlfriend, a woman named Stella, spent a lot of time with Rowland when he was dating his third wife, Violet Hudson. Later my father took a great interest in Rowland's son by Violet, my cousin Lane Dudley. And Lane in his turn took a great interest in my sister and me.

At some point, certainly by 1932, my father and Stella broke up, and my father met Susie Adelia Hall.

❖ ❖ ❖

Susie Adelia Hall was born December 11, 1905, the seventh child and fifth girl born to Tobias Gibbon Hall and his wife Susie Augusta Dunn. Tobias, called "Gib," I believe, by his contemporaries in the family, was a railroad conductor based in Norfolk. With so many mouths to feed, the family was always poor, and my grandmother worked as a seamstress to supplement their income, but the poverty was never grinding. My mother often quoted her father's line that it was cheaper to pay grocers' bills than doctors' bills.

My mother in her late twenties, about the time she met my father.

Thomas Hall, Tobias's great-grandfather, emigrated from County Tyrone, Ireland, in 1788, and settled in Washington County, Pennsylvania. Tobias's father, Austin W. Hall, migrated to Wayne County, Ohio, where Tobias was born in 1867. Austin Hall was a sometime farmer and a Baptist preacher. At some point after 1880, Austin moved his family to Richmond, Virginia. Susie Dunn's family was from St. Mary's County, Maryland, where she was born, though I am not certain how long the family lived there. I do not know where or when Tobias and Susie met.

Tobias and Susie Hall encountered considerable sadness in raising their burgeoning family. Their first child, a boy named Austin for his grandfather, who was his parents' pride and joy, died at the age of seven and a half of scarlet fever supposedly brought into the house by a stray cat. The house was quarantined, so Susie had to wash, dress, and lay out her oldest child's body for burial. The second child, Florence, the family beauty according to my mother, died in 1918 at the age of 23, of complications from giving birth to her third child. Florence's husband, Ed Dowdy, who was very close to his in-laws, came to live with them, and Susie undertook to raise Florence's children, Druceil (known in the family as "Red," for her flaming hair), Edward, and Herbert. The next two children, Mildred Louise (known in the family as "Nig") and Bruce Lee survived, but two more daughters, Doris and Katherine, died as tiny infants. The last two girls, Susie Adelia and Audrey

Naomi (known in the family as "Monk"), also lived to be adults.

I don't have much sense of what my mother's father was like. She loved him very much, and he seems to have been a quiet and gentle man, but he was gone much of the time on the railroad, and the responsibility for raising the children fell largely to his wife. Sadly, Tobias Hall died on May 14, 1945, less than two weeks after my parents and I landed in San Francisco following our release from internment and before we were able to come to the East Coast.

Susie Dunn Hall was by all accounts a powerful personality. She was a strict disciplinarian who believed in meting out sharp physical punishment, and she would tolerate no disrespect from her children. My mother recalled an occasion shortly before Grandmother Hall died, at a time when she was essentially an invalid, when Mother had said something that Grandmother did not like. Sweetly, Grandmother Hall lured Mother to come over and bend down to kiss her. That was when the slap to the face came. My mother was nearly 30 at the time. But Grandmother Hall was also a woman with a great sense of humor and a constant twinkle in her eye. She kept the family together and growing in difficult circumstances, and she had the love and respect of all. My mother and all her siblings that I met—except Uncle Bruce—were great talkers, so conversation must have been encouraged in the Hall household, but Grandmother Hall would not tolerate discussions of either religion or politics. In particular, one was not allowed to say anything derogatory about Woodrow Wilson, her personal presidential hero.

I should say a word about my mother's name. She was named for her mother, whose given name was Susie. When my mother was baptized, Grandmother Hall was still recovering from her seventh delivery and was either unable to attend the ceremony, or at least unable to stand up with her new baby at the altar. Thus my mother was baptized as Susan, which made Grandmother Hall furious, and which neither of them ever recognized as her real name.

In the sixteen years between 1893 and 1909 Susie Dunn Hall bore eight children. My mother claimed that they all weighed in at nearly sixteen pounds. I have always been a bit skeptical of this weight estimate, but regardless, Grandmother Hall seems to have borne large children. Between a long and arduous history of childbearing, the sadness of burying four of her eight children, and the strain of raising three grandchildren in addition to her own six, Grandmother Hall was beaten down and worn out physically by the time she was 60 years old. She spent her last several years a virtual invalid, and died in 1936 at the age of 64.

My mother, center, as a young woman.

With all the busy-ness of life in the Halls' house at 930 Moran Avenue in Norfolk, my mother seems to have had a happy childhood. Pictures of her as a young child and as a teenager show a pretty girl with dark hair, large dark eyes, and a ready smile. Throughout her life she was very warm and gregarious, and she made friends easily, especially with men.

She graduated from Maury High School in Norfolk in 1924 and at some point went to work as a dental technician, which pursuit she followed until she left for the Philippines in 1935.

For some eight years my mother dated a young man named Tommy Callahan. He was Catholic, and the Halls were Methodists. At first, her parents disapproved of the relationship because of the religious difference. But apparently Tommy charmed Grandmother Hall, and she relented. As the relationship dragged on with no conclusion, however, the Halls began to worry that young Susie would be an old maid. As Mother put it, "at first my parents were afraid I would marry Tommy, and after a while they were afraid I wouldn't." She didn't, and in 1932 she met Earl Dudley.

❖   ❖   ❖

I believe that my father met my mother's younger sister Monk and had a date or two with her before my mother attracted his attention. Beyond that,

I know nothing of their court-ship, except that they had known each other about two years before they were married. On March 29, 1934, they eloped to Suffolk, Virginia, where they were mar-ried by a local Baptist preacher. America was still in the grip of the Great Depression, and people of ordinary means simply could not afford wedding celebrations. Most of my parents' siblings and friends ran away on their own to be married on the cheap.

I think over the long haul my parents were happily married, but things definitely got off to a rocky

My parents in 1939, home on vacation from the Philippines.

start. In September 1934 my father was posted by the Navy Department to Cavite, and he left for the Philippines alone. My mother did not join him for several months, and all her surviving letters to him date from this period of separation. The letters are full of protestations of her love and desire to be with him, and the references to the state of their relationship are elliptical. But it emerges clearly from the letters that she did not know when, or if, she would be sent for. Apparently he was having serious second thoughts about being married after an extended time of living on his own. He seems not to have written to her. At least, we have not found any of his letters, and hers are full of plaintive requests for answers. In December 1934 he sent a radiogram announcing that he had made arrangements for her to sail to Manila on the S.S. Henderson, embarking from Norfolk in late February or early March 1935. The ship's voyage wound south to Cuba, thence through the Panama Canal and around Baja California to San Francisco, and after a two-week layover, on across the Pacific to Manila. She was thrilled that he wanted her to come, but she had no money for her living expenses on the voyage, and with typical lack of financial foresight, he sent her none. Her father borrowed $100 and gave it to her to see her through the several weeks aboard ship and in San Francisco. Apparently my father, or the Navy, paid for her ticket, but she was responsible for meals, incidentals, and lodging in San Francisco. She wrote to him that she could stay on the ship itself while it was docked in San Francisco for the grand total of $1.50 a night!

As far as I know, my parents were happy together once they had been reunited in the Philippines. At least, after the war there do not seem to have been more than the ordinary stresses and strains of any marriage where children had to be raised and money was a constant source of worry. Both my parents were moody on occasion, but their moodiness took different forms. My mother had a much quicker flash point than my father, but once she had vented her displeasure—with him or with my sister or me—things swiftly returned to normal, and she could be laughing the next minute. He, on the other hand, seldom showed anger, but once he did, long-forgotten offenses and slights rose to the surface and attained major proportions. Thus there were occasional explosions in our house, but the bond between my parents, born perhaps as much as anything out of the wartime internment experience, was extremely strong. My mother was fond of joking that she had never once given thought to divorce—"murder," she would say, "yes, divorce, no."

My mother was not an intellectual person, but she was quite intelligent, and she always encouraged my sister and me to get all the education we could absorb. She never forced reading on me, but she certainly helped stimulate my love of it.

Susie Hall Dudley was a woman of enormous determination and physical courage. The basics of life were always a struggle for her after she was so badly injured in the bombing of Baguio, but she never complained. While the medical care we received after the bombing was excellent, there was no possibility of fitting her with a prosthesis during the war, so she walked on crutches. A year or so after our return to the States she was fitted for an artificial leg, and she was just beginning to learn to walk on it when she discovered that she was pregnant. She was afraid that a fall might injure the baby, so she remained on the crutches, which she had learned to manage quite well. With two small children to care for, there was never time to return to the prosthesis, and by the time we were older, I think she was just not sure enough of her ability to learn to walk again. So she stayed with the devil she knew. And a devil it was indeed. In her later years she suffered from horrible underarm boils where the crutches rubbed most directly, and she underwent extremely painful draining of the infections. Nonetheless, she was a fully participatory mother, she kept an immaculate house, she cooked every night, and she was very active in her community. I learned a lot from her about how to live.

❖   ❖   ❖

I am convinced that both my parents emerged from the wartime experience, not merely stronger, but better people. They had seen the worst and the best of human behavior, and in the process had found their own internal moral balances. They had renewed confidence in who they were and how to face the challenges of the post-war world.

I think the changes were more marked in my father. He had been born in the South only thirty-five years after the end of the Civil War, and he grew up a poor white man in a region where slavery once flourished and many descendants of slaves still lived. He carried to the Philippines in 1934 all the prejudices of his upbringing. My mother once told me of an evening they spent out on the town in Manila in the mid-to-late 1930s. They went to a trendy restaurant/night club operated by an American black man. As my parents were finishing their dinner, the proprietor was table-hopping and chatting with his customers. He approached my parents' table, introduced himself, and held out his hand to my father. As my mother told the story, my father was a bit in his cups, and he refused the proffered handshake, saying, "Where I come from, a white man does not shake hands with a black man." Inebriated though he was, he had the decency to be embarrassed, and he sheepishly added, "but my wife will shake hands with you."

I can honestly say, however, that after the war I never heard my father make a disparaging remark about any human being because of that person's race, ethnicity, religion, class, occupation, or other group affiliation. He had learned the difficult, but genuine, art of judging people as individuals, on their own merits. This was true even of the Japanese. As far as I could tell, he harbored no bitterness toward the Japanese people for the terrible events of the war. At least, he expressed none to me.

On the other hand, perhaps understandably, my mother never forgave the Japanese for what they had done to her and to her baby. She was extremely bitter about the Japanese to the end of her days. No product labeled "made in Japan" was permitted to cross the threshold of her house. With this lone exception, she took away from the war the same lessons in human tolerance that my father did.

❖   ❖   ❖

Both my parents were tough people, in the most complimentary sense of that word. They figured, I think, that if the Depression and the war had not broken them, nothing ever could. They were right. Even when they were dying, they never complained and they never lost their sense of humor. It must have taxed my father emotionally at times, but by some clear, if perhaps tacit, agreement between them, Mother never sought and he never proffered any coddling because of her severe physical handicap. Nor did they cut me any slack because of mine. She and I were expected to do what people with two good legs did. Difficult though it must have been for them, it was one of the best things they could have done for me.

Tough though they were, they never lost their empathy with other human beings. They were kind, generous, and caring, and they instilled in my sister and me values centered on treating others with decency and dignity. They knew what it was to be underdogs, and they always rooted for them. I was very fortunate to have the parents I did.

Note
[1] *Rebirth of the Old Dominion: Virginia Biography* Vol. 4, 165 (1929).

CHAPTER FOUR

Growing up in the States

1945-1957

When we arrived in San Francisco in May 1945, my parents were still showing the ill effects of nearly three years of severe deprivation, and we were kept almost a month in the Oak Knoll Naval Hospital in Oakland. The pictures taken of the three of us at the end of our hospital stay are a stark contrast to the ones taken shortly after our release from Los Baños. After a month at Oak Knoll, we looked like three healthy, normal Americans eager to take on the post-war world. The only note of sadness during our stay in California was sounded by the death of my mother's father, who never saw his daughter and grandson return from the war.

In early June we embarked upon the three-day train trip across the continent to Washington, DC. There was a layover in Chicago, and we went shopping at Marshall Field, the largest retail store in the world. My parents promised me I could have any one toy in their huge toy department. Somewhat to their consternation, I chose a toy carbine. They tried to talk me out of it, but to no avail.

When we arrived on the East Coast, we went to stay with Miss Nettie at her house in Arlington, Virginia. There I met many of my father's relatives for the first time. I recall a big gathering in her backyard, where I was introduced to my father's two sisters, my aunts Rosamae and Janey, and their husbands, Bob Bell and Frank Caulfield. Later I would spend many happy weeks in the summers visiting Aunt Rosamae and Uncle Bob at their house in Norfolk.

Shortly afterward we took an exciting trip by

My parents and I in June 1945, after a month at Oak Knoll Naval Hospital.

airplane (!) to Norfolk to see many more relatives on both sides of the family. (My mother, a true packrat, kept the ticket stubs. The fare was $10.29 each, inclusive of tax.) I met my mother's younger sister, my Aunt Monk, to whom she was quite close, and her husband, Vic Caffee, along with their two daughters, Trisha and Dorothy Sue. I also was introduced to my mother's other two siblings, her sister Louise and her brother Bruce, who were older than she and to whom she was never particularly close. On my father's side I met one of his uncles, Dodson Morrisette, who was actually four years younger than my father (Grandma Morrisette continued having children, eleven in all, even after her eldest daughter, Nettie, began having her own), and Dodson's wife, Mary Frances, and daughter Nancy, along with Dodson's two older sisters, my great-aunts Rosa and Pat.

❖   ❖   ❖

In August my parents took me to New York City for some sightseeing. I remember visiting the Empire State Building and taking the elevator to the overlook at the top. We stayed at the Algonquin Hotel, one of the city's most fashionable, and the nightly room rate for the three of us was $10! Four nights, together with some meals, a telegram, and some phone calls, cost the grand sum of $67.07.

❖   ❖   ❖

After the happy reunions and the relaxation, it was time to return to normal life. My father was assigned initially to the Naval Supply Depot at Mechanicsburg, Pennsylvania, just outside the state capital, Harrisburg. My parents rented an apartment on the second floor of a large house in Harrisburg. I don't recall much of our time there, except that my parents became good friends with our neighbors in the house, the McClearys, whose daughter Jerry Lee was the earliest playmate I can remember. Also, my parents were inveterate real estate shoppers, and we spent many Sunday afternoons driving around the Pennsylvania countryside looking at property. I think my father still harbored visions of returning to farming, and many of the places we looked at were far out in the country. On one of our day trips, I managed to get myself sprayed at quite close quarters by a skunk, an experience my parents, who had to try to clean me up, never let me forget.

The condition of my left leg was a matter of increasing concern at this stage, as the difference between the lengths of my legs was growing significantly, and my left knee was not strong enough to support very much weight. The doctors at Oak Knoll had emphasized the need for swift attention to this problem, and they had referred my parents to Dr. Jesse Nicholson, a former Navy physician, who was then the head of orthopedics at the University of Pennsylvania hospital. We made many trips to Philadelphia to see Dr. Nicholson, both when we lived in Harrisburg and later. Under his supervision I was fitted for a full-length brace on my left leg, with a built-up shoe to equalize the length of my legs. This first

Taken at age four-and-a-half, when we were living in Harrisburg, Pennsylvania.

brace was an awkward affair. There was no knee lock, so I had to sit with my leg fully extended. Later ones allowed me to unlock the knee joint to bend my leg and got rid of the built-up shoe, which put too much pressure on my knee, requiring surgery when I was eleven.

One of the hardest things for me to learn was how to go down stairs. My Aunt Monk was visiting us when I came home with the brace for the first time, and she spent hours with me in the stairwell of our house, teaching me a little skip-step maneuver that has served as my method of going down stairs ever since. At this time, the tendons in my left knee would tighten at night, causing my knee to contract quite painfully, and to prevent this I had to sleep in a cast. The surgery obviated this problem, but throughout my childhood and adolescent growth, my brace and for a time my cast had to be changed with great frequency. My parents and I spent a lot of time visiting doctors and bracemakers.

We did not live in Harrisburg very long, but we did celebrate our first post-war Christmas there. Our Christmas tree was the first I had ever seen, and we still use some of the ornaments that my parents bought to hang on that tree. While I did not grow up in a religious household, the Christmas holiday—and not just the rabid commercialism that came to dominate Christmas in the second half of the 20th century—was always the most important ritual of the year. As a child and as an adult, Christmas has always been for me a time of genuine joy celebrated with family and close friends.

My parents, my sister, and I at Christmas 1946.

That feeling began with our quiet Christmas in Harrisburg in 1945.

In the summer of 1946 my father was transferred from Mechanicsburg to the Navy Department's offices in Washington. Actually, he worked in the "temporary" Navy Annex buildings across the Potomac river in south Arlington, Virginia. The annex was built during World War II to house the overflow from the main Navy buildings on Constitution Avenue in Washington, themselves "temporary" buildings dating from the military buildup in World War I. The very ugly main Navy temporary buildings were finally torn down in the Nixon administration, but the Navy Annex is still in use in the early part of the 21st century.

My parents rented an apartment in the newly completed Barcroft Apartments complex just off Columbia Pike in south Arlington. They managed to get a quite comfortably sized two-bedroom apartment located on the first floor, which I am sure was a great relief for my mother. She was several months pregnant when we moved to Arlington, and on October 12, 1946, my sister Elizabeth Carlyle Dudley was born in Garfield Hospital in Washington. She was named in honor of Bessie Brazee, to whom she was quite grateful in later years after Mother confessed that otherwise she would have been named for Grandmother Hall's mother, Georgiana.

I recall being quite happy to have a little sister, though I am sure I was no nicer to her than most first children are to their newfound competition for parental love and attention. The five-and-one-half years' difference in our ages and the strong bond between my parents and me growing out of the wartime experience made it a tough family in which to be the second child. But Liz and I have always been close, and she and her family have been one of the real joys of my life.

❖   ❖   ❖

Perhaps not surprisingly, one of the major adjustments for me in coming to the States involved food. I doubt I would have been an adventurous eater under any circumstances, but the very narrow band of foods to which I had been exposed in the internment camps also contributed, I am sure, to what was at the beginning, at least, very finicky taste on my part. For example, I took an instant, overpowering dislike to milk, which has remained with me throughout my life. I would rather do almost anything than drink a glass of milk. My mother, desperate to ensure that my bones would grow, tried everything. She put chocolate syrup in my milk. She put molasses in it. Tricked up in this fashion, it was tolerable … sometimes. But I would never drink it straight. I recall once being in essence forced on pain of major discipline to drink milk at lunch at school. It went down and came right straight back up, all over the table. The school officials never tried that again.

I rejected most new foods, including many that kids usually love, such as macaroni and cheese and strawberries. As I grew older, most of these dislikes receded, and my repertoire of enjoyable food expanded greatly. Often the occasion for the discovery that I actually liked something I had been refusing to eat for years was a social setting in which I feared offending someone. For example, when I was twelve or thirteen our family went to visit some friends of my parents named Williamson, whom I liked very much and who had just moved into a new house with enough land for a sizable garden. They showed us around their new place and took special pride in their strawberry patch. After dinner, Mrs. Williamson, of whom I was particularly fond, served up strawberry shortcake. I could not bear the thought of hurting her feelings, so I gritted my teeth and dug into a relatively small portion. Imagine her delight, not to mention my own, when

I discovered how delicious it was and went back, not merely for a second helping, but for a third!

My learning process was not helped by the fact that my mother had a relatively limited range as a cook and very little money with which to try to vary our menus. We ate a lot of beans cooked in a broth with ham hocks. Except for Thanksgiving and Christmas meals, fried chicken and meat loaf were the spiffy dinners. Both my parents had been raised on poor folks' southern cooking, and when we had meat, which wasn't often, it was cooked to the consistency of shoe leather, a reflexive hangover from a time when refrigeration was not generally available and overcooking meat was the only way to be sure it was safe to eat.

Nonetheless, over the years, and especially after I left home and came under the influence of my truly omnivorous wife, I had many epiphanies comparable to my discovery of strawberry shortcake, and I have become a reasonably open-minded eater. Some dislikes, though, principally milk, mushrooms, mayonnaise, and eggplant, I have never been able to shake.

❖　❖　❖

I have mentioned that my father had a gift for music and singing in particular. Unhappily, while I inherited his love for music, I had none of his talent. It was one of the great disappointments of his life that I could not carry a tune in a truck. Over the years, he tried valiantly to teach me to sing on many of our long car trips together, without any real success.

Early on Dad decided that perhaps music lessons of some sort would help. The husband of my cousin June, Aunt Rosamae's daughter, played the violin. His name was Francis Gayle Thomason, but he was known to all as Tommy. Very soon after we moved to Virginia, Tommy undertook to teach me the violin, and my parents bought me an instrument.

The venture was doomed from the start. For a youngster with a poorly developed sense of tone and pitch, a violin is not a good instrument on which to begin trying to make music. On a piano, the player merely strikes the key. The actual tone produced by striking the key is up to the piano. Thus a kid with a good memory, decent manual dexterity, and a fair sense of rhythm—and a well-tuned piano—can become a passable pianist without a great sense of pitch, and can learn gradually to identify the situations in which he has struck the wrong key. A violinist, by contrast, must choose exactly where to place his finger while dragging the bow across the string. A slight misplacement of the finger can produce a sound jarring to the ears of everyone—everyone, that is, except the tone-deaf kid with the bow in his hand.

Not surprisingly, my lessons and practices drove not merely Tommy, but also my parents, to distraction. My mother, after all, had to listen to me practice while trying to care for a newborn infant. I had a very good memory, and my dexterity and sense of rhythm were certainly acceptable, but the precise location of my fingers for any given note was a mystery I was destined never to master. I worked very hard to learn to play "Away in a Manger" for Christmas 1946 with, I must say, utter lack of success. A few months convinced my parents—and Tommy—that I would never be a fiddler.

The early abortion of my musical education was a sad event to me. I have always enjoyed a wide variety of music and would dearly love to be able to produce some. My excellent memory has, however, given me some measure of revenge in singalongs throughout my life. I always remember more verses of songs than anyone else. Thus I have inflicted many off-key renditions of obscure lyrics on my friends and family over the years.

❖   ❖   ❖

Schooling for me presented an issue in the fall of 1946. My mother had already taught me to read. However, there were no public kindergartens in Virginia at that time, and the public schools refused to consider a five-year-old for the first grade. So my parents decided to put me in private school. After considerable looking around, they chose the Maret School, then located on Kalorama Circle in northwest Washington. It was a small school founded some years earlier by three French sisters. French was a required part of the curriculum from the first grade on. The student body was very diverse, with many children of foreign diplomats. I started there in the second semester, in January 1947, and I loved my first-grade teacher, Mrs. Eicher.

The commute from south Arlington to Kalorama Circle was not easy. Today most people would shudder at my parents' solution to the problem, but it seemed quite natural to me at the time, and it never caused any real difficulty. At the age of six I would ride with my father to the Navy Annex on Columbia Pike, from where I took public buses into the District of Columbia and back out to the Navy Annex at the end of the day. I had to transfer buses twice each way. I made friends with the bus drivers and with other commuter regulars, who I am sure looked out for me and made sure I got off at the right stops. Only once did I make a serious mistake. One day when I was about nine and my father was working for the Defense Department at the Pentagon, I somehow got on a bus headed for Alexandria that did not stop at the Pentagon. All turned out just fine, but the story would send shivers up parents' spines today. When I realized that I was on the wrong bus, I began to cry, and a very nice gentleman seated next to me comforted me and took me home to his house. He called my father at his office, and then he and his family treated me to a nice dinner. His daughter, who was three or four years older than I, played the accordion for me until my father came to pick me up.

At the end of the first grade, the teachers at Maret concluded that my mother and Mrs. Eicher had prepared me so well that I should move ahead directly to the third grade. This was something that was routinely done with academically advanced children at the time, with little thought given to social or other developmental consequences. I was a late bloomer physically, and especially given my physical handicap, I think my school years were more awkward and less happy than they might have been had I been with children my own age. But in any event, a year later my education received a major shakeup that was unrelated to age.

To his great credit, my father was determined that I should never endure the handicap of a lack of formal education that he felt so keenly. He made it his special project to see to it that I received as much education as I could or would absorb. Although I was making mostly A's at Maret, which had a fine academic reputation, he decided that I was not being challenged enough. My dad undertook to home-school me. He was familiar from his days in the Philippines with the special home course developed by the Calvert School in Baltimore, which was popular with American expatriates, and he decided to give it a try. Despite what seemed to all appearances a strong start at Maret, I was unable to pass the fourth-grade entrance examination used by the Calvert School. So, as my father never ceased to tease me, I had to repeat the third grade.

It was quite a year. As I think back over the busy-ness that pursuing a career and raising children entails, I am continually awestruck by the dedication displayed by my father. He worked a full, hard day at his increasingly responsible government job, and then spent roughly three more hours each evening teaching me the lessons set out by the Calvert School. It was a marvelous educational experience. I studied world history and geography at levels I did not encounter again until high school, and I read simplified versions of Greek myths that I never encountered again at all until college.

Indeed, I can honestly say—for good or ill—that I did not really learn anything new in school between that year and the ninth grade, when I took algebra and Latin for the first time.

It was not, however, an easy year. While I loved to read, I was not the most self-motivated student, and my father was not the most patient teacher. In theory, I was to do my homework in the morning hours while the other children in the neighborhood were in school, so I should be free to play with them in the afternoons. Sadly for her, it was my mother's job to make sure that I did my work before going outdoors to play. I don't recall actually lying to her about the state of my work, but it is fair to say that my sense of when I had adequately prepared my lessons seldom jibed with my father's. So when he came home and discovered that I had made mistakes that he considered stupid or that I had omitted portions of my assignments, he was displeased—often volubly—with both of us.

One thing I remember quite fondly from my year of home-schooling. My father had a love of language, both for its communicative quality and for the beauty of its sound. He incorporated in my curriculum the beginnings of a training in forensics that has served me well all my life. He required me to memorize and recite fine poetry, an exercise that has given me pleasure ever since. And he made me read aloud at considerable length. Though he was a southerner, he did not like southern accents, and whenever I pronounced a word with a hint of a drawl, he would stop me and make me say it over again. From this I garnered a great sensitivity to accents and, somewhat perversely, a tendency unconsciously to mimic those of the people around me. Whatever forensic strengths I have had as a trial lawyer and teacher I owe to the love of language and the speaking skills my father inculcated in me, during that year and later.

The noble experiment could not, however, possibly be repeated. My father was exhausted and frustrated. My mother was tired of constantly being in the middle. And I was in a state somewhere between trauma and rebellion. So it was back to Maret in the fall of 1949, where I was placed in the fifth grade at age eight.

❖   ❖   ❖

I should say something about religion—or the lack thereof—in my upbringing. Both my parents were raised as conventional southern Protestants, my father as a Baptist, my mother as a Methodist. Mother remained, I think, a vaguely believing Christian, though by no means a deeply religious woman, throughout her life and would, I am sure, have preferred to attend church and to bring my sister and me up in some faith. But Dad rebelled against religion in his twenties. Although he continued to enjoy and to take part in the musical accompaniment of religious services, his intellectual searchings found religious doctrine unsatisfying. Moreover, as the years progressed, he came to see organized religion as a divisive, not a unifying, force in the world and to view the practices of most, if not all, Christian denominations, as laced with hypocrisy. This bent was strongly reinforced by the internment experience, where I know he found a resounding disconnect between expressed religious piety and good Christian practice.

Though he never took my sister and me to church, Dad struggled to avoid appearing anti-religious. He made it clear that he respected anyone's sincerely held religious beliefs, and he gave me and encouraged me to read Bible stories as a young child. The historical Christ, he emphasized, was a figure he admired enormously. In later years he urged me to read about and attend services in various Christian denominations so that I could make an informed choice about what to do. More important, both by his words and his example, he taught us fundamental Christian ethics, and from him I learned that treating others with basic decency, dignity, and fairness needs no supernatural commandment to make it right.

❖　❖　❖

From my preteen years I have many pleasurable memories. Three categories stand out in my mind today.

Having been taught well by both my parents, I developed a love of reading. With a taste guided at first, at least, by them, I read tales of King Arthur and Robin Hood, virtually all of Mark Twain, Robert Louis Stevenson, Kipling, Poe, and other nineteenth-century stand-bys. I think I read *Huckleberry Finn* first when I was seven or eight, and I re-read it every year until I left high school. Prompted by my father's lessons, I developed an ear for the sound of both poetry and prose, and I read as if aloud, with the language reverberating in my head. I moved on later to Hawthorne, de Maupassant, Conan Doyle, and standard nineteenth-century English and American poets. Historical novels, mysteries, narrative poems—I read widely and happily from the good store of books in our house.

Second only to reading was baseball. My father was a universal sports fan, as I came to be, but baseball was his first love, and mine. I can still recall my first trip to Griffith Stadium with my father to see the Washington Senators play in 1947. In those days the Senators and the New York Yankees played a doubleheader every July 4 in Washington, and my parents enjoyed going to those games. Between games in 1948 or 1949 I scampered out onto the field and got Joe DiMaggio's autograph. I can still visualize him. I thought he was the biggest person I had ever seen.

My uncle Frank Caulfield was friendly with a man named Gabe Murphy, who was a part owner of the Senators, and every year Mr. Murphy gave my uncle three tickets to the annual opening-day game, where the president of the United States traditionally threw out the first ball. I actually got out of school every year to go to the game with my father and Uncle Frank. It was a spring ritual of absolute joy to a baseball-mad little boy.

Uncle Frank was also something of a high-stakes gambler, and he took great delight in constructing an annual bet with me on where the Senators would finish in the American League. The Senators were dreadful in these years, as they had been throughout most of their existence, but however bad they were, I never wavered in my hope and my passion. To this day, I tell myself that rooting for such a tail-end team, year in and year out, built persistence into my character. The American League then consisted of only eight teams. Our annual wager provided that if the Senators won the pennant, I would receive something like the then-munificent sum of $150 (I could not imagine possessing that much money), and my projected winnings would decrease with each lower-place finish, until I would win something like $5—still a nice piece of change to a small boy then—if the team finished sixth. Only if my beloved Nats finished seventh or eighth would I owe Uncle Frank any money, and then it was something like fifty cents for seventh and $1 for eighth. The bet was constructed so that I couldn't lose, but somehow nearly every year I did. I can recall only one year when I took some of Uncle Frank's money for sure. That was 1953, the only time in my youth that the Senators finished at .500, good enough for fifth place. Bob Porterfield won 22 games, Frank Shea and Chuck Stobbs won about 17 apiece, and Mickey Vernon won the batting title. And that year Uncle Frank arranged through Mr. Murphy for me actually to go down in the dugout on a game day to meet the players and get them to autograph a baseball for me. I still have a photograph of the opening day lineup of that team in my office.

Uncle Frank also ignited another passion when he gave me for Christmas 1947 a copy of the Spink "Baseball Bible," which contained all the major and minor league statistics for that year and a complete list of all-time major league records. I virtually memorized the latter section of the book, and while I swore off baseball more or less permanently after the major leagues took the Senators away from Washington a second time in 1971, I was up to that time known as the "court of appeals" in baseball trivia games.

I recall many happy outings to Griffith Stadium with my father to see the Senators play. He was a connoisseur of pitching, and he used to watch the papers to see who the starting pitchers were when the Senators were in town. We would go when he spotted the best matchups. I learned from him that good defense, in baseball or any game, is every bit as exciting as good offense. I still think that the ideal score in a baseball game is 1–0. I have never cottoned to the insane number of home runs produced by the juiced-up ball and the even more juiced-up players of recent years.

On one occasion Dad took me to see Satchel Paige pitch. Paige, perhaps the greatest pitcher of the old Negro League, was in his forties (or maybe older) when the Cleveland Indians brought him in for a season or so in the major leagues. On another occasion, when we were watching the best pitching matchup that the sad-sack Philadelphia Athletics and the Senators could produce, my father spotted Connie Mack, the legendary former manager and then owner of the A's, sitting behind the Philadelphia dugout in back of third base. It was one of those steaming hot July nights for which Washington is justly famous, but Mr. Mack, who was then over 90, was wearing a black three-piece suit and a straw boater hat. Dad urged me to go over and get Mr. Mack's autograph. I approached him tentatively and stuck out my scorecard with a mumbled request that he sign it. Although he was watching two of the worst teams in the major leagues play a meaningless game, he glowered at me as if I had interrupted an important religious observance, which in a way I suppose I had. "Sit down until the inning's over," he growled. So I watched half an inning of baseball with the great Connie Mack, after which he very kindly signed my scorecard and chatted with me for a few minutes.

My favorite summer ritual, though, was my annual visit to my Aunt Rosamae's house in Norfolk for two weeks. I think my first visit by myself was in the summer of 1945. Both sides of my extended family were then still in Tidewater, so there was a lot to do. I would always go over to Hampton for a night or two with Aunt Monk and Uncle Vic. Sometimes I would visit my cousin Herbert Dowdy and his wife Mildred. Herbert was the son of my mother's older sister Florence, and he grew up with my mother and Aunt Monk after his mother died. I would also spend a night or two with my great-uncle Dodson. I developed over the years a crush on his daughter

Nancy, who was about three years older than I and who I thought was beautiful. Despite the difference in our ages, Nancy was always very nice to me and included me in whatever she was doing. I would also always see Dodson's sisters, Pat and Rosa. Aunt Pat, who never married, and who was as addicted to sports as I was, was a lot of fun. Uncle Bob and Aunt Pat would always take me to see the Norfolk Tars play a couple of baseball games. The Tars were at that time the New York Yankees' Class B farm team, and many Yankees stars came through Norfolk on their way up to the big leagues. I still recall seeing Whitey Ford pitch a shutout for the Tars before he ever put on a Yankees uniform.

Mostly, though, I just hung out with the children in Aunt Rosamae's neighborhood. I got to know many of them quite well over the years, and the long summer days and evenings were a constant blur of baseball, Monopoly games, trips to "Doc Zed's," the local pharmacy, for specially concocted fountain cokes, and twilight games of kick the can. These were genuinely happy times for me, and I remained close to Aunt Rosamae for the remainder of her long life. She lived to be 97.

Travel to and from Norfolk for these visits and many others was sometimes an adventure. On more than one occasion, my mother and I took the overnight steamboat that then ran between Washington and Norfolk. It was an exciting trip, and I still recall discovering my love for Norfolk spots in the steamboat's dining room. One year, when I was ten or so, my parents and Aunt Rosamae decided that I was old enough to make the return trip from Norfolk by myself on the steamboat. I have little recollection of that trip, but apparently I had an extremely good time, as both I and my clothes were quite filthy when my parents met me the next morning. That experiment was not repeated.

In those days one could not drive from Northern Virginia to Norfolk without taking either an extremely long detour around Hampton Roads and the Norfolk harbor, or a ferry boat across one of the many intervening bodies of water. We always took the ferry. There were several, including one across the James River at Yorktown, and another across Hampton Roads from Old Point Comfort to Willoughby Spit. Indeed, my great-grandfather Tully Morrisette, Miss Nettie's father, had been a ferry boat captain in the Norfolk area for many years. It was a pleasant and exciting change from the monotony of riding in a car to get on the ferry boat, smell the salt water, and watch the destination grow gradually larger as we approached.

In the summer of 1949, when my parents and my sister drove down to retrieve me from Aunt Rosamae, my father announced with great pleasure that they had just bought a farm. As it turned out, "farm" was a bit of an exaggeration, but it was an exciting purchase nonetheless. They had bought a little more than twenty acres, approximately half of it wooded, in Fairfax County, Virginia, roughly midway between the little hamlet of Colvin Run and what is now the village of Great Falls, which was then called Forestville. There was a small, somewhat dilapidated two-bedroom house on the property. The four of us moved into that house in the late summer or early fall.

I still smile ruefully whenever I think of the economics of that purchase. My parents paid $250 an acre for what was to become prime Fairfax County real estate in the later boom times of Northern Virginia. We lived there for ten years, and my parents built a nice new house on the property, which was completed in 1955 or 1956. Unhappily, my father's health began to deteriorate, and they sold the house and land in three parcels. The last sale, of raw land, brought $2,000 an acre in 1959, and my father was convinced he had made the biggest killing in history. If only he knew. I do not know what the land is worth as I write this almost fifty years later, but I do know that if we still owned it, my sister and I would be very well off today.

When we moved there, that part of Fairfax County was still dairy-farming country. It was pristine, beautiful rolling countryside, very sparsely populated. There were a few farmhouses, some of them quite old and lovely, and a few shacks where the poor working folk lived. The one truly enjoyable feature of the house we moved into was an enormous picture

My parents, my sister, and I in 1955 or 1956 in front of the house my parents built near Great Falls.

window in the living room, from which we could look out over seven miles of green hills and woods.

The house was located half a mile from the nearest paved road, Walker Road, which runs between Route 7 and Route 193. Between Walker Road and the house was a plain dirt country lane, which was quite bumpy at the best of times and impassable for ordinary cars in really wet or snowy weather. We had a name for it—the "bumpadiddies"—though of course it is now paved and has the grand name of Harriman Lane. The man who sold the property to us had an old World War II army Jeep that he tossed into the deal to sweeten the pot. The four-wheel-drive Jeep, which had no cover, was made to go anywhere. My sister's and my favorite weekly ritual was a Saturday morning Jeep ride with Dad. He would take us over the bumpiest parts of the land at a rapid clip, as we squealed with delight. When the weather was good the family car had no trouble making it up the lane to the house. In bad weather, our wonderful neighbors Marvin and Laura Sanders, whose White Pines Dairy Farm fronted on Walker Road, would let us park our car in their yard and use the Jeep as a ferry from the paved road to the house.

My father garnered great satisfaction from just owning some land. He worked happily every weekend clearing the land of brush and rocks so that he could plant vegetables. What began as a modest and sensible vegetable garden of half an acre or so blossomed over the years into wild and unmanageable agricultural projects. For these projects, of course, Dad needed a tractor. Never one to do things by halves, he bought the largest tractor John Deere made—larger even than Marvin Sanders' tractors—to work perhaps six or seven arable acres.

One year Dad planted 150 tomato plants. Even assuming that you plan to put up tomato juice and can lots of tomatoes for the winter, fifteen or twenty tomato plants will do your average family of four very nicely. That summer, which was, by the way, a bumper year for growing tomatoes, my mother was exhausted from canning them and making juice. And I spent what seemed like the entire summer picking them. When the tomatoes began

My parents on my father's big John Deere tractor.

to ripen in earnest, it would take me several hours to get through the whole enormous patch, by which time there were newly red ones already waiting at the starting point. Everyone who came to visit us was forced to take a bushel of tomatoes home with them. We ran out of bushel baskets to hold the tomatoes, so at one point we all had to use the shower stall in my parents' bathroom, because both bathtubs were full of tomatoes.

Another year Dad planted five acres of corn. That comes out to an acre and a quarter for each of us. And, yes, I picked most of it by hand. For a time, my sister ran a little vegetable stand on Walker Road, selling corn and tomatoes. This has always been a sore subject between us, for Dad gave Liz half the proceeds for sitting there doing nothing until a customer stopped, while I received nothing whatever for picking the corn and tomatoes, which was at peak periods close to a full-time job. I have hated the idea of farming ever since.

In some ways, it was a beautiful, idyllic setting for my sister and me. Fresh air, lots of open space, lovely vistas, regular but relatively undemanding chores. But it was also a fairly lonely existence, especially in the summertime. We had few playmates, and our house was quite inaccessible. Our lack of social intercourse was exacerbated by the fact that Dad was gone at work all day, and our mother never learned to drive a car. And Liz and I were too far apart in age to be real playmates for each other. We sort of divided the side yard in two, and we each had our own "plot." In mine, I developed an elaborate imaginary baseball game, in which I drove my mother nuts by endlessly throwing a tennis ball against the porch of the house and then spent hours hitting fungoes with hickory nuts and small rocks. And I read a lot.

The purchase of the old house on the property did bring us one delicious new form of entertainment. The previous owner, who had served extensively overseas in World War II, called the place "Aching Acres" and used it to decompress from his wartime experience. When he was finished with that phase of his life, he wanted to leave it behind. Hence the inclusion of the Jeep. He also left all his furniture behind, *and* a seven-inch black-and-white television set (there was no color TV then). This was before most people had television. I had seen a little TV at my Aunt Janey's house. They had money from Uncle Frank's very successful plumbing and heating contracting business, so they had every material thing before we did. I had never dreamed that *we* would get a TV set. The screen was tiny, though the set was large, and the reception wasn't very good. We struggled constantly with indoor and outdoor antennas. Washington, however, had four local television stations, an unusually large number in those days. In the afternoons Liz and I would watch a local show for kids, "Pick Temple," which ran old Westerns endlessly. Dad and I watched a lot of baseball. For reasons that now escape me, we also watched a lot of boxing, wrestling (!?), and variety shows. It was a big deal when my parents said I was old enough to stay up on Monday nights to see "I Love Lucy."

What little social life we had, other than family birthday and holiday gatherings, strange as it may seem today, revolved around events sponsored by the Great Falls Grange. The Grange was an old farmers' advocacy organization that achieved some real power in the Midwest and West in the populist days of the late 19th century. The Grange Hall, located atop a small hill, dominated the village of Forestville. The Grange property consisted of several acres, including a baseball diamond with a few bleacher seats, where semi-pro teams played on Sundays in the summers. My parents swiftly joined the Grange and became quite active in both its local and statewide affairs. They encouraged me to join the "Juvenile Grange," which met twice a month on Friday nights and held dances in the Grange Hall on the non-meeting Fridays. The dances were pretty simple affairs. There was a 78-rpm record player and a fair sample of popular records, and you could buy cokes for a nickel. Since I was still attending Maret School for the first three years we lived in Forestville, the Grange meetings and dances were my only contact with local children of my age, but I soon came to know some of them and to look forward eagerly to Friday nights. The activities of the Juvenile Grange were supervised by a wonderful brother and sister, Berwin Babson and Beulah Moorland. They had been born and raised in the area, and they lived in an old farmhouse with their mother and Beulah's husband, Bill Moorland. Berwin never married, and Bill and Beulah had no children of their own, but they threw much of their considerable energy into giving the local children a good time at the Grange Hall.

Every year the Grange held a fund-raising carnival in the picnic area between the hall itself and the baseball diamond. For two weekends each summer people would come from all around to try their luck at hitting targets with baseballs, playing roulette, raffles, bingo, and a whole variety of other games, and just to socialize. There was also a dance with a live band inside the Grange Hall on the last Saturday night of the carnival. My sister and I "worked" at whatever stall my parents were in charge of each year, which meant among other things that we got to stay up much later than usual. The carnival was a genuine highlight of the summer.

Some people in the area resented the Grange, which was seen as the gathering place of those who were somewhat better off financially. The opposite social pole in Forestville was the Volunteer Fire Department. I think my father took great delight in the fact that he was the only person anyone could remember who served both as master of the Grange and as president of the Fire Department.

❖   ❖   ❖

The move to Fairfax County coincided with the end of my home-schooling year and my return to Maret. If the commute to school was problematic before, it was now a nightmare. I had to ride with my father, not just a few blocks from the Barcroft Apartments to the Navy Annex, but at least three-quarters of an hour—on good traffic days, more on bad ones—from outer Fairfax County to the Pentagon, and I still had to transfer public buses twice each way. At the end of the day, I had to wait until my father was finished at his office, and then we faced the long drive home. There was much less traffic in those days, but there were also fewer and narrower roads, and even then they sometimes became clogged with cars. Finally, in bad weather, when we reached the Sanders' farm, we either had to switch to the open Jeep for the last, rugged half-mile, or, if the Jeep was up at the house, we walked to the house in the rain or snow. Indeed, on some days when the weather was threatening, or if the car was not working well, Dad and I would leave the house in the Jeep and drive all the way to and from the Pentagon in it. Given that the Jeep had neither roof nor sides nor heat, those days could be very wet and cold.

It was a very long day for an eight- to ten-year-old, and it was hard to find a good place to concentrate on my homework. We tried different arrangements. For a time I met my father at his office. This was always an adventure, as I have never had a very good sense of direction, and all the corridors in the Pentagon looked exactly alike. Many was the time that I got lost and had to walk all the way around that enormous building. Dad would try to find a place in his office for me to do my homework, but the Department of Defense was not constructed for fifth graders. Then for a while I took the bus to Miss Nettie's house in Arlington. She would fix me a cup of tea and a snack, and I think the idea was that this would be a better place for me to get my homework done. But I was always tired by the time I reached her house, and grandmothers have never been the best enforcers. So I spent much time talking to Miss Nettie and very little doing homework. This arrangement also added significantly to my dad's homeward commute, as he had to traverse much of Arlington County to pick me up.

I enjoyed my last three years at Maret. I was in a very small class—about thirteen children, as I recall—and I had made many friends. My last year I had a crush on Margaret Corcoran, the very cute daughter of Tommy "the Cork" Corcoran, a prominent Washington lawyer and former Franklin Roosevelt "brain truster." Margaret went on to become quite a beautiful young woman, and she was the first female law clerk in the history of the Supreme Court, serving Justice Hugo Black, in the 1966-67 Term of Court. Sadly, she had also become a drug addict, and she died of an overdose not very long thereafter.

❖   ❖   ❖

Even though I was happy in school, the commute was simply too much. And I could seldom see my school friends outside of class hours, because all of them lived in Washington. So my parents decided at the end of the seventh grade, in 1952, to enroll me in public high school in Herndon. In those days in Fairfax County, at least, there was no middle school. Elementary school ran from the first through the seventh grades, and high school started in the eighth grade. At that time, there were only three high schools in all of Fairfax County, which is an enormous geographic area. Two of them, Fairfax and Mount Vernon, served the more populous southern and eastern portions of the county. Herndon served all the rest, the then-great rural swatch of northern and western Fairfax County. The major program for the boys at Herndon High was agriculture, and the biggest organization was the FFA (Future Farmers of America). For the girls, it was home economics and the FHA (Future Homemakers of America). While the school was tiny by today's suburban standards—there were 56 members of my graduating class, the largest in the history of the school—it was several times the size of Maret.

Herndon is today a sizable, bustling town in the high-tech corridor that western Fairfax County has become. In 1952 it was essentially a village of little more than 1,000 people. There was an old train station, though I don't think any trains had stopped there in years, a drug store, and precious little else. I began the eighth grade in a tiny old school house dating probably from the early years of the 20th century, but we moved into the new high school, just next door, that year. I remember we had to help move our desks from one building to the other.

The commute to Herndon High School, while a lot better than the commute to Maret, was sometimes no picnic. We lived seven miles from Herndon, and I took a school bus whose route ran along Walker Road. I had the choice between getting up early enough to catch a ride with my father—and I have never enjoyed waking up early—or walking the half mile down to Walker Road. Coming home, there was no alternative to walking, regardless of the weather. Walking long distances was not the easiest thing for me. Often the brace would rub open sores on my leg. But it was good for me. My sister claims that I would often make her carry my books as we walked up the bumpadiddies together, but that surely was not the case!

I recall feeling awkward and out of place in high school, especially in the first two or three years. Several factors, I think, contributed to that. Age and size were among them. Having in effect started school a semester early and then skipped a grade, I was almost two years younger than many, if not most, of my classmates. And I was always small for my age (I grew four inches in college). My physical handicap also made me different and hindered my competition in the arena I valued most, sports. I was at this time very sensitive about my leg and about being physically different. I remember that a boy called me "peg-leg" once on the playground at school. I hauled off and hit him, but got what I deserved when I lost my balance and fell, while striking him only a glancing blow. (He later became a good friend.)

There was, too, a large cultural gap between me and many of my schoolmates. They tended to come from working class or farming families, and education—at least higher education—was not high on the agenda for most of them. On the other hand, I had been drilled from the very beginning about the value of education, and even though we were hardly well off, it was clear that I would go to as good a college as possible. I believe I was the only member of my high school class to take the SATs, then better known as the College Boards. Only seven of us went on to college. Moreover, even then it wasn't cool for a boy to be a good student, which I had to be, in sheer self-defense at home. The result was that, with one exception, I had no real friends among the boys in my class. In the tenth grade, a new boy, Nick Capozio, entered the school, and he and I were fast friends for the rest of the time. His family had no money, and Nick was not headed for college, but he was smart and loved to read, and his friendship helped me through a lot of the tougher times.

I got along better with the girls, but I seldom dated girls in my class. Most of the girls I dated were a year or two below me in school, nearer my own age. There was, however, an exception. For a time I dated a very bright and sweet girl named Winnie Lee Brown, who was actually two years ahead of me in school, and thus almost four years older than I. I often wondered why she had the time of day for someone so much younger.

✧ ✧ ✧

On May 17, 1954, near the end of my ninth-grade year, the world changed forever for people in sleepy little southern towns like Herndon, Virginia, and for people all over the country for that matter. That was the day the Supreme Court handed down its famous decision in *Brown v. Board of Education*[1] holding that legally imposed racial segregation in public schools violated the Equal Protection Clause of the Fourteenth Amendment to the Constitution.

Legal scholars have pointed out, correctly, that *Brown* did not achieve much in the way of immediate change. It was widely disobeyed, and for over a decade virtually no progress was made in the desegregation of southern schools. Indeed, the decision created a huge political backlash in the South, which stiffened resistance to racial progress and undermined the position of southern moderates who favored change in racial policies.[2] Only when Title VI of the Civil Rights Act of 1964, passed in the tidal wave of national guilt following the assassination of President Kennedy, threatened a cutoff of federal funds to non-complying school districts was any real measure of desegregation achieved.[3]

Nonetheless, the impact of *Brown* was staggering. It transformed the topic of race from America's dirty little secret to the most important subject on the domestic agenda, and it permanently awarded the moral high ground to the advocates of greater civil rights for the nation's black population, still suffering many hardships almost a century after the Civil War was fought to put an end to human slavery. I lived through this transformation, and it was stunning indeed.

Before the decision in *Brown*, I don't recall race having been much of an issue in any phase of my life. I knew that Jackie Robinson's historic breakthrough as the first black major league baseball player was important, but by 1954 even the most retrograde teams had black players, and many stars were African American. Nobody was trying to argue that Willie Mays didn't belong in the big leagues. I had heard other people disparage blacks as "niggers," but I had learned from my parents that they were "colored ladies and gentlemen." In my parents' post-internment world, race and ethnicity counted for nothing, and my own brief experience was of great diversity. Maret had been a little melting pot, with children of all races and many nationalities. On the public buses I took every day in my commute, I met and became friendly with black children in the District of Columbia. Just across the Potomac River in Virginia, however, things were very different, and even though I lived there, I did not really understand the difference at the time. Though in Fairfax County, as in most of the rural South, there was no real residential segregation—blacks and whites lived side by side, one legacy of the slavery era, in which the blacks lived on and worked the land owned by the whites—everything else was rigidly segregated, mostly by law. Blacks could not go to the same restaurants or theaters as whites, were often not welcome in the same stores, seldom voted in elections, and, of course, were shunted off to inferior schools, which received only a fraction of the financial support from the state and localities that the white schools received. Even worse, the black schools were widely dispersed, and young black children often were forced into commutes even more grueling than the one I had endured voluntarily for three years. For example, black students were bused from McLean all the way to Manassas to maintain the system of segregation, and many of them stayed throughout the week away from their homes, with friends or relatives, to avoid the lengthy busing ordeal.

On the day *Brown* was decided, it dominated the news coverage, and we discussed it over dinner at home. My parents explained to me that the Supreme Court had obviously gotten it right, that slavery had been a terrible thing, and that even after slavery was abolished, blacks had not been treated fairly. They said that everyone was equal before the law, that black children should have the same chance for education and advancement as white children, and that separate schools never had been, and could not be, equal. It all seemed clear and right to me.

I learned the next day just how southern Fairfax County really was. I am sure there must have been other students at Herndon High School whose parents told them what my parents had told me, but I never found one. On the playground before classes started, the only topic of conversation was the Supreme Court's decision. When I said it was clearly right, I was hooted at, called a lot of names, and actually punched.

My ninth-grade civics teacher was a wonderful woman named Patricia Alger, who decided to seize the moment to do a little educating. She announced that we would have a debate on the merits of the decision a few days later, and she asked for volunteers for the debate. Many students wanted to take the side opposing *Brown*, but I was the only one who volunteered to defend the Court. Mrs. Alger asked for another volunteer because she wanted to have two debaters on each side. Finally, a very pretty and smart girl in the class, with the marvelous name of Dixie Lou Simpson, said she would argue with me in defense of the decision. Dixie was from Alabama. Her parents had only recently moved to Northern Virginia, and I don't believe she had been told at home that the Court got it right. But she was a good sport and had an innate sense of fairness. So Dixie and I worked together on our arguments, and on debate day we gave it our best before a hostile audience. When Mrs. Alger asked for a vote as to who had won the debate, Dixie and I garnered a solid majority. I don't mean we made converts. But the Supreme Court and Mrs. Alger got us talking about the issue of race, and Dixie and I gave the others something to think about. The dialogue has really never stopped to this day.

At first the dialogue was not very pretty. In the months and years immediately after *Brown*, the discussion, in the South at least, was dominated by the reactionaries. The air was blue with racial slurs and dire predictions of the impending fall of civilization. Congressmen rushed to sign the so-called Southern Manifesto, which asserted a version of John Calhoun's pre-Civil War doctrine that states could nullify federal law. State officials drew lines in the sand. The Herndon High School band took, for the first time, to playing "Dixie" before football games. Friends and relatives shocked me with some of the things they said.

I think perhaps this unpleasant phase of the dialogue was necessary, that only through constant repetition could the banality and emptiness of the pro-segregation arguments be revealed, at first to those who genuinely wavered on the issue, but ultimately even to the fire-breathers themselves. Gradually some sanity returned, even to southern politicians. J. Lindsay Almond was attorney general of Virginia when *Brown* was decided, and he spewed forth some of the most arrant nonsense in an effort to get himself elected governor on the crest of the backlash. But I shall never forget the sight of Governor Almond taking physical possession of the Virginia standard at the 1960 Democratic National Convention to prevent its being dragged onto the floor as part of a last-ditch pro-segregation demonstration.

We were all, however, so naive. Of course the claim that letting black and white children go to school together would mean an end to civilization was preposterous. But almost equally lacking in foundation was the progressives' jubilation at the decision. Even Thurgood Marshall, the great advocate who achieved victory in *Brown*, believed that white southerners would now recognize and obey the law, and he failed to argue with sufficient force in the second, remedial phase of the case the following year. The

Court, unhappily, signaled its institutional understanding of the South's problem with the phrase "all deliberate speed."[4] And most of the decision's supporters, both black and white, thought that race was only skin deep, that both races shared essentially a common culture, and that once legal barriers to advancement were removed, a new day of equality would arrive. We had a lot to learn.

❖   ❖   ❖

Not all of high school was social awkwardness. I had many good times, especially as I matured and fit in better, and as I gained some respect among my classmates for my abilities. Steered by my father, as well as by my own developing inclination, I was very active in forensic competitions. I was a member and later president of the debate club, and I competed in prose and poetry reading and a variety of public speaking contests. My sophomore year, I was boys prose reading champion of Virginia. I got to go to the University of Virginia in Charlottesville to compete with students from all over the state. I was also on the newspaper and the yearbook and joined the chess and stamp clubs. I was the manager of the baseball team my sophomore year, and after many hours of practice learning to throw a curve, I made the JV team my junior year and the varsity my senior year as a pitcher. I didn't get to play much on the high school teams, but I did have one summer of real joy and success in Pony League, where I had a 5–1 record and started the All-Star game. I never had the vaguest excuse for a fastball, but I could throw three different kinds of curves, and I could get the ball over the plate. This was enough to get most fifteen-year-olds out.

My last two years in high school I had a fairly active social life, dating several different girls, though from the middle of my senior year I had a steady girlfriend named Ginny Anderson. My parents certainly encouraged me to date, but transportation was a very big problem. The kids who lived in a town like Herndon could hang out together in the evenings and walk to each other's houses. But the isolation of our house meant that every social event was a project. Also, being young for my grade meant that I was unable to get a driver's license until after all the other boys in my class. This was, naturally, quite galling to me. If I wanted to go somewhere with a girl, either I had to find someone with a car to double-date with, or my father had to drive us. I can attest that the latter arrangement can put a serious crimp in one's dating style. I doubt it was much fun for Dad either. Fortunately for me, however, Virginia in those days granted driver's licenses to fifteen-year-olds. With my father's strong encouragement, I took the test the first available day following my birthday, so I was on my own (at least when I could get the family car) from the middle of my junior year on.

This led to a number of adventures, but the most memorable was a Saint Patrick's Day dance my senior year at the church in Fairfax City attended by my cousin June and her husband Tommy. I was driving my father's car, and there were three couples on the ride. The evening did not start very well. I first picked up my friend Larry Flannigan, who lived just outside of Herndon, and as I was backing down his steep and muddy driveway, the tailpipe of the car became stuck in the mud and broke loose from the bracket that held it in place. Larry and I got some wire and restored it to roughly its proper position. Before we could go to Fairfax for the dance, we had to attend a locally sponsored fashion show at the high school in Herndon, as Ginny Anderson was modeling something in the show. As soon as the show as over, we tossed Ginny's crinoline underskirts and other gear from the fashion show in the trunk of the car and headed for the church. When the dance was over and we emerged from the church social hall, we discovered that an extremely thick fog had descended over the area. Despite my most careful efforts, I managed to back into some object in the church parking lot that was obscured by the fog. This put a dent in the rear fender of my father's car. The next two hours were among the most harrowing of my life, as I traversed a great deal of Fairfax County in total pea soup, responsible for the safety of five others, who lived in widely dispersed places. Of course, I took Ginny home last, and, grateful that everyone was safe and concerned about the extreme lateness of the hour, I forewent my usual amorous lingering and headed swiftly home. I finally got home at around 2:30 in the morning, and as I went to bed I made a mental note to myself that I had to get up before Dad did, because I had a lot of explaining to do about the car. I was not smart enough, however, to set an alarm clock, and being a normal teenager, by the time I woke up, my father had been up for hours and had driven the car up to Colvin Run to get the Sunday paper. With great trepidation, I approached him at the kitchen table, where he was drinking coffee and reading the paper. I was sure I was in for it. But all he did was cock his head, give me what he thought was a terrifying look, but which was betrayed by a twinkle in his eye, and say, "Look, I don't mind the broken tailpipe, and I don't even mind the dent in the fender, but what the hell is Ginny Anderson's underwear," which, of course we had forgotten to retrieve in our haste to get home, "doing in the trunk of my car?" Whew!

❖ ❖ ❖

My parents seemed to overcome the privations of the internment years and to return to relatively robust health throughout my childhood and early teenage years. But the combination of extended malnutrition, years of heavy cigarette smoking, and hard work—in my father's case, very stressful work at the Department of Defense during the height of the Cold War—began to take their toll. It showed first in Dad. In the fall of 1956 he began to suffer severe chest pains, but he refused either to slow down at work or to see a doctor. Finally, he had a massive heart attack. Still unwilling to call a doctor—country boys born in 1900 thought that seeing a doctor was a sure prelude to dying—he suffered through a night of fear and agony. Ironically, perhaps, my mother nursed him through it with a bottle of brandy, which probably saved his life. The next day he was hospitalized. He remained in the hospital for a couple of weeks, and when he came home he was confined to bed for more weeks. Gradually, he returned to some semblance of health, though he was forced to retire early from the government.

It was all very scary for my sister and me. In our isolated country existence, our family was everything, and our dad was what made it tick in many ways. We were, of course, happy that he recovered, but his health was never again the same. Not only could he no longer perform his job, but he was now unable do much of the heavy farming exercise that gave him so much pleasure. Indeed, in less than two years, he and my mother sold the house and land they loved and moved to a small house in McLean.

Dad did not really do much to help his long-range survival prospects. He couldn't give up cigarettes; indeed, he seemed to smoke more the worse his health became. And he continued to give in to another lifelong addiction—to ice cream. He would look pleadingly at Mother every few days and say that he really did not eat ice cream very often. Of course she could not resist serving him some.

We were fortunate. Dad actually overcame the heart disease and lived four more years. When he died of cancer in 1960, his doctor told me that he had not believed Dad would long survive the heart attack.

❖ ❖ ❖

My father lived long enough to perform one more act that powerfully influenced my life for the good. It was a given that I would attend some college, but I had not a clue which one or how to go about making the choice. Colleges did not market themselves to prospective students in those days, and there were no guidebooks to provide comparative information. Particularly if one's parents had not attended college, one was at the mercy of the vaguest of reputational information. The guidance counselors at Herndon High, while very nice and well-intentioned, were of little help. I was their prize student, and they just assumed that any college would want me, so all I had to do, they said, was choose one and apply. And they had a heavy bias in favor of southern, and particularly Virginian, schools. Feeding that bias from my perspective was my relationship with Ginny Anderson, about whom I had become very serious in the manner of sixteen-year-olds. She was a year behind me in school, and I liked the idea of being near enough to come home frequently to see her.

My parents from the beginning steered me away from large schools, such as the University of Virginia. They thought that the quality of education was much better at smaller liberal arts schools, and they were worried that, young as I was for my grade, I might simply get lost on a large campus. I accepted that, but decided for some reason that Hampden-Sydney in Farmville, Virginia, sounded like a good choice. Hampden-Sydney was and is a decent, but less than first-rate, academic institution, and it was set in deeply conservative and rigidly pro-segregation Prince Edward County. My parents were less than impressed.

My father had somewhere along the line absorbed great admiration for small, New England liberal arts schools, and he began reading about them. He settled on Amherst College, which had just been ranked the number two men's liberal arts college in the country in an early *U.S. News* survey of American colleges and universities. I did not like the idea of being that far away from home and girlfriend, and I was not charmed by the thought of New England winters. It came down to a contest of wills between Dad and me. He won, thank goodness. The decision was not made until the very end of the application period. And, heeding the ignorant praise of the school counselors, I applied to only one school—and that a day late. I had no clue that, even then, Amherst received roughly ten applications for each place in the class.

Fortunately, I was accepted by Amherst, and fortunately, I won a National Merit Scholarship (the program was then in only its second year), which in those days provided a need-based stipend. That scholarship allowed my parents to afford to send me to Amherst, despite my father's significantly reduced retirement income. I still recall my father tearing his hair out filling out the torturous parents' confidential financial statement on which the amount of the scholarship was based. Tuition, room and board my first year at Amherst were just under $1,500—and the comma is not misplaced! The National Merit Scholarship paid $1,000 of the cost.

My father's intervention in favor of an Amherst education enriched my life in more ways than I know how to count.

Notes
[1] 347 U.S. 483 (1954).
[2] See, e.g, Michael J. Klarman, *Brown, Racial Change, and the Civil Rights Movement,* 80 Va. L. Rev. 7, 141-50 (2000).
[3] See James R. Dunn, *Title VI, the Guidelines, and School Desegregation in the South,* 53 Va. L. Rev. 42 (1967).
[4] 349 U.S. 294 (1955).

CHAPTER FIVE

Amherst

1957-1961

My father's choice of a college for me could not have been better. Amherst then was a very small—1,000 students—all-male liberal arts college set in the beautiful rolling country of western New England. It had a "new"—*i.e.*, post-World War II—core curriculum carefully designed both to acquaint students with the literary traditions of Western society and to introduce them to scientific method and independent thought. The faculty was small and intensely dedicated to teaching. The school had a tradition of feisty introspection that was perfectly suited to my temperament and intellect. And it was located seven miles from Northampton, home of Smith College with its 2,400 women, and about fifteen miles from South Hadley, where roughly 1,600 Mount Holyoke women resided. The ratio was hard to beat.

I still look back on my years at Amherst as among the most exciting and enjoyable of my life.

❖ ❖ ❖

My father and I drove alone together from home to school, and quite a send-off it was. We broke the lengthy trip with an overnight stay in New York City, where Dad took me to see a Broadway play. Perhaps without any sense of irony, he chose Eugene O'Neill's *Long Day's Journey into Night*, which sported a magnificent cast that included Frederic March, his wife Florence Eldridge, and Jason Robards, Jr. I still recall the performance vividly. I was transfixed by Robards' portrayal of the powerful, roiling, but deeply flawed brother Jamie, based on the older brother whom O'Neill both adored and resented. Somehow Jamie reminded me of my father.

The next morning we drove the roughly four hours from New York to Amherst. Along the way, Dad decided to have a major father-son talk. He told me that he was proud of me and that as of that day I was really on my own. I would be making my own decisions and would be responsible for the use of my time, for good or ill. He then laid out a suggested weekly schedule of study. He acknowledged that he had put considerable pressure on me throughout elementary and high school to get good grades, which he said was because he feared I was "mentally lazy" and apt not to work up to the standards of which I was capable. That, he said, was a thing of the past. He would never pressure me about grades again but would trust me to do the best I could. Just as I was getting comfortable with that idea, he added, "Of course, I would be disappointed if you didn't make Phi Beta Kappa."

It was a memorable, but perhaps not entirely reassuring, introduction to life on my own.

❖ ❖ ❖

Partly because I was deeply concerned that my rural Virginia high school education had not prepared me for the academic big leagues, where I now realized I was playing, I took my father's admonitions to heart and threw myself intensely into my studies from the very beginning of freshman year. And though I never lost my intellectual self-confidence, I did not find the going easy at first.

At the heart of Amherst's core curriculum lay two courses, Science 1-2 and English 1-2. Though the setting of the former was rather simple Newtonian physics, it really was a course in scientific method. One could not simply memorize formulas and apply them, for the labs and the tests required one to explain their derivation. To help in understanding this, we were also given a course in introductory calculus, Math 1-2. English 1-2 was purely a composition course, in which we wrote three short essays each week based on a carefully coordinated set of assignments (which changed every year) designed to challenge our assumptions about virtually everything and to force us to look inward and explain the bases of our thoughts.

There were also courses in Humanities and World History. The former covered great books of Western civilization, beginning with the *Iliad* and stretching through the Bible to *The Brothers Karamazov*. "World" History was, in the fashion of the day, quite Eurocentric. The "world" seldom stretched east of the confluence of the Tigris and Euphrates rivers.

I was in deep water from the start, at least in Science 1-2. Whereas many of my classmates from prep schools or urban public schools had already had courses in physics and calculus, Herndon High had offered neither. Thus the subject matter was as unfamiliar to me as the method of instruction. I found the labs especially puzzling. I recall one in which we were given two little cars of different weights on rollers, connected with a rubber band, and a yardstick and were required to calculate the relative difference in the weight of the cars and to explain our calculation.

The playing field was relatively more even in English 1-2, as I was already a reasonably good writer, thanks mostly to my father's critiques of my high school papers and speeches. However, many of my classmates again seemed at the start, at least, more comfortable than I with the underlying intellectual structure of the course, though by the end I counted it the best educational experience of my life—and still do. The class was divided into sections of about 25 students, and my teacher was perhaps the finest instructor I have ever encountered. His name was Theodore Baird. He was the most senior professor in the English Department, and he had invented English 1-2. Professor Baird was a terrifying presence to an easily intimidated freshman. Somewhere in his sixties, he was tall, and his head consisted of an enormous, completely bald, shiny dome. He wore rimless *pince-nez* glasses, and he had prominent, arched eyebrows that could express exquisite contempt for a student's argument, written or oral, with the merest flick. He had what seemed to be ill-fitting false teeth, for he spoke with his jaws clenched tightly, and his consonants were forceful and liquid.

All students in all sections were given the same assignments at the same times, so there was much talk about them over meals and in the dorms across sections. The classroom drill was for the instructor in each section to reproduce one or two papers for each class to serve as exemplars for discussion of the assignment. The students whose papers were chosen were required to read them aloud at the start of the class. At the outset, we thought it was an honor to have one's paper selected, but we soon learned better. A few were praised as showing significant insight into the assignment, but most were torn to shreds before the authors' very eyes. In the first week of the course, one of my classmates, Ed Barber, who became a lifelong friend, read his paper aloud in proud and sonorous tones, only to have Professor Baird remark, "I don't quite know what to say about this paper. It's in English. But the hell with it!" I am not sure Ed has ever quite recovered.

History was mostly a lecture class, and the professor was an Amherst legend, Dwight "Bucky" Salmon, a feisty bantam of a man who had served as one of the U.S. Army's chief historians in World War II and who proudly displayed in his office a picture of himself in uniform standing next to General Eisenhower. He would write a detailed outline of his lecture each day on the blackboard, so that students could get there a few minutes early, copy the outline, and then sit back and let the lecture roll over them with sheer pleasure. His wonderful descriptions of the "big, barrel-chested, ginger-bearded Teutonic hordes" that overran the Roman Empire and then charged about Europe for several hundred more years are indelibly imprinted on my memory. This course, like all the other freshman courses, also broke up into small sections, and I was lucky enough to be included in Professor Salmon's section first semester. He was a caring and encouraging man, and I recall him with much fondness.

I took my father's suggestion of a study schedule to heart. I was in class all morning, from Monday to Saturday, and, with the exception of Physics lab days, I spent my afternoons and evenings in the library. For the most part, I limited myself to an hour for dinner, and I usually studied until at least 11 or 11:30 p.m. Saturday afternoons I also studied, except when there were home football games. Sundays I pretty much slept in and relaxed, unless I had an unfinished English paper due on Monday. I was, in short, a real grind.

Despite my strenuous efforts, when "practice" grades came out at the end of the first six weeks, I was both disappointed and scared. I did fine in History, Humanities, Spanish, and Math, but I had a low C in English, and a high D in Physics. I recall vividly the evening of the day those grades were placed in our mailboxes. My roommate, another product of a rural semi-southern high school, had an even worse cold bath than I did. He took each one of his books and threw it across the room. I decided I was not working hard enough.

My intense effort paid off in the next few weeks. Somewhere around Thanksgiving I had an epiphany. I saw that English 1-2 and Science 1-2 were really the same course being taught in two different languages, that one could not simply accept the offerings of others but had to struggle to observe, construct, and justify one's own conclusions in whatever arena. I worked very hard on my Science 1 final paper, which required one to restate some of Newton's essential work on gravity based on the antecedent work of Galileo and Kepler, and while it was not my finest hour, it was reasonably good. I wrote a better, more elegant final essay for English 1. I finished the semester with a B plus average, which included the highest grade in the entire freshman class in History. This earned me an invitation to dinner at Professor Salmon's house, the first of my many enjoyable social encounters with Amherst faculty members. I went on to do even better second semester. A special source of pride to me was Professor Baird's comment on my last English 2 paper. He wrote, "I have enjoyed reading your papers. You have style. Watch out!"

❖ ❖ ❖

Freshman year was not all about grinding on my studies. I made many new friends, with some of whom I have remained in close contact throughout my life. Nonetheless, I missed my family and especially Ginny Anderson. Virtually every day I wrote at least two letters, one to Ginny and the other to someone in my family. Ginny and I were "going steady," so I was not dating anyone at school the first year. My parents liked Ginny very much, but they were worried that I was missing out on a great deal of the fun of college life. So they insisted that I should get a date for prom weekend in the spring, and they underscored their seriousness by sending me a white dinner jacket, tuxedo pants, a cummerbund, and a bow tie. Reluctantly I gave in, and someone fixed me up with a blind date, a freshman at Mount Holyoke, whose father was a very fancy chocolatier in New York. I tried to have a good time, but we really didn't hit it off.

❖ ❖ ❖

Believing heartily in the old Roman adage *mens sana in corpore sano*, Amherst required all freshmen to take physical education. Because of my handicap I was placed in the slowest group, which we all called Spastics 1, which consisted mostly of floor exercises. After a while I was allowed to move on to the swimming pool, where the swim coach, Hank Dunbar, took an interest in me and worked on my strokes. I actually learned to swim an entire length of butterfly, and I was never in better shape than I was that year. All Amherst students had to pass certain physical tests in order to graduate. Some found it virtually impossible to swim the requisite fifty yards. Another test required us to run 300 yards. I claimed and was granted an exemption from this test on account of my handicap, but when I presented my written excuse to Coach Dunbar, who was timing the runs, he expressed great disappointment that I was not even going to try. (It was a source of great pleasure to me that a generation later the same Hank Dunbar recruited my son, albeit unsuccessfully, to come to Amherst to swim.)

Spastics 1 was not my first encounter with the athletics establishment at Amherst. We were given a physical examination during orientation week before classes started. Part of the exam required us to wander about the gym in the nude while being poked, prodded and observed in different ways. Amherst's long-time athletics director, Al Lumley, who was also the college chess champ, approached me as I listed along on my uneven legs. He put his arm around me and said, "Son, I'll bet you're a real good student."

❖   ❖   ❖

The cafeteria food at Amherst was pretty dreadful—par for the course, I think, in colleges during the 1950s. The only reliably good meal was Sunday brunch. For the most part we were served some kind of overcooked, grey-colored, unidentifiable meat, which we called, of course, "mystery meat." This led to one of my most embarrassing moments. I had become good friends freshman year with a student from Newton, Massachusetts, just outside of Boston, named Cush Anthony, who was later to be my sopho-more-year roommate and the best man in my wedding and who remains one of my closest friends. In between semesters we had only three days, not enough time to justify a long ride (or expensive plane flight) home to Virginia. Cush invited me to go home to Newton with him. The Anthonys were quite well-to-do (Cush's father was president of an insurance com-pany) and much more proper and formal than my family had ever been. As I recall, Cush and I wore jackets and ties for dinner each evening. The first night four of us—Mr. and Mrs. Anthony, Cush, and I—gathered around their large dining room table. While Mr. Anthony was busy carving some-thing to my right, his wife engaged me in conversation on my left. Searching, I suppose, for some reliable and reliably neutral topic of conversation, she asked me about the food at school. Being on my best behavior, I was reluc-tant to give it the description it deserved—I certainly wasn't going to talk about "mystery meat" to these rather proper adults. So I said, "It's okay, I guess, except that they give us roast beef"—a grandiose and wholly inac-curate description—"about four times a week." At that point, Mr. Anthony said, "Oh, if we had known that we would have had something else tonight." For the first time I noticed that he was carving a very elegant roast of beef at his end of the table. I wanted to find a little hole and crawl into it. I looked to Cush for help, but he was laughing much too hard at my gaffe. I guess my reputation with the Anthonys survived this rocky start, as I saw them often over the years and they were always very kind and caring to me.

❖   ❖   ❖

The dining hall was the source and scene of an amusing student protest at the very beginning of my freshman year. Unhappy with the generally grubby state of students' attire, the college administration announced that henceforth students would be required to wear jackets and ties to dinner in the dining hall on Saturday nights. Part of the rationale was that many guests—mostly dates, of course—came to dinner on Saturdays, and the students should spiff up a bit for them. This order was met with howls of protest all across campus. The newspaper, the *Amherst Student*, fulminated against it in editorials. Student compliance took some very humorous forms. Some showed up for Saturday dinner in nothing but a jacket and tie (no shirt and no shoes or socks) plus boxer shorts for minimal decency (fortunately for them, the weather was still quite warm that early September). Some others showed up in formal attire, with their dates wearing evening gowns, spread tablecloths on the normally bare tables, and added lighted candles to the decor. The administration knew when it was beaten, and it surrendered after only two weekends. The students from that point on rather reveled in their grubbiness.

❖   ❖   ❖

As I mentioned before, I was in my youth very sensitive about my leg and what I thought was my awkward appearance because of it. I was jarred out of that freshman year by a student in the class ahead of me named John Raye. John had been a good athlete until he contracted polio sometime during high school. He had no real use of his legs, and he walked on metal crutches, the kind that looped bands around the wrists. He had great upper body strength and could really move on his crutches. As soon as we met, he began teasing me unmercifully about my handicap. I could hardly resent it coming from him, so I soon got used to it and began giving back as good as I got.

John and I even raced each other a couple of times in the infamous "chapel dash" on the Friday morning of prom weekend in the spring. The only real holdover from Amherst's beginning as a denominational Christian college was compulsory chapel attendance. Each student was required to attend two sessions each week in Johnson Chapel, the college's most prominent building and its largest gathering place. There were four chapel sessions each week, given at 9 a.m. on Monday, Tuesday, Thursday, and Friday. To avoid offending non-Christians, two of the weekly sessions were given the oxymoronic title of "secular chapel." The only difference between "secular chapel" and "religious chapel" was that we sang a version of the Doxology at the start of the latter sessions. Otherwise, every chapel session consisted of a ten-minute talk by some faculty member, guest speaker, or the college chaplain. These talks were generally devoid of religious content, though I think the speakers did make efforts to choose uplifting themes.

Each student had to check in with a designated chapel monitor in order to have his attendance counted, and the doors to the chapel were closed promptly at 9. There was a traditional race on prom weekend to see who could be the last person to leave the dining hall, which was on the other side of the campus, and still manage to check in with the chapel monitor. John and I must have made a curious sight trundling along, he on his crutches and I on my brace. I don't recall who won our races, but it was a lot of fun. I learned from John Raye how to deal with my handicap with good humor.

❖   ❖   ❖

Actually, compulsory chapel played an ironic role in my father's choice of Amherst as a college to urge upon me. Students at Amherst had for many years chafed against the requirement to attend chapel. As far as I recall, the opposition was based, not so much on principled disagreement with what could be seen as an effort to force-feed the students a little religion, but rather on a dislike of being forced twice a week to get up and go to chapel at 9 even if one did not have an early morning class. Even on early class days, the fifteen minutes that chapel took could be much better spent, or so we thought, in bed or lingering over coffee in the dining hall. So many students dodged the requirement as much as they could. One year my roommates and I proudly displayed on our bulletin board two sets of letters, one congratulating us on making the Dean's List and the other notifying us that we were on "chapel probation" because of our poor attendance. (I think I made "chapel pro" every semester, but nothing ever happened to me because of it.)

The year before I arrived, Amherst broke ground for a new classroom and office building, which was designed, among other things, to provide a home for the Religion Department and a private, non-denominational chapel where students could come to pray or meditate. The night after excavation began, a rowdy group of Amherst students came out with their trash baskets and filled in the hole. They were said to be protesting against the continuation of compulsory chapel. The so-called "chapel riot" received a brief smattering of amused attention in the national news media. (Actually, it turned out that the students did the college a big favor, as the initial hole was dug in the wrong spot, and it was going to be filled in in any case.) My father saw the news coverage and decided that the students' spirit was eminently compatible with his own attitude toward organized religion. He never seemed to have realized that the college won and made no alteration in its compulsory chapel policy. In any event, I believe this is one reason why he pushed Amherst, which was ranked only number two by *U.S. News and World Report*, on me. The top-ranked liberal arts school was Haverford, which still had a strong Quaker tradition.

❖   ❖   ❖

After hitting my academic stride in the middle of freshman year, I found the Amherst experience intellectually bracing and thoroughly enjoyed my studies. I remained a diligent student but did not need to resort to the intensely organized and rigid regimen of the first few months. I took a wide variety of courses, though I mostly avoided science and math and concentrated heavily on history and English. Much of my learning took place outside the classroom in often intense discussions with my friends. In addition, I found that most of my friends and classmates had read more widely in good literature than I had. I heard my professors and my peers talking about important books that I had heard of but never read. So in my spare time I played an enjoyable game of catch-up. It was made easier for me because I was not dating anyone at college for the first two years, and I whiled away many a weekend afternoon or night with a good book.

The two courses that have contributed the most long-range pleasure to my life were the introductory survey courses in fine arts and classical music. I had had some acquaintance with art at home and in school—I had been numerous times to the National Gallery of Art in Washington—but had no real idea about the historical development of Western art or the styles of famous artists. I was wholly ignorant about classical music. My father, as I have said, loved music and singing in particular, but he knew no classical music, and I heard none at home. I had no idea how to listen to a piece of music or of the formal structures within which composers worked. I found the going pretty tough at first, but after almost flunking the first hour test, I determined to put as much effort into the course as I could. We spent a number of class sessions on a detailed analysis of Beethoven's Third Symphony, the *Eroica*. I bought a recording of the work and drove my roommate, Cush Anthony, to distraction by listening to it over and over, outline in hand, for weeks. I was rewarded, not only by high marks the rest of the way, but by countless hours of pleasure listening to classical music throughout my life.

I thought, naively as it turned out, that I had left ugly racism behind in Virginia and come to a place where all people were judged, as Martin Luther King later said, "not by the color of their skin but by the content of their character." I was swiftly disabused of this notion. To begin with, there were a lot fewer black people around than I was used to. While the school administration always denied having quotas, it soon became obvious that each class contained among its 250 entering students exactly five African Americans, all of them products of the middle class who wanted to and easily did assimilate to the predominantly white, WASPish culture. Worse, on the occasion of perhaps my second haircut in the town barbershop, I heard two of the barbers speaking derisively of a basketball team with five "jigs" on it.

I soon learned that racial integration of the fraternities was a hot issue. I have never been a fan of fraternities, and the Amherst system of that day was the only setting in which I would have considered joining one. The college provided dormitory housing for all freshmen and sophomores, but it was heavily dependent on the fraternities for upper-class housing. More important, women, house parties, and alcohol were forbidden in the dorms, while those living in fraternities could entertain women, not only in the public parts of the houses, but in their personal rooms as well, and there were several "house party" weekends each year, at which alcohol was served without regard to age. On non-party Saturday nights, each fraternity tapped a keg of beer in its social space. There were thirteen fraternity houses, which were then maintained in excellent shape, and one "social dorm," where nonfraternity upperclassmen could also entertain female guests and have parties. The social dorm was not nearly as nice as the fraternity houses, and most of its occupants were thought of as a bit nerdy. So upwards of ninety percent of Amherst students, including me, joined a fraternity in the spring of their freshman year.

Most national fraternity organizations were heavily dominated by southerners, who were fighting a desperate battle to keep the organizations all-white. Not before the early 1950s did an Amherst fraternity admit an African-American member, and by the time of my freshman year, only four of the thirteen houses had done so. In most cases, the national fraternities had immediately suspended the charters of the local chapters upon learning that they had admitted a black student. There was a big divide between the four "liberal" houses and the nine more conservative ones, which during my school years showed no interest in integrating.

The fraternity I joined, Alpha Theta Xi, had been part of a national, Theta Xi. The year before I entered Amherst, the house had admitted a black student by the name of Jimmy Jackson. Jimmy was a wonderful person who became one of my good friends. As soon as the national learned of Jimmy's admission, it suspended the Amherst chapter's charter for three years, making it plain that once Jimmy had graduated and the house had not repeated its dereliction, it would be welcomed back into the fold. That way the "brothers" around the country would be spared the taint of having such an "intimate" relationship with a black person. The members of the Amherst chapter responded that they had no interest in being reinstated to such an organization, adopted the new name, and operated thenceforth as a purely local fraternity.

There was humor to be found even in the midst of all this silliness. I had, of course, told my parents the story of my fraternity's rejection by the national, and they were quite pleased that I had chosen to join a more progressive group. On Parents' Weekend of my sophomore year, they attended a reception at the fraternity house, where I introduced them to Jimmy Jackson. I casually said, "Jimmy is our celebrity," assuming they would immediately catch my meaning. I was wrong. My mother looked blankly at Jimmy and asked, "And what are you celebrated for?" Jimmy smiled, stretched himself to his full six-feet-three-inches, and replied, "Well, ma'am, I put the Alpha in Theta Xi."

On another occasion, a member of Delta Kappa Epsilon from a southern school found himself in Amherst one Saturday night, probably visiting a young lady at Smith or Mount Holyoke. He asked for and was quickly given a couch to sleep on in the local DKE house. (It was a tradition for men from other schools who were dating women at Smith or Holyoke to show up late on Saturday night at a dorm or fraternity house at Amherst, where they would be happily accommodated.) Down in the darkened bar of the fraternity house, this young southern gentleman found himself in conversation with a member of the house named Roscoe Lewis. Roscoe was a very light-skinned African American, and in the dark I am sure it was impossible to discern his race. The southerner said, "Hey, I understand you guys pledged a nigger. Would you point him out to me?" (DKE, to its credit, had not kicked the Amherst chapter out for its transgression.) Roscoe, who was also a very tall fellow, pulled himself up to his full height and said, with exquisite grammatical precision, "Sir, I am he."

As my time at Amherst wore on, I had the opportunity to meet the parents of many of my friends and acquaintances. Most of the parents I met were from New York or New England, from which the Amherst student body was then still predominantly drawn. A pattern swiftly developed to our conversations, though there were exceptions, of course. As soon as the parent learned that I was from Virginia, he or she would give me a stern lecture about how badly we treated our Negroes down there, as if this had never crossed my mind. They were as good as anyone, I was told, and had a right to go to school with whites. The lecture, however, almost always ended with words to the effect of "Of course, I wouldn't want to live next door to one or have my daughter marry one." I came to wonder if these people could actually hear what they were saying. After a while, I decided to counter with a little attempted humor. Why, I would ask innocently, weren't black people entitled to live wherever they wanted, and why shouldn't anyone be allowed to marry whomever he or she pleased? At this point the parent would look at me very seriously and ask, "Do you have a sister?" "Yes," I would say, "I have a sister." "You wouldn't want her to marry one, would you?" I would respond that my sister's choice of a husband was her business, and that my only criteria were that he love her and treat her well. That always put an end to the conversation. The parent would need to refresh a drink or would see some long-lost friend across the room.

The sad part of all this was that the parents and the members of the all-white fraternities would have roundly and sincerely denied that there was any racism at all in their attitudes. Only the long, and still continuing, national dialogue sparked by the *Brown* decision has illuminated the layers of unconscious racism with which even the best-intentioned among us are burdened.

In the spring of my junior year, groups of young African Americans in several southern cities began "sit-ins" at drug-store lunch counters to protest the refusal of these facilities to serve black customers. Their protest movement resonated deeply with many young people all around the country. One evening I was discussing the sit-ins with two friends, Peter Berek and Harold Varmus. The three of us were the top officers of the *Amherst Student*. Harold was the editor-in-chief, and Peter and I were the two principal deputies. We were disappointed by what we saw as the utter failure of the Eisenhower administration to support civil rights. We came up with the idea of a peaceful demonstration at the White House to express our solidarity with the blacks seeking equal treatment. We publicized the idea in the *Student*, which sparked a lively debate on campus.

The demonstration idea went forward, a date was chosen, and somehow

I wound up in charge of logistics. We had some 200 Amherst students and another 50 or so from other schools. I had to find enough cars to transport the group to Washington and back and enough beds for them to sleep in. Several faculty members offered to let us use their cars. I contacted the Amherst Alumni Association in Washington, and they eagerly took care of finding places for many of the students to stay. The faculty and alumni reaction was overwhelmingly positive and very heartwarming. I recall approaching Henry Steele Commager, the best known historian on the faculty, to see if he would let us use his car. He said he would like to help but his insurance would not cover our use of the car. As we were gathering in front of the college library to caravan down to Washington, Professor Commager and his wife, who was a lovely lady from an upper-crust South Carolina family, came tootling up. She presented us with a very large batch of homemade baked goods and apologized for not letting us use their car, saying, "I told Henry I just couldn't let you all go down there empty-handed."

I was also in charge of getting a parade permit from the Washington police. We were determined to look like a serious adult group, so we required all those participating in the march to wear jackets and ties, and we designated one person to be the lone spokesman to the press. Dressed up and carrying picket signs calling on the government to come to the aid of the blacks, we marched silently up and down the sidewalk between the White House and Lafayette Park for several hours. When it was over, the police captain who had issued us a permit came over, shook my hand, gave me his card, and said, "If you ever want to come back, we'd be happy to have you."

The 1960s became known as a decade filled with demonstrations and riots on all sorts of subjects, but our march took place on April 18, 1960, and it was then a very unusual event. We got a lot of media coverage; the *New York Times* ran a picture of the march—in which I was identifiable—on its front page above the fold. Some of the alumni expressed joy that what they called the "silent generation" was beginning to speak up.

The march—or at least my role in it—caused a bit of a ruckus in my family. As I said above, my parents were the only ones in the family with a progressive outlook on racial and civil rights issues. Through a bit of bad luck, I happened to call my parents to tell them of the march and to ask them to put up several marchers right in the middle of a family gathering. My news did not go over well. After the march my mother rather puckishly asked Miss Nettie if she had seen me walking in front of the White House on the local TV newscast. She replied, "I did not, thank God!"

❖   ❖   ❖

One of my happiest memories from college days is of my ride back to school at the beginning of sophomore year. Once again, my father and I drove up together, but this time we gave a ride to my friend Ed Barber, who also lived in Northern Virginia. Ed had a singing voice as good as my father's, and for almost the entire time in the car the two of them sang old songs, while I listened, enchanted.

❖   ❖   ❖

As my second year at Amherst wore on, I was increasingly troubled by a sense that my high-school girlfriend, Ginny Anderson, and I were moving in very different directions. She was attending Madison College (later James Madison University) in Harrisonburg, Virginia. Madison's student body was then all female, and the school's avowed mission was to turn out elementary and secondary school teachers. The atmosphere was very southern, the academics were not very challenging, and Ginny did not seem to be experiencing the sort of intellectual awakening that I was undergoing at Amherst. Nor did it help our relationship that we were several hundred miles apart for most of the year and that long-distance telephone calls were then relatively expensive and viewed—by our families, at least—as a major extravagance.

I didn't date anyone during sophomore year, but once again, more or less to please my parents, I got a blind date for prom weekend. My close friend, then and to this day, Peter Berek had a cousin, Lillian Sharf, who was then a freshman, I think, at Hunter College in New York. Peter fixed me up with her, and to my surprise I had a wonderful time all weekend. This changed things between Ginny and me.

That summer my parents and sister took an extended trip by car through the South to Mexico, then to California and back East. Because of my father's previous heart attack, I went along for part of the trip to do most of the occasionally arduous driving from Virginia to Mexico City. I flew back from there while my parents and sister continued on, as I had a summer job and needed the money. I was gone for about three weeks, and thus Ginny and I had less time together that summer than we ordinarily would have. She noticed a change in my demeanor, and I confessed to having developed something of a crush on my prom date. Ginny and I did not formally break up before I left, but things were rocky between us, and I determined that I would now embrace an active social life in college.

As soon as we returned to school, I told Peter Berek, then my roommate, that I was definitely interested in seeing more of his cousin. Very shortly thereafter he and I hitchhiked to New York City one Friday afternoon, and I stayed with him and his parents in Brooklyn and had a date with Lillian that Saturday night. I thought it went quite well, and she seemed to share my interest in seeing more of each other. I was surprised, then, when a couple of weeks later Peter said that he had been deputized by his family to tell me that her parents did not want Lillian dating anyone who was not Jewish and that I should leave her alone. I felt sorry for Peter, for it must have been a very awkward and difficult assignment, one which he handled with sensitivity and aplomb. I wasn't crushed—and I certainly wasn't interested enough in Lillian to want to buck such strong family feelings—but I felt for the first time something of the sting of discrimination that exclusionary practices always entail.

Especially after this rebuff, I was determined to create for myself something of a swinging social life. As it turned out, September 19, 1959, was one of the most important days of my life, though I didn't know it then, or for some time thereafter. I was the president of an organization called Sphinx, which was the honorary society for juniors at Amherst, one of whose traditional activities was to help with freshman orientation. The group annually cosponsored a mixer at Smith for freshmen at the two schools. So I spent the early part of that Saturday evening herding several busloads of Amherst freshmen over to Northampton. There was recorded dance music at the mixer, and I spent at least two hours doing what I saw as my duty—approaching every terrified-looking Smith freshman with no one to talk to and asking her to dance. Chatting away as best I could, I encountered a number of the most monosyllabic women I have ever met. Finally, I decided I had done enough, and I sat down to rest next to the punch bowl, which was being worked by a very attractive young dark-haired woman, who turned out to be a junior at Smith. Her roommate, she told me, was part of the organization at Smith that was helping to put on the mixer, and the roommate had talked her into coming and serving punch. Her name was Louise Merrill and she was from Tacoma, Washington. I chatted with her for a long time, enjoying myself enormously, and the two of us danced and listened to the live entertainers who performed late in the evening. I really wanted to ask her out, but I was too shy. So we parted at the end of the mixer.

As I was walking down the stairs to leave, I experienced a life-changing moment. Cursing my shyness, I told myself that if I was ever going to be

My Amherst College picture at age 19.

Louise's Smith College picture
at about the time I met her.

the swinger I wanted to be, I had to learn to take my chances when they presented themselves. I turned around and retraced my way back up the stairs, going against the heavy traffic like a salmon swimming upstream to spawn. Fortunately, I found Louise still there, and I breathlessly said, "Want to go to the football game next Saturday?" She said it sounded like a nice idea but she had to check with her roommate. I must have shown that I was puzzled by this, so she explained that they had tentative plans to go to her roommate's parents' home in Vermont the following weekend. She ultimately accepted my invitation, and that was both the beginning and the end of my swinging social life.

The following Saturday Louise and I had a thoroughly traditional Smith-Amherst date. We went to the football game, had dinner in the dining hall (they did try to improve things a bit on Saturday nights), and then went back and hung out at my fraternity house. I had a great time and would almost certainly have asked her out again anyway, but the clincher was that she beat me in ping pong. I couldn't let that go unavenged, so I asked her out again the next weekend. With one exception, I never had a date with another woman.

I found Louise delightful, a breath of fresh air, and I soon was wandering around whistling the old tune, "Every Little Breeze Seems to Whisper Louise." She was extremely bright and shared many of my intellectual interests. Our conversations and letters to each other were full of talk about religion, philosophy, history, literature, and contemporary politics. She was herself a National Merit Scholar, and she was a good sport, a fine athlete, and very competitive. In addition to our running ping pong matches, she would come over to Amherst early on nice weekend days and beat my friends at tennis, which was her principal sport, and at which she was quite good.

My final date with someone else occurred one weekend in the late fall of that year. Perhaps to show that she was not totally committed, Louise announced one day that she was going to Harvard the following weekend to see some guy she had gone to high school with. I was stung, and I retaliated by asking one of my friends to get me a blind date for the same evening. I had an okay time with this young lady, another Smith junior, who as I recall was very funny, but I was not smitten. (Even if I had been, it was a non-starter, as I learned years later that she was exclusively a lesbian.) The following weekend I asked Louise out again, half expecting to break up with her. But I was so glad to see her (and I think she felt the same way) and we had such a wonderful time that all was forgiven and we were thenceforth definitely an item.

I gave Louise a long woollen scarf bearing Amherst's purple and white colors that Christmas (getting "scarved" was sort of a sign of "going steady" in those days). She made a Christmas stocking for me and filled it with fun small presents. A few months later I gave her my fraternity pin, and in the spring I took a huge step and invited her to visit me and my family at home in McLean over break. She came, though she stayed with the family of a Smith professor in Washington. My parents instantly loved her. Unfortunately, it was the only time she ever saw my father. He died of cancer that September, just before I returned to school for my senior year.

The following March, on the evening of the day I received a Woodrow Wilson Fellowship to graduate school at Harvard and thus knew I would have enough money to live, I asked Louise to marry me. She said yes, and after we had caught our breath and got over our nervous giggles, we began to discuss a date. Since we were both headed to graduate school in the fall and would probably both be at Harvard, we agreed that early September would be a good time. Then she said, "It will have to be September first, because I know the church is taken on the second." I said, "Wait a minute. I thought this was a surprise!" She *said* she knew the date because a friend of hers was already scheduled to be married in the church the evening of the second.

That night one of Louise's close friends at Smith said she knew something big must have happened because we were holding hands when I dropped her off at her house.

✧　✧　✧

One of the subsidiary benefits of dating Louise for all of my last two years in college was that I became practically an honorary member of Chapin House, her dormitory at Smith. She was part of an extremely close-knit group of friends in her class at Chapin House, and they became my good buddies as well. Indeed, we are still in close touch with a number of them.

As a regular couple Louise and I were often importuned to "fix up" one of her friends or mine with a blind date. We did this fairly often, with complete lack of success. Well, almost complete lack of success. We brokered a date senior year between Ed Barber and Edie Smith, one of Louise's close Chapin House friends. They both enjoyed the experience and said they would like to see each other again. A couple of weeks later Ed called and asked Edie for a date on a coming Saturday night. Edie had two big papers due the following Monday, so she said she would love to see him but would have to pass on that particular evening. Ed began looking for a blind date. It turned out that the Saturday night in question was part of a big dance weekend at Smith. Edie's roommate, Ellen Stover, had a date with an Amherst student who, unbenownst to either of them, was a fraternity brother and good friend of Ed's. Ellen's date began putting pressure on her to find a blind date for a friend of his. Ellen put the arm on Edie, very hard. Edie at first refused, but then relented, saying she could spare only the time of the actual dance itself. That Saturday, I arrived at Chapin House in the middle of the afternoon to hang out with Louise. Edie came up to me in a panic and asked, "Who is a senior History major in Phi Psi?," explaining that that was all she knew about her new blind date. I knew several, but I told her, correctly, "The only one it could be is Ed Barber." So she had a few hours to think of how to handle the situation. When Ed, who knew nothing about his blind date except that she was a member of Chapin House and a friend of Ellen Stover's, arrived with his fraternity brother, Edie went up to him and said, "I'm Mary Smith. I think you have met my twin sister Edie"—a pretty good attempt at saving face, I thought. Ed, who had been terrified in his turn that he would run into Edie, said, "Sure, sure," and grabbed some dressed-up freshman who was waiting for her date and dragged her toward his car, with her protesting all the way. After the embarrassment was over, Ed and Edie confessed what had happened and enjoyed each other's company again. They continued to date for a while, even sporadically after college, but they ultimately went their separate ways.

Among my fondest memories of Chapin House was an evening in which I found myself in an intense debate with the house's resident faculty member, Helen Bacon, who was in the economics department and was very conservative. The McCarthy era in American politics was a recent and vivid memory, and though the redbaiting fervor of the late 1940s and early 1950s had begun to wane, the House UnAmerican Activities Committee still cut a powerful swath. Miss Bacon was a supporter of HUAC and rather inclined to find communists in all sorts of places. I had grown up watching Richard Nixon, Joe McCarthy, and HUAC strike terror into the hearts of government officials like my father, who never knew when their loyalty— and hence employability—would be called into question because of some ancient friendship or association with a person or group now thought to be too radical. I thought that the demands of political conformity imposed by the anticommunist crusade undermined our freedoms and said so. We argued in polite but intense terms for an hour or more in the parlor at Chapin House with a large number of the student residents listening and occasionally chiming in. Many of the women came up to me afterward to say they agreed with my position.

❖   ❖   ❖

The fall of my junior year was the occasion for a pleasant and exciting brush with celebrity. The great American poet, Robert Frost, had a long and close connection to Amherst, having taught there for a number of years, and he returned every year to deliver a talk—and to "say" some of his poems—in Johnson Chapel. (He hated the term "read" in this context.) In 1959 the United States Information Agency was doing a film on Frost for overseas consumption. The filmmakers accompanied Frost to Amherst in the fall, where they wanted to film him talking to a small group of students in a seminar-like setting. I was invited by the English Department, along with several others, including Peter Berek, to take part in the filming. It was certainly an enjoyable experience, though I have no idea whether any of it made it past the cutting-room floor. I still have my copy of Frost's poems that he autographed for me on that occasion.

The session showed that Frost could be quite contrary when he wanted to. The director told us that he had once heard Frost talking about George Washington and had been very unhappy that no camera was trained on him at the moment. He encouraged us to ask questions that would lead Frost to enlarge on his views of our first president. Frost, I think, had wind of this and was determined not to be drawn in. No matter how we phrased the question, Frost would turn it aside with some answer that pointed in another direction. I don't know whether the director ever captured Frost on film on the subject of General Washington.

❖ ❖ ❖

The evening I arrived home at the end of my junior year, my parents told me that my father had been diagnosed with colo-rectal cancer and would be operated on in a few days. I knew that his health had been gradually going downhill since his heart attack in the fall of 1956, but I was shocked nonetheless. They put a hopeful face on it, but I saw through the brave front and was very discouraged. After the operation the surgeon said he thought he had excised the entire tumor, but my father remained in a good deal of pain, and it soon became clear that the cancer had metastasized and spread to his liver and other organs. His doctor did not give him long to live.

As I have written above, it was a rough summer for all of us, though one that brought me closer than ever to my father. Dad was dying, and I am sure he knew it, though the doctors kept up a cheerful front with him. Since he could not sleep at night and craved company, my mother and I would each take a four-hour shift talking to him each night. She was also trying to run the house on her crutches, while I was working all day at my summer job and doing the shopping and laundry. We were both exhausted. My sister Liz, who was not yet fourteen, was very close to Dad and was very scared, but she pitched in as best she could with the housework and nursing.

There was tension in the extended family, as my father's sister Janey, who was an incorrigible alcoholic and barbiturate addict, came totally unglued and accused my mother and me of not seeing that Dad got proper medical care. She in effect forced people in the family to take sides, and as a result for several years I was estranged from my grandmother, who was never able to face Janey down on any issue. Janey also poisoned my hitherto close relationship with my great-uncle Dodson, though his wife Mary Frances continued to be the soul of kindness to my mother, my sister, and me. My Aunt Rosamae and Uncle Bob stood staunchly by us, as did their daughter June and her family. The day before he died, my father, whom we had tried to shield from all this turmoil, said to my mother, "Now you can tell all of them to go to hell." My daily correspondence with Louise sustained me through this terrible period.

Adding to the strain of the summer was real financial concern. Medical expenses were heavy, and my father's impending death would mean the end of his retirement pay, though my mother would still receive a much-reduced widow's pension. Tuition, room, and board at Amherst had gone up to almost $1,900, and my National Merit Scholarship covered barely half of the cost. Mother simply did not have the remaining money to send me back to school. Swallowing pride and bowing to necessity, I wrote a letter to one of the assistant deans at Amherst, John Esty, with whom I had had very pleasant interactions, explaining the situation and asking if I could apply for additional financial aid from the college. By return mail I received a hand-typed reply from him that he had stayed late to get out, assuring me that Amherst would make it possible for me to return, but suggesting that I first approach the National Merit Scholarship Corporation about an increase in my stipend. So I wrote another letter to the NMSC explaining my situation and asking whether there was a procedure by which I could apply for additional funds. Again virtually by return mail I received a letter from the NMSC doubling my stipend to $2,000, with nothing asked beyond the letter I had already sent. I was deeply moved by these responses, and they have played a major role in channeling my charitable giving throughout my adult life.

My father died on September 12, 1960, a scant few days before I was scheduled to report for my senior year. I still don't know what I would have done had he lingered longer. I could not in good conscience have left Mother and Liz to cope with the mess at home. As it was, I still was uncertain about going back, but Mother insisted. I asked one of my father's closest friends, Toby Shipp, who had been a rock throughout this ordeal, to drive me back to school.

I was glad to have a lot of work to throw myself into at school and even gladder to see Louise, who hugged me a lot that fall.

❖   ❖   ❖

My biggest project at school was my senior thesis. I was a candidate for honors in the History Department, and all honors candidates were then required to produce a senior thesis based on original research. I had chosen to major in history, even though I also had enough credits in English to satisfy the major requirement, for two reasons: first, the History Department would let me do the kind of thesis I wanted to do, viewing some literary figure against the backdrop of his or her times, while the English Department was heavily oriented toward the "new criticism," which insisted upon focusing on the text of a piece of literature in isolation; and second, I had decided that I wanted to work with one of the history professors, John Halsted, from whom I had already taken several courses. It was a choice that has continued to pay dividends throughout my life. Halsted, whose field was 19th-century European history, had done his Ph. D. thesis on Walter Bagehot, a major commentator on political, social, and cultural trends in Victorian England, and Bagehot's many essays constituted a veritable fount of potential thesis topics. More important, John Halsted is one of the most intelligent, kindest, most balanced people it has been my pleasure to know, and we have remained in touch throughout the more than 45 years since my graduation.

After reading numerous Bagehot essays on figures in Victorian England, I decided to do a study of Arthur Hugh Clough, a poet in whom many—including Thomas Arnold, the legendary headmaster of Rugby; his son Matthew, the great poet who was Clough's closest friend; Ralph Waldo Emerson; and Alfred Lord Tennyson—had seen the promise of greatness, but who never quite joined the pantheon of truly outstanding poets of his age. He seemed paralyzed by a kind of introspective doubt, caught between a desire to remain a believing Christian and the empirical scientific spirit of his times, exemplified by Charles Darwin, whom Clough knew, and unable to shake his revulsion at what he saw as the hypocrisy of the self-styled Evangelicals who so thoroughly exploited the capitalist system in pursuit of worldly wealth.

I buried myself in Clough's charmingly ironical introspective poetry, his voluminous letters to family and friends, and the many views of him expressed by his contemporaries. He had a burst of creative activity during and after his time at Balliol College, Oxford, but seemed at some point to give up, took a humdrum job in the Education Department, and supported the efforts of Florence Nightingale, whose niece he married, to bring better medical and nursing care to the Crimean War front.

One of Clough's problems as a poet was his firm belief that dactylic hexameter, the meter of much classical Greek and Latin poetry, could be made to sustain narrative poetry in English. Clough's long poem, *The Bothie of Tober-na-Vuolich*, proved that he was wrong. (If any further proof be needed, I suggest the works of Longfellow.) The meter is simply too sing-song and draggy to work in our strange language.

From my personal perspective, the thesis was a great success. For one thing, it took my mind off my sadness over the death of my father. I learned a tremendous amount about Victorian England. I also explored some aspects of the connection between doubt and action, skepticism and creativity. At times I saw a lot of Clough in myself. I had the experience of doing original research and drawing my own conclusions from the evidence. And I thoroughly enjoyed the long talks with John Halsted, whose gentle guidance and careful editorial suggestions were a vital help.

The final draft of my thesis was almost exactly a hundred pages long, and I asked Louise, who was an excellent typist, if she would type it for me. I fully intended to pay her, but when she was done, I had no money. So I used to tell her that I married her because I couldn't afford her typing fee.

❖ ❖ ❖

Naturally, a major preoccupation of senior year was figuring out what to do with my wonderful Amherst education. When I was in high school my immersion in forensic activities and the heady presence nearby of most of the federal government, especially the Congress, led me to think that I wanted to be a lawyer and perhaps someday run for elective office. It had not yet dawned on me that my solidly liberal views, especially on racial issues, would disqualify me for any such office in staunchly conservative Virginia, which was the only place I had any roots or family. During most of my time at Amherst I put aside any thoughts of the long-range future and simply let the pleasures of liberal education wash over me. I had now reached the point where I could no longer postpone serious thinking about my career.

At Amherst my role models were my professors, and I had come to know and admire a number of them—John Halsted, Theodore Baird, Bucky Salmon, Renaissance historian Richard Douglas, and in my last two years, American Literature professor Leo Marx. I enjoyed both the life of the mind and the lifestyle of a small liberal-arts campus. I could see myself as a professor in a small school like Amherst. So I decided to apply to graduate school.

The question was in what field? European and especially English history had been my principal interest for most of my time at Amherst. But I had thoroughly enjoyed my three courses with Professor Marx, the last a seminar in which I wrote two papers that engaged my interest a great deal. The first was a critique of a draft chapter of Marx's book on the pastoral theme in American literature. The book was later published under the title *The Machine in the Garden.* I was genuinely heartened and flattered when the professor praised my critique and incorporated some of my suggestions in a revised draft. For the second paper I read most of the major works of William Faulkner. As a southerner who detested slavery and the racial oppression that had followed its abolition, but who also saw some aspects of gentility and nobility in the civilization of the South, I was deeply conflicted. I had no illusions about white racism in the South—or in the North for that matter—but I felt an urge to explain through works of literature the good and bad strands of southern culture. Thus I made a last-minute switch in my program. I applied for graduate study, not in history or English, but in the interdisciplinary field of American Civilization.

I do not now recall how many or which graduate schools I applied to, but I knew from the beginning that my sights were set on Harvard. More sophisticated students now understand that few universities have strong programs across the board and that some of the best departments exist in universities that are not ranked at the top overall. But I had absorbed in my years at Amherst the sense that Harvard represented the acme of academic excellence, and I knew that the American Studies movement had originated at Harvard. So all my emotional eggs at least were in the Harvard basket.

I was fortunate to be admitted to Harvard's relatively small American Civilization program and to receive a Woodrow Wilson National Fellowship. The Woodrow Wilson program was almost as new as the National Merit Scholarship program had been when I was coming out of high school. It offered full tuition and a $1,500 stipend. As I said before, I proposed to Louise the night I learned that I had this munificent sum to live on my first year after college. As things turned out, she was admitted to Radcliffe (then technically still separate from Harvard, though the students attended the same courses), but interestingly she switched from American Studies, her undergraduate major, to history, and she received a fellowship that provided full tuition plus $600. So we would have a total of $2,100 to live on in our first year of marriage. I hoped it would be enough.

As I left Amherst, I looked forward to marriage, to a new intellectual experience, and to living a new lifestyle on our meager joint income.

❖   ❖   ❖

I should close by saying that several of my teachers at Amherst, including John Halsted, predicted that I would dislike graduate school and that I would not be able to replicate the warm, friendly, collegial atmosphere of a place like Amherst. I smiled but ignored them. After all, all of them had made it through. I had no clue how right they were.

CHAPTER SIX

Marriage, Graduate School, and Journalism
1961-1964

Louise and I graduated from college the same weekend in June 1961. It was the first time I had met most of her family, and the weekend was full of introductions and get-togethers. The following weekend we attended a large reunion of her mother's family (Louise's mother was the youngest of five siblings) at the beach cottage of her Aunt Louise and Uncle George Clapp in Avalon, New Jersey. I felt fully welcomed and really enjoyed my prospective new relatives, though Aunt Louise later said she was worried about the future of our marriage because Louise did not make my bed when we arrived!

The summer seemed to me to drag on. Louise was in Tacoma, and I was in McLean, and I wanted nothing more than to be with her. Again, we corresponded virtually every day, but it wasn't the same as being together. Being home also meant that I missed my father more. I had a summer job at the Pentagon in his old area, and I found what little work I could do interesting, but it was mostly makework. At long last it was time to leave for the wedding.

We—Liz, best man Cush Anthony, usher Ed Barber, and I—arrived in Tacoma two or three days before the wedding, having driven across the country in my mother's car. Mother had planned to come with us, but she fell and broke her hip the morning we were scheduled to leave. She had to have surgery and flew out later, accompanied by Uncle Vic, arriving the night before the wedding.

There was one embarrassing thing about getting married in Washington State. I had to get a note from my mother to do it. I was only twenty years old, while my bride was an ancient twenty-one. In Washington a woman was legally emancipated at age eighteen and hence could make all her major life decisions for herself. But a man was not emancipated until he was twenty-one. Thus when we applied for our marriage license, I had to present a letter from my mother signifying her permission. I got over it. (Many years later, when I was teaching Constitutional Law, I would point to this as an obvious instance of gender discrimination, but ask the students which

Louise's wedding picture.

sex was getting the short end of the stick.)

All went smoothly at the wedding, though my prospective father-in-law took me out to lunch on The Day (the ceremony was at 8 p.m.), plied me with bourbon, presumably to steady my nerves, and then gave me a major tour of the Tacoma area, of which he was quite proud. When we hadn't returned by 4 p.m., Louise's mother was ready to send out the army looking for us.

Louise and I began our honeymoon in a cottage on Hood Canal that belonged to a friend of Louise's family. It was a beautiful spot, but we stayed only the weekend, as we were planning to drive my mother's car back across the country. We had breakfast Sunday in a rustic little restaurant in the woods and took great delight in the fact that, to keep out the bright sunlight, the owners had pinned in the window a page from the bridal section of the newspaper with Louise's picture on it. When we left Tacoma, Louise's mother said in a forlorn voice, "Have a nice life." Our trip across country was wonderful, and we arrived in McLean in time to stay a day or two before heading for Cambridge and graduate school.

❖ ❖ ❖

My introduction to Harvard was not prepossessing. I had been warned not to expect the kind of close and supportive relations with faculty members I had experienced at Amherst, but I was not ready for the speech the dean of the Graduate School of Arts and Sciences gave to the assembled new students. "You may think," he said, "you are here to continue your education. You are not. You are here to get a degree. Get A's and get out!" It may have been good advice, but it jarred my sensibilities quite severely.

I was assigned a faculty advisor, who gave me about three minutes of his time and perfunctorily approved my proposed schedule without bothering to tell me that it would not make me eligible for a master's degree at the end of the year. To get a master's I needed two seminars. I thought I was signed up for two, but one of them was the year-long introductory seminar required of all entering American Civilization graduate students, which it turned out did not count for some reason as a seminar, even though we had to produce not one but two fairly substantial papers. When I sought to rectify this by taking a second seminar in the spring semester, I was told by the bureaucracy that no one was allowed to take two seminars in a single semester.

I found graduate school at Harvard a dispiriting, almost anti-intellectual experience. For the most part I sat in huge lecture classes with hordes of Harvard undergraduates (more than 300 students in one course). With one exception, the Harvard faculty I encountered made it perfectly plain that they wanted nothing to do with students. And almost everyone I met seemed terribly self-important. I was not a happy camper.

The one professor whom I found welcoming and encouraging was named William Taylor, and he was a student of southern literature, which I hoped to make my field. I had numerous talks with him in his office and liked him a great deal. The experience that ultimately soured me irretrievably on Harvard involved him.

The American Civilization seminar was taught by the famous scholar Perry Miller, who claimed, with some justification, that he had invented the interdisciplinary field. The first important document in the American Civilization movement was Henry Nash Smith's book *The Virgin Land*, which began life as a Ph.D. dissertation under Miller's supervision. *The Virgin Land* was a study of numerous late 19th-century Western novels and what they revealed about attitudes and trends in America at the time. Miller talked about it a lot.

In 1961 Miller was in his late sixties or early seventies, he drank a lot, and he was well past his prime. In the middle of the academic year, William Taylor published a book called *Cavalier and Yankee*, which was a study of pre-Civil War novels from the North and the South and the attitudes they revealed about sectional differences. It owed a lot in conception to *The Virgin Land*. Taylor was up for tenure, and this was his obligatory book. I read it when it came out and thought it was very well executed. Shortly after I read it, the book was reviewed in the *New York Times* by Perry Miller, who savaged it, thus effectively ending Taylor's chances for tenure at Harvard.

(Taylor went on to a fine career at, I believe, Minnesota.) I was upset, and I decided to stick it to Miller a little. One of the exercises in Miller's seminar required the students to write papers on some of the major works of the American Civilization movement. I had drawn *The Virgin Land*. I did what I thought was a workmanlike analysis of the book, and then I closed the paper with a comparison of it with *Cavalier and Yankee* in which I said a lot of nice things about the latter. The students in the seminar read their papers aloud as a prelude to discussion. When I finished reading mine, Miller said, "Well, well, what you say is very interesting. I'll have to reread *Cavalier and Yankee*. I haven't read it since it was a dissertation eight years ago." I almost fell out of my chair. It was inconceivable to me that someone of Miller's stature, whose opposition could doom a person's career at Harvard, would trash a tenure book that he had not read in eight years and that had probably changed a great deal since it was submitted as a dissertation. I am still furious as I write this more than 45 years later.

Shortly after this incident, I decided to leave Harvard and quit graduate school. I made the decision on my twenty-first birthday, January 8, 1962, as I was pulling on my pants in the morning and listening to the stirring *coda* of the last movement of the *Eroica*. I suddenly said, "I don't have to take this [stuff]. There are better things to do with my life." That night over a special birthday dinner, I announced my decision to Louise. She cried but was very supportive. I think she liked graduate school better than I did, though she was not in love with it.

❖ ❖ ❖

Our year at Harvard was schizoid. I came to detest Harvard, graduate school, and Cambridge, in which I was continually getting lost. But I enjoyed the material I studied, and I was extremely happy in my personal life. Louise and I were very much in love. We did virtually everything together. We lived in a pleasant, spacious furnished apartment on the second floor of a large house, which we rented for $90 a month. The landlord, who was about 90 years old, lived on the first floor, and there were two other student apartments in the house.

Because we had the grand total of $2,100 in fellowship money on which to live for the entire year, we made up a strict budget, and we stuck to it religiously. At the beginning of each month, we stuffed a series of marked envelopes with the cash allotted to each category of expenditure. "Haircuts and newspapers" was one; "mad money," for which we did not have to account to each other, was another, though it was tiny, only $5 each. When the cash was gone from the envelope, we spent no more on the particular kind of item until the money had been replenished at the start of the next month.

We enjoyed the cultural life of Cambridge and the Boston area, attending plays and concerts. We got to know Louise's father's cousin, Helene Lee, a Mount Holyoke graduate who had spent her career in nursing administration. Cousin Helen, as we called her, was then well into her seventies and had never married. She lived in her family's old house (vintage 17th century) in Peabody, and she came into the city quite often. Despite her sheltered, spinster existence, she believed in "exposing herself" to all sorts of modern trends in music, art, and the stage. She was extremely kind and generous to us and took us to a number of events.

We wrote letters to our families regularly (there wasn't much room for long-distance calls in our budget), and we saw a lot of our college friends, some of whom were studying at Harvard or MIT and some working in the area.

So, aside from my unhappy experience at Harvard, it was a year of which I have many fond memories.

❖ ❖ ❖

Having reached a negative decision to leave graduate school, I faced the question of what I wanted to do next. I still felt a keen interest in public affairs, and as I thought about it, my best and most marketable skill seemed to be my ability to write. I devoured newspapers and in particular their editorial pages. I decided to try my hand at journalism. Having not a clue about how one entered the field, I compiled a list of the best newspapers around the country, probably about twenty in number, and wrote each of them a letter of application describing my education, my skills, and my interests. I got only three responses. An editor at the *Boston Globe* called me in for an interview, but said that they would not consider hiring me without experience elsewhere. He suggested that I apply to one of the suburban papers in the Boston area and come back to see him in a couple of years. The *Providence Journal*, which had perhaps the only real training program for aspiring newspaper writers in the country, offered me a place at a salary of $75 a week. And the *New York Times* offered me a job as a copy boy in its newsroom at $60 a week. The *Times* had a practice of hiring graduates of top colleges as copy boys and promoting them slowly through the ranks.

I had no interest in working for a suburban Boston area paper, especially as I never felt comfortable in Boston or Cambridge. The choice was between the *Providence Journal* and the *New York Times*. Louise and I talked it over. At the *Journal* I would be covering stories sooner, and it paid twenty-five per cent more than the *Times*. On the other hand, neither of us particularly wanted to live in Providence. New York was a much more attractive place, where many of our friends from college had settled, and the job market for Louise would be much better there. Plus, it *was* the *Times*. So I signed on to be a copy boy, starting in mid-June.

We found an apartment on the bustling upper East Side of Manhattan, a fourth-floor walkup in a converted brownstone at 406 E. 83rd Street, which we rented for $125 a month. It had only one bedroom and was much smaller than our Cambridge apartment, but it was very convenient, the building had recently been redone, and the neighborhood, which was called Yorkville and which retained a lot of the flavor of its history as a home for German and Czech immigrants, was good. Before I had encountered the realities of the job market, we had bought a car on the assumption that I would need to be able to drive myself to reporting assignments. It was a horrible old clunker of a Plymouth. It broke down on our first scouting trip from Cambridge to New York, and of course, it was utterly useless in the city, particularly in my new life as a copy boy. Even after we had it repaired, it refused to haul our rented trailer down to New York, so we had to rent a car to pull the rented trailer. After several months of moving it from side to side of the street to comply with the alternate-side street-cleaning rules, we sold it to the superintendent of our building for $50.

We had no furniture and no money with which to buy any. So we borrowed an old daybed from one of Louise's Smith friends and slept on it (and sat on it and ate on it) until we had a few paychecks under our belts. Louise soon found a job as an assistant librarian at the American Newspaper Publishers Association (ANPA) Foundation. I went to work as a lowly copy boy.

❖ ❖ ❖

I don't think newspapers have copy boys any more, but in the days before computers and modems, reporters would compose their stories on typewriters, using carbon paper to make enough copies for all the editors who had to review the story plus one for the reporter to keep. When the reporter was finished with a draft of all or a portion of the story, he or she (then mostly he) would rip it out of the typewriter, mark where it was to go, toss it in an out-basket, and yell, "Copy!" A copy boy would come running over, pick up the papers and distribute them to the appropriate recipients. Sometimes one or more editors, having made suggested corrections, would forward them to the editor with the final say, again via copy boy/carrier pigeon. Copy boys also had other duties of a general gofer nature.

My first evening on the job—things didn't really heat up until the late afternoon at morning newspapers like the *Times*—I arrived, I think, around 6 p.m. The man in charge of the copy boys was a diminutive Irishman named Steve, who was almost completely inarticulate, or at least spoke with an impenetrable (to me) New York accent that amounted to the same thing. He showed me what to do, and I happily stumped around the newsroom for an hour and a half or so. Around 7:30 Steve called me over and told me to go get "danoose and damirrahs." I hadn't the foggiest notion what he was talking about. I interrogated him for a few minutes, translating feverishly as best I could, and finally figured out that there was a newsstand nearby that set aside several copies of the early editions of the *Daily News* and the *Daily Mirror* for the *Times*, presumably so that editors and reporters could look them over to see if the *Times* had missed some important story or an angle on a story. I nervously asked him *which* newsstand I was to go to, recalling that there must have been 30 or 40 of them in Times Square. All he would say, with considerable exasperation at my ignorance, was that it was the one "down in da subway." This was not a lot of help, since there were probably a dozen different subway entrances in Times Square, and at least 25 news-stands underground. Figuring, however, that I had pushed my luck as far as I dared and hoping that I would think of something, I set off into the *terra incognita* that was Times Square in the sweltering heat of a humid summer evening. Close to an hour later, when I was no nearer locating the perti-nent newsstand, Steve sent another copy boy out to find me. He located me wandering aimlessly underground, showed me the proper newsstand, and guided me back to the newsroom. Steve looked at me with withering con-tempt, and I was sure I would be fired on my first day. Fortunately, nothing happened to me.

Even more fortunately, by the end of my first week I was the senior copy boy in the newsroom, as the result of several departures and promo-tions. Within another week a slot had opened up for a news clerk, the next step above a copy boy, and I was promoted. A news clerk was sort of a sit-down copy boy, charged with keeping track of the papers flowing through a given desk and making sure that the editors had what they were supposed to have. The promotion was a godsend, for two reasons. Walking around the newsroom for seven or eight hours a night, coupled with the nightly excursion for danoose and damirrahs, had rendered my leg one large open sore, rubbed constantly by my brace. It was heaven to be able to work sitting down. Equally important, the promotion came with a 50 percent increase in pay, to $90 a week. The raise was withheld during a probationary period of a month or two, but after my work had been approved, the raise was retroactive to my start in the new job. So I got a nice raise and one really fat paycheck.

❖ ❖ ❖

When my big paycheck came through, Louise and I went on a furniture-shopping spree. We bought a hide-a-bed couch so we could have visitors, a comfortable black chair for the living room, and a card table and four chairs for our dining area. We returned the daybed to its owner and made a trip to Villanova, Pennsylvania, to retrieve a very nice double bed and bureau that Louise's Aunt Louise contributed to us. We also bought some unfinished bookshelves and an unfinished chest of drawers, which I spent two or three weeks finishing during the days. A couple of prints from the art shop at the Metropolitan Museum, and we were ready for company!

We had a very active and enjoyable social life in our new city. Louise's Smith roommate, Tina Schafer, and another of her Chapin House friends, Ellen Stover, had taken an apartment a few blocks from us with two other classmates, Julie Kayan and Susie Haller. We visited a lot back and forth with them, and we saw many other friends from college days and earlier. With both of us working, despite our meager individual salaries, we had enough money for occasional evenings on the town, and we actually began to save some for the future.

The major drawback to our life at this point was that we saw much less of each other. Louise had a regular 9 to 5 job, while I was working nights. Moreover, my days off were not always on the weekends. Sometimes, with the connivance of her boss, Louise would sneak out a few minutes early, and we would meet for a cup of coffee somewhere in midtown before I began work. But we were happy, and our confidence was growing.

❖ ❖ ❖

My assignment as a news clerk was to the radio news desk. The *Times* owned a radio station, WQXR, which had a number of affiliates. The radio news desk supplied the WQXR network with hourly five-minute news summaries and a more comprehensive fifteen-minute newscast at 11 p.m. The editor of the radio news desk was an experienced, affable, and relaxed man named Herb, who was very easy to work for. I would get copies of the stories that the *Times* was running, plus wire service stories, sort them, and give them to Herb and the others who worked on the desk. I became friendly with a veteran newsman named George Miller, whose job it was to prepare the 11 o'clock newscast. I would gather all the stories that he might be interested in, sort them in order of apparent importance, and do whatever else he asked me to do. After a while, George offered me the opportunity to draft a few items for the newscast. He would correct my drafts, usually shortening the sentences radically, and go over them with me, teaching me how to write "radio copy." I enjoyed this and appreciated the mentoring. After a while, as George began to trust my writing more and more, it became an arrangement of mutual convenience. George was something of a *bon vivant* and ladies' man, and the hours he put in writing the 11 o'clock newscast cramped his style considerably. My eagerness to write and my progress as a writer gave George some added flexibility in his evenings. I didn't mind, as I was learning a lot.

I did have one other opportunity to exercise my writing skills while at the *Times*. The paper allowed news clerks and copy boys to cover what seemed likely to be major church sermons in the city. They could see if a youngster could write, and if he/she botched the job, it was no great loss. I put my name in the hopper for an assignment. One week I was told to stand by for an assignment that Sunday. I was to call in on Saturday morning. When I called, I was told that the church was at 125th Street and (I think) Fifth Avenue, in the heart of Harlem. It turned out to be a very high Episcopal service to celebrate the independence of Trinidad and Tobago from British rule, and it was attended by lots of diplomats and Caribbean bigshots. I took careful notes on the sermon and attended a reception afterwards. A junior British diplomat, upon learning that I was covering the event for the *Times*, asked me, "Do you specialize in West Indian affairs?" I told him no, that I was just a news clerk trying my wings. He gave me a completely deadeye look and walked away. My story ran in the Monday paper with little or no editing.

❖ ❖ ❖

George Miller made another major contribution to my career. One day over a drink in the fall of 1962 he advised me that I should leave the *Times*. First, he said, career progress at the *Times* was very slow, and it would be years before I could hope to be even a very junior reporter. He urged me to go to one of the wire services, where I could get better experience immediately, and then return to a paper, perhaps even the *Times*, after I had a portfolio of stories. Second, he warned me that the Newspaper Guild was about to go on strike against all seven daily papers in New York, that the strike would likely be protracted, and that I, along with all the *Times'* employees, would be without pay until the strike was over. The Wire Service Guild was not going to strike against the Associated Press or United Press International. George offered to contact people he knew at UPI and recommend me. I thought it over, talked to Louise about it, and took him up on his offer.

George got me an interview with a UPI editor named Don Dillon, who ran the service's international desk. The name "international desk" did not signify that it covered foreign news, but rather that it covered all news for foreign clients. UPI had many clients and bureaus all over the world, and the job of the international desk (code-named NXI) was to gather, edit, and transmit the stories those bureaus and clients would be interested in, with careful attention to the differing deadlines around the world. Don Dillon was a very pleasant man, and he offered me a job at NXI. It even came with another raise to something just above $100 a week.

George Miller was certainly correct in his advice to me. The Guild strike was indeed protracted and bitter, and when it was over, it had killed four of New York's seven daily papers. And my learning curve at NXI was a lot steeper than at the *Times*. Within a very short period of time I was taking a regular turn running the desk's major outgoing wire, which was for some reason called "Bromleigh." It was a radio teletype broadcast that went world-wide. The Bromleigh editor sat in a horseshoe-shaped area surrounded by nine incoming teletype machines. He was responsible for following all the output of those machines, selecting the stories to go out on the big wire, editing them for the international market, determining in which order they would be sent, and feeding them to the teletype operator. He also peeled off stories that were likely to be of interest primarily to European clients and fed them to a separate cable wire to London. It was always a busy and hectic job, but when there was a major breaking story, it was a madhouse, as we had to balance the feed on that story against the somewhat specialized interests of overseas clients and bureaus. Running Bromleigh was further complicated by the vagaries of atmospheric interference with the radio signal. We often got messages that Manila, or Tokyo, or London, or Riyadh had lost a major segment of the broadcast, which had to be repeated as and when we could fit it in.

❖ ❖ ❖

Sometimes the world is a very small place indeed. Don Dillon's immediate boss at UPI was a grizzled veteran reporter, by then a senior editor, named Francis McCarthy. I met him when I started work—indeed, it is possible that I had a *pro forma* interview with him after Don Dillon had recommended my hiring—but we did little more than shake hands. I happened to mention to my mother that the big boss's name was Francis McCarthy. She immediately said, "I'll bet it's the same man who bought you your first pair of shoes." It seems that after we were liberated from Los Baños and moved to the staging camp at Muntinlupa, a wire-service reporter covering the Philippines campaign by the name of Francis McCarthy had taken a shine to me. One day he piled me and some other children into a Jeep and somehow found a place to buy me a pair of canvas shoes. I had had no shoes in Los Baños. After talking to Mother, I went to see Mr. McCarthy, who broke into a huge grin when I told him who I was. He was indeed the same man, and we had a very pleasant talk. He was helpful to me later when I was making a serious career decision.

❖ ❖ ❖

The fall of 1962 produced perhaps the most frightening few days of my adult life. When the United States and the Soviet Union squared off over the latter's placement of missiles in Cuba, it was the closest the world has ever come, thus far at least, to a nuclear holocaust. There was a feeling of absolute helplessness, as the lives of millions of people in both countries— around the world, for that matter—were dependent upon the good sense of a very few men in both camps, and we had no reason to trust those on the other side. Until the Soviets backed down, I kissed Louise goodbye each day on the way to work with real fear that we might never see each other again.

❖ ❖ ❖

At NXI I was learning the valuable skills of editing, rewriting, and news judgment in a situation where I had to exercise those skills under the pressure of time and with a lot on the line. But I still craved opportunities to write my own stories. While NXI was not primarily a news-gathering operation, Don Dillon took care to give me a few chances to write my own material. For a time, I wrote a weekly financial column designed for overseas consumption. I also got to cover some events of interest to some of our foreign clients.

The most memorable of the latter was an interview with then Crown Prince, later King, Faisal of Saudi Arabia. NXI had a special relationship with Saudi Arabia. At the time the giant Arabian-American Oil Company (Aramco) employed thousands of Americans at its pumping and refining operations in the desert of Saudi Arabia. It published a daily newspaper for the benefit of these employees, emphasizing coverage of events in the States, and it had a contract with UPI to provide that coverage. Each day NXI would send a special two-hour radio teletype broadcast, known as the "Saudicast," especially for Aramco. Indeed, I cut my teeth at NXI doing the Saudicast. Every day I would go through what seemed like miles of teletype copy from the "A wire," the main domestic news wire, and elsewhere, select the stories I thought the Aramco employees would be interested in, and then edit them down to a 7,200-word news summary.

I have forgotten now why Crown Prince Faisal, who was the *de facto* head of the Saudi government, came to the United States or even exactly when, but I had been at NXI long enough that Don Dillon trusted me to conduct an interview which, while not earth-shatteringly important, was still of considerable interest to a major client.

I made arrangements for the interview through Faisal's private secretary, a man with the surname of Shawaf. I mention this because it did not register with me at the time that I had known an Arab student at Amherst named Saud Shawaf. Faisal was staying in an enormous suite at the Waldorf-Astoria Hotel. I arrived at the appointed time wearing my best suit, was announced as Mr. Dudley of the United Press International, and was shown into a very large waiting room where a great many Arabs, all of whom I guessed were there to petition the prince for some favor, sat or paced nervously as they awaited an audience. After a while Mr. Shawaf came out and introduced himself. At this very moment I heard from across the room a cry of "Boootch." It was my old college friend Saud, who was Mr. Shawaf's much younger brother. He ran over and gave me a hug, and we chatted for a couple of minutes. I don't think my stature in Mr. Shawaf's eyes was exactly the same after that.

Mr. Shawaf showed me into a cavernous bowling alley of a room, lavishly furnished, where we sat and chatted until the prince entered a few minutes later. While Mr. Shawaf and Saud were dressed in Western suits, Prince Faisal, a tall, gaunt man, was wearing flowing Arab robes and headdress. Though I began to believe as our conversation wore on that Faisal's English was actually very good, the interview was formally conducted through Mr. Shawaf, acting as interpreter. I would ask a question in English, Mr. Shawaf would translate it into Arabic, Faisal would reply in Arabic, and Mr. Shawaf would translate the answer into English. I suspected that this dance was mainly designed to give Faisal extra time to ponder his answers. I no longer remember most of what I discussed with Prince Faisal, but one exchange stands out in my mind. One of the youngest of Faisal's many, many half-brothers (his father the King had many wives) had recently run away from Saudi Arabia to Cairo to sit at the feet of Egypt's President Gamal Abdel Nasser, an Arab socialist who had overthrown King Farouk and was no friend to any Arab royalty. I asked Faisal for a comment on his brother's action. Faisal fully understood my question in English, for it produced an involuntary grunt of dismay before Mr. Shawaf had begun his translation. When Mr. Shawaf had finished, Faisal turned full face to me and flashed me an almost goofy, toothy, false grin. Mr. Shawaf said, "His Majesty is giving you an enigmatic smile." It was time to go.

❖ ❖ ❖

After a year or so at the ANPA, Louise began to look about for something more challenging to do. Her Chapin House friend Ellen Stover was working at the *Ladies Home Journal*, a sister publication of the *Saturday Evening Post*. The latter was then in its heyday as a national magazine that published everything from muckraking journalism to good fiction. Ellen introduced Louise to some of the executives at the *Post*, and she was hired as an assistant editor in the fiction department. Her job was to read the unsolicited short stories that authors submitted for consideration, to flag those that might have some merit, and to send them on to the senior editors. It was a heavenly job for a college graduate in her early twenties who had a keen interest in American literature.

❖ ❖ ❖

As our time in New York wore on, we continued to enjoy almost constant interaction with friends, and as our financial situation continued to improve, we immersed ourselves more in the cultural life of the city, attending plays, concerts, and movies on many of the evenings when I was not working. And we enjoyed baseball. We went to the old Polo Grounds to see Stan Musial, nearing the end of his illustrious career, play against the Mets. He obliged by hitting three home runs. In October 1962 I went to my first World Series game with Ellen Stover, a Yankees fan. Despite Ellen, I cheered Juan Marichal of the San Francisco (*nee* New York) Giants to a shutout of the Yankees. I also attended the Mets' inaugural game at their new home, Shea Stadium in Queens.

We entertained some of our siblings and showed them around New York. My sister Liz visited us in the summer of 1963. We took her on the Circle Line sightseeing boat around Manhattan and that evening to a Broadway play. Not having read the reviews closely, but having seen that it was hailed as a brilliant comedy, I got tickets to Edward Albee's *Who's Afraid of Virginia Woolf?* It *was* a great comedy, but a seriously adult one, which I realized about two minutes into the first act. Liz was not yet seventeen and had led a very sheltered southern life with Mother, who had moved back to Tidewater to be near her sister Monk after Dad died. I leaned over and swore Liz to secrecy about the play. She was happy to comply. On the same visit we took Liz to a performance of *Hamlet* on Broadway starring Richard Burton, Alfred Lunt, and Lynn Fontaine. Burton was playing a dark and brooding Hamlet—quite convincingly—but about an hour into the performance, he walked off the stage in the middle of a scene. Someone came out and announced that Burton had bursitis and was unable to continue and that the theater would offer the patrons a choice between a full refund of their money or tickets to a later performance. We chose the latter, though the later date would mean that Liz would miss the play. Having gotten out early on a mild summer evening, we headed to a nearby sidewalk café. We were with another couple of friends. When the waiter came we ordered four gin and bitter lemons and one straight bitter lemon. Without hesitation the waiter set one of the gin drinks down in front of Liz and the bitter lemon in front of Louise, who at this stage looked like she was under the New York drinking age of eighteen. I don't know which of them was more flattered.

Several weeks later, when Louise and I attended the make-up performance of the play, Burton played a wildly different Hamlet, milking the role for every piece of wit and humor. He was equally convincing. Equally remarkable, the cast around him was so good that they didn't miss a beat.

Louise's brother Gregg and her sister Ros, who was attending Wheaton College in Massachusetts, also visited us in Manhattan. Gregg was about fourteen and we took him to his first major league baseball game. Ros had friends of her own in the city that she sometimes hung out with.

At this time, unsurprisingly, we spent a lot of time going to and participating in weddings of our friends. It was all great fun.

❖ ❖ ❖

By the fall of 1963 I had begun to contemplate my next career move. The learning curve at NXI had flattened considerably, and I did not want to become stuck as a deskman, which was something of a dead-end job. The long-range prospect struck me as boring. I still hankered for the opportunity to be a full-time reporter, but I had begun to have doubts of two kinds about such a path. First, I saw that reporters were on their feet a lot and took a considerable physical beating. I was afraid that my handicap might make this aspect of a journalist's life very difficult. Second, and perhaps more important, I was beginning to feel that I might be better suited temperamentally to a career of advocacy rather than one of observation. Politics was what interested me and what I would want to cover, but I had strong political views and was uncertain about whether I could sustain what I saw as the necessary degree of objectivity. I began to think about law school.

In late October President Kennedy paid a visit to Amherst to dedicate the college's new Robert Frost Library. His speech was scheduled for a Saturday afternoon, and Louise and I decided to go. We spent Friday night in New Haven with my close friend from Amherst, Marty Lowy, and his wife Pam, a Mount Holyoke graduate whom we had known since she and Marty began dating. (I had been an usher in their wedding, a very fancy affair at the Sherry Netherlands Hotel just off Central Park.) Marty was in his first year at Yale Law School, and he was loving it. This was in distinct contrast to my friends who had attended Harvard Law School, all of whom had detested the experience. (This, of course, didn't surprise me, given my views of Harvard.) I listened to Marty talk about his courses and about the intellectual feast he was finding at Yale. I asked a lot of questions, and we stayed up late talking.

❖ ❖ ❖

My most unforgettable day at NXI was November 22, 1963, the day President Kennedy was assassinated. It was after 1 p.m. Eastern Time, and I was looking forward to my relief from Bromleigh at 2:45. It had been a slow news day. NXI was covering the president's political fence-mending trip to Texas, but not in excruciating detail, as it held little interest for our foreign clients. Suddenly we heard five rings, the signal for a bulletin over the A wire. It was a new lead from our White House correspondent, Merriman Smith, to the effect that shots had been fired at the president's motorcade in Dallas. Only a few weeks before, extremists in Dallas had spat upon former Democratic presidential nominee Adlai Stevenson, who was President Kennedy's ambassador to the United Nations. Not realizing that the president had been shot, we shook our heads, and said, "Those crazies in Dallas will do anything." But the A wire desk in New York held the wire open for further developments from Smith. It was not long before we saw "FLASH President Kennedy wounded seriously perhaps fatally" by the attack. Soon Smith had dictated a new lead to the story, confirming that the president was dead.

The news of the assassination hit me, as it did almost everyone, like a punch to the solar plexus. But I had no time to grieve. I was running an international news wire with the biggest story in many years. Given the magnitude and pace of events, there was no time for a transition to a new editor, so I remained in the Bromleigh slot for most of the next shift as well. The next few hours are largely a blur in my memory, but I do recall marveling at the job Merriman Smith was doing. We were several minutes ahead of the AP with the story, and with evening newspapers all over the country on deadline, that was a crucial margin, which resulted in a large majority of those papers running the UPI coverage. I later learned that Smith had been in the "pool car" following the president's limousine and had beaten the AP reporter to the car's lone telephone. He hung onto it and dictated away. What was truly amazing was that he managed over the course of a couple of hours to dictate a coherent and informative story about rapidly breaking events over an open phone line directly to a teletype operator in the Dallas bureau. He received a well-earned Pulitzer prize for his efforts. I simply operated on instinct and somehow made it through the crisis without panicking.

President Kennedy was shot on a Friday. On Sunday I worked the 6 p.m. to 1 a.m. shift. I read up on what had gone out on Bromleigh and took over the desk around 7 o'clock. Within minutes all hell broke loose once again, as Jack Ruby shot and killed Lee Harvey Oswald, the only suspect in the Kennedy assassination, in the basement of the Dallas Police Department, of all places.

Monday was a day of national mourning, and I was off during the day. Louise and I were glued, along with the rest of the nation, to the TV set where the sad ceremony of the president's funeral was broadcast to the world. We watched with several of our friends, all of us weeping. It was a terrible moment for our country, one from which in many ways I think we have never recovered.

For every American of my generation, the assassination of President Kennedy became an indelible, defining moment. All my contemporaries I have ever met can relate exactly where they were and what they were doing when they heard the terrible news. While I was still in the grip of these events, I wrote an account of my day in the newsroom when the president was killed and of what I was feeling at the time and sent it to Amherst, where it was published in the *Alumni News*. This is how I summed up my feelings then:

> I will not dwell on these emotions which all Americans felt on learning the news, except to say that for the second time in my life—and for the second time in two months—I was ashamed for my country. The race riots at the University of Mississippi last year did not fill me with the shame I felt for America upon the occasion of the attack on Adlai Stevenson and the assassination of President Kennedy.
>
> This shame was largely inarticulate. I could find no words to express it. I could only agree dumbly with *New York Times* correspondent James Reston that for one brief and horribly irrevocable moment, "the worst in the nation had triumphed over the best."
>
> Still I could not bring myself to grapple with the reality of the end of this human life. So I turned instead to thoughts more easily handled, thoughts of externals, thoughts of what we—more personally felt, what *I*—had lost....
>
> The only word—perhaps a poor one, certainly an overworked one—of which I could think to describe this loss was "style." ... I am haunted by the recollection of a passage from the talk of Archibald MacLeish on the occasion of the late President's visit to Amherst. Mr. MacLeish said that we should be grateful and proud that "a young

and gallant President of the United States, with the weight of history heavy upon his shoulders, should somehow find time to come to our small corner of the world to talk of books and men and learning."

We should indeed. Mr. MacLeish unwittingly gave expression before the tragic event to the essence of what I think we have lost.

We have lost a young and gallant President. Not that Mr. Johnson is old or ungallant. He is neither. But Mr. Kennedy's youth and gallantry were a special inspiration to the young of this nation and to the would-be gallant of my generation, too many of whom stand bewildered and paralyzed in a seemingly chaotic world.

Nor can any other man carry the weight of history upon his shoulders in the way John Kennedy did. He combined the feel of command with the flavor of grace, the pathos of humanity with the winning flash of humor and the ability to laugh, a broad and educated perspective on our times with an attention to the small details of human needs and deeds in a way that no public figure in my conscious or historical memory has done. On the same trip to Europe he could stand before The Wall and say, "*Ich bin ein Berliner*," and sit in the humble parlor of an aging woman in Ireland and happily eat her homemade cake.

Finally, and perhaps most tragically, we have lost a man who cared enough to come to a small corner of the world and talk of books and men and learning. In honoring Robert Frost, John Kennedy paid homage to the aspirations and values of all of us who love books and men and learning. He carried that tribute into his every act of wisdom, grace, and intellect. For us there will never be another to take his place.

The moment at which the full realization of the finality of this man's passing was borne most piercingly into my consciousness came when the honor guard bearing his flag-draped casket paused on the steps of the Capitol while the Navy band played *Hail to the Chief*. Drained from the always stirring march were all its joy and triumph; it was slow and sad and majestic. The memory of his vitality when they played this song for him so recently at Amherst was almost unbearable.

I for one am grateful and proud that he was our President, even for so tragically short a time.[1]

❖   ❖   ❖

Louise and I talked a lot about my possible career change, but for a time our discussions were inconclusive. Meanwhile, my impulse toward public service (and hence law school) was quickened by the assassination of the president, who had done so much to attract idealistic young people to government service. In December I went to see Don Dillon and Fran McCarthy and told them that I was restless. I asked McCarthy if UPI might have some assignment for me that involved covering politics at least part of the time. He said he would give it some thought and see what he could do. Not too long thereafter, he called me into his office and said that I could have the job of bureau chief (actually, he meant I could *be* the bureau) in Little Rock, Arkansas. I thanked him for his help and said I would think it over.

It was in some ways remarkable that McCarthy was willing to offer this job to someone in his early twenties (I was not yet 23) with no real reporting experience. It was either a testament to his and Don Dillon's confidence in me or an example of UPI's legendary parsimony (I would be a lot cheaper than an experienced reporter)—probably a little of both. It also presented me with a tough decision. One the one hand, Little Rock was likely to be a news hotspot as the sixties wore on. It was a southern capital city, a hotbed of racial controversy, where the governor, Orval Faubus, had been for almost a decade one of the firebrands of the segregationist backlash to the *Brown* decision. President Eisenhower had called out the National Guard to enforce a federal-court school-desegregation order, but the whites of Little Rock were still in a surly and rebellious mood. A young journalist who did the job right could really win his spurs there. On the other hand, the AP had a three-person bureau in Little Rock, and I would be up against them all by myself, with only a limited budget for stringers. The prospect exacerbated both of my fears about a career as a reporter. I wasn't sure I had the physical stamina to do what the job was likely to demand, and I certainly had well-developed views on the segregation controversy that would not be popular in Little Rock's white power structure. I agonized for a while, but ultimately chose law school.

❖   ❖   ❖

The question of where to go to law school then reared its ugly head— ugly because Louise really loved her job at the *Post* and our social life in New York. She didn't want to leave and asked me if I couldn't go to law school at Columbia or NYU. Neither of them had a reputation as a happy place to attend law school, and in any event I preferred to be in a university town rather than a big city. Besides, I thought New York would be a difficult place to raise a family in the long run. I felt strongly that I wanted to attend either Yale, where Marty seemed to be having such a terrific experience, or the University of Virginia, which was located where I had my only family and political roots. They were both at the very top rank of national law schools.

In the 21st century's world of two-career couples we are used to valuing the aspirations of both partners to a marriage equally and to arrangements that compromise or postpone the gratification of the desires of one to accommodate the other's. Today I suspect strongly that I would honor Louise's desire to pursue her career at the *Post* and attend law school at Columbia. But both of us in 1963 still operated on the old-fashioned assumption that it was my career that was paramount, that Louise was likely to be out of the work force for a substantial time when we had children, and that it was at the end of the day my call to make. I confess to some remorse over what even then could be seen as my selfishness, but that remorse is lessened by how well the ultimate choice worked out, for Louise as well as for me. In any event, she was her usual good sport about it.

By Christmas time I had made it clear that I would attend either Yale or Virginia, assuming I got into one or both, but had not decided which I preferred. Louise at this point harbored a strong preference between the two for Yale. New Haven was close to the cultural orbit of New York, and we would know some people there. Moreover, as a westerner, Louise looked upon the racial ugliness then playing itself out in the South with considerable distaste. She had spent almost no time south of Washington, and I think she would have been happy to leave things that way.

We spent Christmas 1963 at my mother's house in Hampton, Virginia, surrounded by my family. Louise was happy with that, as she got along very well with Mother, Liz, and the rest of my relatives. But a couple of days after Christmas, Mother decided to invite all the little old ladies with blue hair in the family and the neighborhood over for tea to meet her wonderful new daughter-in-law. While they were all assembled, my pending career choice naturally became a topic of conversation. Mother, with a distinct lack of subtlety, launched into a forceful monologue about how the University of Virginia School of Law was one of the great educational institutions in the Western world. Mother was, of course, an unabashed advocate of my attending Virginia, largely because it would bring us closer to home. I looked sympathetically at Louise, who was desperately trying to figure out what to say. Being a thoroughly gentle and genial person, and not wanting to offend her mother-in-law, she said, "I know it's a fine law school. After all, Bobby Kennedy went there." Louise had failed to focus on the fact that the president's brother Robert, his attorney general, was anathema in the South, largely because he had seriously beefed up enforcement of federal civil rights laws. Even my mother, who admired President Kennedy and was generally sympathetic to the struggle of black people for equality, drew the line at Bobby. There ensued a frozen silence in the room that lasted for what seemed like several minutes before Mother spoke up and changed the subject.

In January I applied to Yale and Virginia. I got into Yale by return post card. Virginia kept me hanging for months. I later learned that this was for two reasons. First, the regular chair of the faculty admissions committee (there was then no separate professional admissions staff) was on leave, and his replacement, a young professor named Walter Wadlington who later became a dear friend, was new to the job and feeling his way along. Second, there was a big question whether I could qualify as a Virginia resident for purposes of paying in-state tuition, and Walter was fighting the good fight for me. The difference was all of $400: out-of-state tuition was $1,200, and in-state $800. Ultimately I was accepted as a Virginia resident, despite the fact that I had been married for more than two years and living with my wife in Massachusetts and New York.

After considerable agonizing, I chose Virginia, again disregarding Louise's stated preference. I still harbored the fantasy (some might say the delusion) of perhaps running for public office some day, and the pull of my roots in that regard was overwhelming. And even if I did not run for office, I cared how my home state fared on the major issues of the day and did not want to leave the field entirely to the troglodytes.

Interestingly, despite my recognized status as a Virginia resident, money played no role in the decision. Tuition at Yale was, I think, only slightly higher than out-of-state tuition at Virginia, and we thought that either one was manageable. Indeed, remarkable as it may seem today, we managed to save enough money in barely two years of living and working in Manhattan, with our joint income not much more than $10,000 a year, that, with Louise working full time and me working in the summers, we came out dead even at the end of law school. We were completely broke, but we didn't owe anyone a penny, and I had not received any scholarship assistance. We were fairly proud of that.

❖ ❖ ❖

Thus in August 1964, after two very good years in New York, we said goodbye to our friends, packed up our stuff, jumped into our new baby blue Chevy II, and headed for Charlottesville. It was a course that neither of us has ever regretted.

Note
[1] Earl C. Dudley, Jr., "Crisis in a Newsroom," Amherst Alumni News, Winter 1963-4.

CHAPTER SEVEN

Law School
1964-1967

Louise and I arrived in Charlottesville several days before my classes began, to give ourselves a chance to settle into our new environment. We had rented an apartment in a large house called "Betsy Belle Farm" about three miles west of town, in the beautiful rolling countryside of Albemarle County, which is set in the foothills of the Blue Ridge Mountains. The house was the home of real estate broker Roy Wheeler and his wife Betsy. It was set on the crest of a hill that rolled sharply away from the house in back. There were two stories in front and a third down the hill in back. The latter level had once been given over entirely to a stable for the horses that Betsy Wheeler rode in competitions. She was now in her sixties and no longer rode competitively, so they had enclosed half the stables and converted them to student apartments. Our apartment consisted of two former horse stalls and their surrounding space. The horses had lived very well. We had a large living/dining room, a reasonably sized kitchen and a spacious bedroom with its own charming Dutch door. The interior was a combination of pine paneling and stucco. Across the way in an identical apartment were Tom and Niki Williams. Tom was also entering law school. Upstairs the Wheelers lived on the first floor, and another student couple, John and Betty Hollister, lived on the second floor. John was a second-year law student.

It was in many ways an idyllic setting, and we were fortunate to have found it. The Wheelers never advertised, and the apartments were essentially handed down from one generation of law students to another by word of mouth. We learned of Betsy Belle Farm from Evan Kemp, a member of the law school class of 1964 who became a close friend. Evan was dating Margie Steck, another Smith graduate, who had moved in with Tina, Julie, and Susie when Ellen Stover got married. Evan had visited Margie in New York, and we had hit it off immediately.

One idiosyncrasy of the Wheelers was a distaste for animal (including human) reproduction. Every animal on the place—horses, dogs, cats, and Roy—had been neutered, and they made it clear that any students who had babies were to move out as swiftly as possible. Shortly after we all arrived for the start of law school, Niki Williams discovered that she was pregnant. The Wheelers allowed the Williamses to stay to the end of the school year, but then they had to leave. Louise and Niki became good friends, and the two would go grocery shopping together every week. They developed a contest to see who could buy a week's worth of groceries (staples didn't count) for the least money. The winner often came in under $5 for the week.

❖ ❖ ❖

Despite my very deliberate choice of law school over Little Rock, I was not actually looking forward to the next three years. With the exception of Marty Lowy, none of my friends who had attended law school had liked the experience. And if academic graduate school was no fun, how could a grubby trade school be intellectually stimulating? I knew I wanted a law degree, but I had no burning desire for a legal education. So I was prepared to grit my teeth, lower my head, work hard for three years, and move on—in short, to quote a certain graduate school dean, to "get A's and get out." In particular, I was unhappy with the prospect of certain parts of the heavy core curriculum that then dominated legal education. For example, we had to take two semesters—six full credit hours—of property law. I may not have known what I wanted to be, but I knew for certain I was never going to be a real estate conveyancer, so why did I have to waste so much of my time studying this dry and dusty stuff?

The day before classes began we convened for a welcoming speech by the dean and other things attendant on registration. The dean of the law school was Hardy Dillard, a nationally known scholar in the fields of contracts and international law, who later went on to a seat on the World Court in the Hague. Dean Dillard was a magisterial presence with perhaps the finest speaking voice I have ever heard. His enthusiasm for the law as an intellectual discipline was infectious. I have never forgotten the opening line of his address to the incoming students. "Welcome," he said in his syrupy southern baritone, "to the last of the learned professions." He went on to describe in moving and elevated terms both the legal profession's long tradition of public service and its stirring intellectual ferment. He made it all sound pretty interesting, but I kept my skeptical eye on that damned Property course.

I returned to the regimented approach to study that had marked the first semester of my freshman year at Amherst. I stayed at the law school all day, doing my reading and religiously briefing my cases when I was not actually in class. At night I would go over my reading again and type my case briefs, leaving half the page blank to take notes on in class the next day. I would relate the facts of the cases to Louise and discuss them with her. That year at least she came close to getting a free legal education.

About two weeks into classes I realized to my great surprise that I was having more intellectual fun, was more intensely engaged, than I ever had been, even at Amherst. I had some wonderful teachers, among them Dean Dillard for Contracts and a first-year faculty member and 1963 graduate of the law school, Peter Low, for Criminal Law. Peter and his wife Carol became lifelong friends. And to my utter amazement, perhaps my favorite course was Property, taught by a puckish Irishman named Tom Bergin, whose darting, lightning-fast mind illuminated the kaleidoscopic quality of legal concepts and brought home the rigor of legal analysis. Our first case in Property, *Pierson v. Post*, involved the question of who owned a fox captured in a hunt in 18th-century England. Tom would begin class with a tart question—"Did Pierson win because he had possession of the fox, or did he have possession of the fox because he won?"—and use it as the platform for an illuminating discussion of just what "possession" might mean in different legal contexts. I was hooked for life.

My three years in law school were among the best years of my life, intellectually and personally. I grew and matured tremendously, and I learned concepts and skills that formed the basis of my whole career. Virginia had a reputation as a very pleasant, as well as a challenging, place to study law, and it fully lived up to that reputation.

❖ ❖ ❖

As I settled into law school, I began to meet and interact with my classmates, and a wonderful crew they were. Walter Wadlington, the faculty member who admitted our class—the only one he ever did—had assembled a very interesting group, with more people who had had substantial work experience before coming to law school and more married students than were the norm. They were a stimulating bunch to be with, and they carved out many very distinguished careers. I did not know it then, of course, but among them were a future governor of Virginia, a future speaker of the Virginia House of Delegates, a president of the College of William and Mary, a rector of the University of Virginia, judges of numerous federal and state courts, and more prosecutors, managing partners of law firms and general counsels of corporations—and just plain great lawyers—than you could shake a stick at. Among them I found many lasting friends.

It was not, however, a very diverse group demographically. Only five of the 230 or so members of the class of 1967 were women, and only three of them made it to graduation. There was only one African American in the class, and, I believe, one Asian-American student. This was not the result of discrimination. Virginia was already looking hard for good minority and female students. Not until several years later did they begin to attend law school in larger numbers.

❖ ❖ ❖

Louise began looking for a job as soon as we arrived in Charlottesville. As was—and is—typically the case in a university town, there was a surplus of "trailing spouses," then mostly wives, of graduate students and young faculty members, which made for a very tight job market. Many of the wives of my classmates taught school in Charlottesville or one of the surrounding counties. Louise's first job, running a slide projector for lectures in the Art Department, was not very stimulating and paid very poorly. Before too long, however, she landed a job in the University News Service, which was to have major ramifications years later. She was mostly employed writing and editing press releases about events at the university for the local and state press. She enjoyed the job, and it taught her a lot about what was going on at the university.

❖ ❖ ❖

1964 was, of course, a presidential election year, and Louise and I decided to become involved in the Democratic campaign in Charlottesville. We rang doorbells for the Lyndon Johnson-Hubert Humphrey ticket in the Belmont area of town, then inhabited largely by an aging, rather poor, white population. As we canvassed, we saw the first signs that the national Democratic Party's support for civil rights was beginning to put a strain on the old New Deal coalition that had been so powerful from 1932 to 1960. Johnson carried Virginia on his way to a huge landslide win over Barry Goldwater, but we were astounded at how many Goldwater supporters we found in Belmont. Many of its citizens were ripe for Richard Nixon's "southern strategy" four years later, which began a very substantial realignment of lower-income white voters in the South and elsewhere in favor of the

Republican Party's conservative social agenda.

Working for the Johnson ticket we met and became friends with a number of like-minded people, including my law school classmate Dick Dunnells and his wife Geni and Tom and Judy Connally. Tom was the co-head resident at the university hospital. He was and remains one of the few active liberal Democrats among the doctors of my acquaintance. Tom went on to become a member of the university's Board of Visitors, and he was our physician for many years. Judy had a distinguished career in the Virginia House of Delegates and in many Arlington civic initiatives. Along with the Dunnells and the Connallys, Louise and I became part of an upstart group of former Johnson bell-ringers that called itself the Citizens' Democratic Council, bringing a new liberal face to the Charlottesville Democratic scene.

❖ ❖ ❖

As my first year wound on into the spring semester, I began looking for a job for the summer. I spread my resume around among lawyers in Charlottesville, but it attracted little interest. Charlottesville has always had too many lawyers—mostly people who fell in love with the place when they were in law school and couldn't bring themselves to leave—so even the summer job market was not good. However, among the friends we had made first year were a young man from Richmond named Lee Davis and his wife Misty. Misty, it turned out, was the daughter of one of my political heroes growing up in Northern Virginia. State Senator Armistead Boothe, a scion of one of Virginia's oldest families, had led the fight in 1959 against the effort by the Byrd Machine—the dominant force in Virginia politics since the 1920s—to close down the Virginia public school system in the wake of the *Brown* decision to avoid integration. It had been a near-run thing, the debate lasting for weeks and the vote very close, but the schools were not closed statewide, although some few jurisdictions did shut down for months. Later, in 1961, Boothe had run in the Democratic primary for lieutenant governor on a ticket that stood for progressive racial policies. They put up a good fight but lost.

I had told Lee and Misty how much I admired "Army" Boothe. One day Lee called me out of the blue and said, "Would you be interested in working for my father-in-law this summer?" I said a very quick yes. Thus began my first tentative steps down a road that ultimately I did not take but that attracted me a great deal.

Army Boothe was the senior partner in the Alexandria firm of Boothe, Dudley (no relation), Koontz, Blankingship & Stump. Mr. Boothe paid me $60 a week—the same as my salary as a copy boy—and I am sure I was not worth even that, as I had almost no practical skills after one year in law school devoted almost entirely to the basic theory and structure of the common law. But he was extremely kind to me, invited me several times to his home, and made me feel more useful than I could possibly have been. It was the beginning of a wonderful relationship between our families, which has continued to this day. His grandson, Lee and Misty's son Evan, roomed with our son Will in college and remains one of Will's closest friends.

Louise remained in Charlottesville that summer, working at the News Office, and I roomed with Evan Kemp in Alexandria, commuting home on the weekends.

❖ ❖ ❖

When I returned to school in the fall of 1965, I threw myself into the fascinating work of the *Virginia Law Review*. Law reviews are unique institutions in the scholarly and professional world. The legal profession is the only one whose scholarly journals are operated and edited by students. The tradition goes back to the late 19th century. The law reviews publish both articles written by faculty members or practitioners and "notes" written by student members of the review staffs. Until fairly recently law reviews have been highly elite organizations, with membership limited to the students at the top of the class. At most schools there are now other ways besides having very high grades to become a member of the law review, but they still retain much of their old elite status. At Virginia in my day, grades alone were not enough; one also had to survive a rigorous tryout that lasted for several weeks and involved the preparation of two pieces of scholarship and the intense critique of two done by others. In the spring of first year, the students with the top ten GPAs in the first semester of law school were invited to try out for the *Review*. I spent six or so weeks of that semester working harder than I had ever worked, writing two papers on recent court decisions, one by the Supreme Court and the other by a federal appeals court, while desperately trying to stay on top of my studies. I succeeded on both counts. My grades actually improved second semester, and both my "recent decisions" were published in the *Review*.[1] In the fall another twenty-five students in the class were invited on the basis of grades to try out.

My major project for the *Review* in the fall of my second year was to write my note. Each student member of the *Review* was required to write one, a scholarly treatment of some issue or area of the law, though not all of them were published in the journal. I began working on a critique of a recent Supreme Court case, *Swain v. Alabama*,[2] which had made it much harder for black criminal defendants to prove what everyone knew was going on, especially, but not exclusively, in the South: blatant racial discrimination in the selection of juries in controversial cases. My research carried me far into the history of "peremptory challenges"—generally unreviewable challenges to individual jurors exercised by lawyers on the basis of their hunches developed during the questioning of prospective jurors, known as *voir dire*. The prosecutor in Robert Swain's case had done what southern prosecutors routinely did in "salt and pepper" rape cases: he struck all the black jurors, which was facilitated by considerable underrepresentation of blacks on the jury list. I became convinced that the Court had made a major error when, over the dissents of three justices, including Chief Justice Earl Warren, it had imposed a virtually impossible burden to prove discrimination on defendants like Swain and sent young Robert Swain to his death. I had the satisfaction many years later of seeing the Court overrule *Swain* in the case of *Batson v. Kentucky*.[3] Though I wrote, and the *Review* published, a lengthy and detailed critique of *Swain*,[4] my project took a different turn and expanded greatly when the Johnson administration proposed and Congress seriously took up legislation designed to try to eliminate the blight of discrimination in the jury selection process. This much longer analysis of jury discrimination took up more than 90 pages in the *Review* when it was published the following year under the title "The Congress, the Court and Jury Selection: A Critique of Titles I and II of the Civil Rights Bill of 1966."[5] I was pleased that it was cited with some frequency and that parts of it were, for a time at least, reprinted in some criminal procedure texts.

I was also pleased that during my two years on the *Review* staff we published numerous pieces calling for broader interpretation of civil rights laws and constitutional provisions to give greater protection to the civil rights of minority citizens. My note was one of those pieces. So was an article on jury discrimination in Virginia by Samuel W. Tucker, one of the state's outstanding and courageous African-American lawyers, who, along with his partner Oliver Hill, led the fight for civil rights in Virginia for decades.[6]

❖ ❖ ❖

In the second semester of my second year, the *Virginia Law Review* was in considerable trouble. Like the journals of most other major law schools, the *Review* published—or was scheduled to publish—eight issues a year, averaging between 200 and 250 pages of legal scholarship per issue. Gradually over the preceding three years, however, the *Review's* publication schedule had slipped, to the point where it was fully five issues behind. The publication deficit was a source of embarrassment, but even worse, it made the *Virginia Law Review* a much less desirable place to publish their work for outside authors, who were often concerned to get their commentary on current or pending issues before the public with dispatch.

The responsibility for the operation of a law review is committed to a "managing board," a relatively small subgroup of the membership. A new managing board is chosen during the second semester of their second year in law school, and they operate the review for a year until a new board is chosen to replace them. Our class's managing board, of which I was chosen the editor-in-chief, was determined to eliminate the publication deficit. In an effort to help achieve this goal, the previous board created a new office, associate editor, which was filled by my close friend Rick Lowery. Beginning in March of our second year, ten of us regularly worked eighty- or ninety-hour weeks. We sacrificed our bodies, our grades, and our social lives to catch up. And catch up we did. With a lot of satisfaction, we were able to put an advance copy of the *Review's* October 1966 issue on Dean Dillard's desk on Halloween, which took him by considerable surprise. At the end of our year, we had published thirteen issues of a scholarly journal with, I think, no diminution in quality, and to my knowledge it has been a point of honor for the *Virginia Law Review* to remain on schedule ever since.

The faculty knew what we were doing and tolerated our extensive absences from classes. Indeed, there were times when my work on the *Review* paid off academically. First semester of third year I was enrolled in a class in Federal Courts given by a visiting professor from another law school. I went to the first session of the course and then never made it to another. It was embarrassing because I encountered this man a couple of times at cocktail parties, and he asked, "Aren't you in my Federal Courts class?" The exam he gave was considered perhaps the hardest any of my classmates had seen. It contained an extremely complex and difficult two-hour essay question that just happened to have been the subject of a student note that I had spent the preceding two weeks editing, so I was one of the most up-to-date people in the entire country on that subject and aced the exam, to the dismay, I was told, of the poor professor. While this experience was unique, the benefits of my work on the *Review* were extensive. I learned the value of attention to every detail. I was in on the cutting edge of legal scholarship in all sorts of fields at the time. I learned something about running a large and complex organization. And all of us won the gratitude and esteem of our classmates and the faculty. The latter came in very handy more than twenty years later.

The managing board experience also created an indelible bond among the ten of us. We generally worked until late Saturday afternoon and then took that night off. On any given Saturday evening, there would be two, or three, or four groups of members of our board relaxing together with our wives or girlfriends. By early Sunday afternoon we were back to the grind. At our twentieth law school reunion, nine of us (the other member of our board did not make it to the reunion) got together with our wives for a wonderful celebratory dinner. I still count most of the members of that board among my closest friends.

❖   ❖   ❖

I was genuinely uncertain about where I wanted to practice after law school. In the mid-1960s the major California firms were just beginning to see themselves as part of a national recruiting market and to seek students at eastern law schools. Louise was from the West Coast, and I was certainly open to the idea of moving there. Washington State was still seen as a bit on the provincial side, though Seattle became a hot market a few years later, but I interviewed for a summer job after my second year with firms in Los Angeles and San Francisco. Louise's family, indeed, had roots in Pasadena, where both her parents had grown up. So I took a brief job—I could spare only about half the summer from my duties on the *Review*—at the Los Angeles firm of Gibson, Dunn & Crutcher. I later learned that Louise's grandfather on her mother's side, James S. Bennett, a Los Angeles lawyer, had been invited to join Gibson, Dunn at the time of its founding. Gibson, Dunn was in 1966 one of only two "large" firms in Los Angeles. It is difficult to believe in light of today's giant firms, often containing well over a thousand lawyers spread over several cities, indeed several countries, but then there were very few law firms in the entire country with more than 100 lawyers. There were several in New York and one or two in Houston, but that was it. Gibson, Dunn and O'Melveny & Myers, the other big Los

Angeles firm, each had about 90 lawyers, as did Covington & Burling in Washington. Latham & Watkins and Paul, Hastings, Janofsky & Walker, both multi-city behemoths today, were confined to Los Angeles and had about thirty-five and a dozen lawyers respectively.

Louise and I flew out to Los Angeles in time to join a family gathering that had celebrated the graduation of her brother Jim and his girlfriend (later wife) Jan Harkness from Occidental College. We rented an apartment in Pasadena and were loaned a car by Louise's Aunt Kay and Uncle French Fogle who lived in nearby Claremont, where French was on the English faculty of Claremont Graduate University. We enjoyed ourselves in Los Angeles, though our time together was quite brief, as Louise could spare even less time from her job in the University News Service than I could. I liked most of the people at Gibson, Dunn, but could never quite shake my sense that I was far away from the political action. Actually, I was wrong about that, as an actor by the name of Ronald Reagan was then running for governor of California, with the active support of a number of Gibson, Dunn lawyers who later became prominent members of his administration, in particular the Justice Department, when he became president. But my politics were very different from those of the Reaganauts. I crossed paths in an odd way with one of them, a young lawyer named Ted Olson who was a couple of years older than I, many years later in Washington.

While I slammed no doors in California, I returned to Charlottesville pretty much convinced that I could not live without the *Washington Post* on my breakfast table and the federal government all around me.

❖ ❖ ❖

In the spring and summer of 1966, Army Boothe ran in the Democratic primary for a seat in the United States Senate. Harry Flood Byrd, Sr., who had dominated Virginia politics since his election as governor in the mid-1920s, resigned from his Senate seat in 1965 for health reasons, and governor Mills Godwin appointed his son Harry Byrd, Jr., known all his life as "little Harry," to serve on an interim basis. A special election was held in 1966 to choose someone to fill out the remainder of the elder Byrd's term. Though I was too occupied with my duties on the *Review* to be of much actual help, I was the titular head, at least, of the Charlottesville chapter of "Youth for Boothe." Little Harry was not the brightest of fellows, and Army ran a great campaign. It was the toughest challenge the old guard of Virginia politics had ever faced. Army came very close to a stunning upset, but in the end fell a few thousand votes short. Had he won, I am sure I would have gone to work for him in the Senate on graduation from law school.

❖   ❖   ❖

During the summer of 1966 Louise and I decided that it would be a good time to start a family. I would be graduating from law school and taking a real "permanent" job the following June, so we could afford it. And the move to a new city would be a good point in Louise's career to take some time off to be a mom. In the fall we learned that she was pregnant, due in late May. We were very excited, as were the prospective grandparents. My mother had always claimed that she dreaded being a grandmother because she had always criticized her friends for being so gushy about their grandchildren, but she showed every sign of being prepared to outdo them. Louise's mother had written us when we began our marriage in graduate school that she did not want to see any children until there were two doctors in the family, but more recently had been bemoaning the fact that all her friends had grandkids, while she ....

It just happened that Louise and Rick Lowery's wife Gail became pregnant at about the same time. Gail was due a little earlier in May than Louise. As the due dates began to loom closer, the four of us spent a number of enjoyable evenings bandying about possible names. Rick delighted in teasing Gail by championing utterly implausible names—Mron and Torg were two examples. Rick and Gail already had a two-year-old named Kirk, who was my little buddy. Gail worked as a secretary for Graham Lilly, a recent Virginia law graduate who was teaching in the Army's Judge Advocate General's School next door to the law school and who soon joined the Virginia faculty. After work, she would pick Kirk up from day care and bring him down to the *Law Review* office in the basement of Clark Hall, the law school building. Kirk and I would play for a few minutes each evening before the Lowerys departed for supper. So it was natural that Louise and I agreed to babysit for Kirk whenever Gail went into labor. The call came early in the evening of May 9, and Louise and I settled ourselves into the Lowerys' living room while Rick drove Gail to the hospital. Shortly before midnight Rick returned and announced that they had another little boy. After making the happy calls to his and Gail's parents, Rick cracked open a bottle of Virginia Gentleman, and we shared a celebratory drink. While sipping his bourbon thoughtfully, Rick returned to the question of names. "You know," he said, "you could insult an entire religion and call the kid Allah."

I replied, "That would be wrong, but how about Mohammed Ali?" referring to the great heavyweight boxing champion. Ali, of course, had begun life as Cassius Clay until he joined the Black Muslim sect. That started Rick thinking.

"How about Cassius?" he offered.

"No," I said, "Clay." And that, so help me, is how Clay Lowery was named.

The next morning Rick went to the hospital and announced to Gail the name he had chosen, which she greeted with a great sigh of relief.

Ten days after Clay was born, on May 19, Rick and I were at our apartment preparing to study for our examination in Corporate Tax the next morning. I mentioned earlier that our class attendance had suffered because of our duties on the managing board of the *Review*. I must confess, however, that when we laid down the burdens of office in late March of our third year, most of us on the managing board had not returned to being the model law students we once had been. Physically and mentally exhausted after a year of completely nonstop work, and facing the prospect of working similar hours as entry-level lawyers, we kicked back, played a lot of tennis and golf, and spent our evenings enjoying each other's company. Thus Rick and I literally took the cellophane wrappers off our brand new Corporate Tax books that afternoon and began to try to figure out which sections of the Internal Revenue Code we would be responsible for on the exam. Sometime between 10 and 11 p.m. Louise emerged from our bedroom and said, "I hope you guys know all the Corporate Tax you need to know, because things are starting to happen."

This was before the time when most educated young couples attended pregnancy and birthing classes together, so in the age-old manner of prospective first-time fathers, I flew into a lather of excitement and began telling Louise to relax and breathe deeply. I called the hospital and spoke to an Ob-Gyn resident, who upon learning that this was Louise's first child said, "Relax, you have a lot of time. Bring her in when the pains get real regular." Well, Louise had a contraction, then another about fifteen minutes later, a third ten minutes after that, then another in five minutes, and then two more at three-minute intervals. I figured they were getting pretty regular.

For some reason, Rick had not driven his car to our apartment that afternoon, so the three of us piled into our car and headed off, with Louise doubling over quite predictably every three minutes. We came to an intersection where to take Rick home I would turn left, while to go to the hospital I would turn right. Even I knew that taking Rick home was out of the question, but he with his great experience in these matters was even surer. So we agreed I would head for the hospital. When we got there the same resident I had spoken to on the phone took Louise into a room and examined her. He emerged, quite shaken, saying, "It is quite remarkable, but your wife is about to have a baby." I didn't seem to find that remarkable, so he added, "I mean right now!"

I was afraid that I would miss the birth if I tried to take Rick home at that point, so the two of us headed for the fathers' waiting room, with our Corporate Tax books and copies of the Internal Revenue Code in hand. The nurses looked at us a bit strangely, and I heard one of them say rather snidely, "Isn't it nice? He brought his friend with him." We ignored them and tried to study.

At a little after 2 a.m. Louise's doctor, a grizzled older gentleman with iron grey hair, emerged from an elevator and approached us. He was still in his scrubs and was blood from the knees down, with a cigarette hanging from his lips with at least an inch of ash on it. Given his appearance, I was sure everyone had died. But he calmly announced that I was the father of a healthy baby boy and that Louise was doing fine. He said they would clean the baby up and bring him for my inspection soon. I waited nervously for more than an hour. It seems that there was an emergency in the maternity ward. A very obese woman had been brought to the hospital suffering from severe cramps. She was so fat that she had not realized she was pregnant until after she went into labor. She occupied the attention of all, and so it was some time before young William Carlyle Dudley, named for his two grandfathers, was brought forward, wrinkling his brow and blinking curiously in the light.

I took my Corporate Tax exam later that morning and somehow managed to pass. And I slogged my way through my remaining final set of exams while Louise and Will remained in the hospital. Her doctor was quite old-fashioned even for that day and insisted that she stay in bed for a week after giving birth. I brought them home the afternoon after I had taken my last exam.

I entertained quite romantic notions about fatherhood. I had decorated Will's bassinet with a welcome home sign and carefully placed a brand new baseball inside it. That evening the three of us settled down in bed, Louise nursing Will, and I drifting off to sleep holding her hand. KAPPOWW!!! The young man suddenly voided his bowels with considerable force. Another of the doctor's old-fashioned notions was that he was against rubber pants, as they tended to promote the proliferation of diaper rash. Thus the product of Will's mighty effort was spread all over our bed—not exactly the dreamy homecoming I had envisioned. Also, the lack of rubber pants meant that every time he peed, he soaked through not only his diaper, but his nightgown and all the bedclothes. I spent the first few weeks of father-hood almost entirely at the laundromat.

❖ ❖ ❖

Mother and Liz drove over from Hampton a couple of weeks after Will was born to attend my graduation from law school and to meet the young addition to the family. After the ceremony, we went to a graduation party given by my tax teacher, Ed Cohen, who had joined the law faculty my first year after a lengthy and very distinguished career in the tax field, includ-ing a substantial hand in the preparation of the Internal Revenue Code of 1954. Mr. Cohen had a son, Dinny, in my class. Dinny had been three years behind me at Amherst, and we had become good friends in law school. The Cohens had entertained us, along with numerous other of Dinny's friends, more than once at their home. They generously gave a party to celebrate Dinny's graduation and invited several other graduates and their families. I had taken Federal Income Tax from Mr. Cohen my second year as well as his Corporate Tax course my last semester. After my adventure becoming a father, I had received a "gentleman's" 2.5 (a C-plus) on his exam. As we were leaving the party, Mr. Cohen took my mother aside and said, "You know, I really agonized about Earl's grade. I knew his wife had had a baby the night before the exam, but I also knew that he hadn't been to class once the whole semester, and I just couldn't figure out which one to take into account." My mother's jaw dropped, as her last illusion about her diligent law-student son was blown away.

❖ ❖ ❖

Although Louise and I were debt-free at the end of law school, we were flat broke. I had planned to take the summer after graduation off, except for studying for the bar examination. I hadn't had a real vacation since before we left New York, and I wanted some time to get acquainted with my new son. I would be starting a judicial clerkship in the late summer, and it seemed an ideal time to relax a bit. But as we looked at our finances, we decided it would be better to postpone the vacation for a year than to go into debt. So in March or April, I called the head recruiter at the Washington firm of

Covington & Burling and asked if they might have room in their summer program for a graduate waiting for his clerkship to start. I had an offer of permanent employment at Covington and was seriously considering going there after my clerkship. To my relief, the firm gave me a summer job. Not only did it help financially, but it allowed me another glimpse of life inside a major urban law firm. Covington was the largest, and very possibly the best, firm in Washington, and it had a rich and varied practice. I enjoyed my summer there and made a number of very valuable contacts.

Notes

[1] See 51 Va. L. Rev. 692 (1965), *commenting on* City of El Paso v. Simmons, 379 U.S. 497 (1965); 51 Va. L. Rev. 973 (1965), *commenting on* American Dredging Co. v. Local 25, Marine Div., Int'l Union of Operating Eng'rs, 338 F.2d 837 (3d Cir. 1964), *cert. denied*, 380 U.S. 935 (1965).

[2] 380 U.S. 202 (1965).

[3] 476 U.S. 79 (1986).

[4] Comment, Swain v. Alabama, *A Constitutional Blueprint for the Perpetuation of the All-White Jury*, 52 Va. L. Rev. 1157 (1966).

[5] 52 Va. L. Rev. 1069 (1966).

[6] S.W. Tucker, *Racial Discrimination in Jury Selection in Virginia*, 52 Va. L. Rev. 736 (1966).

CHAPTER EIGHT

Clerking for the Chief Justice
1967-1968

The institution of the judicial law clerk is an invention of American judges in the late 19th century. Beginning in the late 1880s, Supreme Court Justice Horace Gray and later Justices Oliver Wendell Holmes and Louis Brandeis began hiring bright young law graduates to serve as their "legal secretaries." These young men would perform legal research for the justices, help them with their correspondence, and occasionally assist in the drafting of opinions. The idea caught on, and soon most, if not all, Supreme Court justices were hiring legal secretaries, who at some point began being called "law clerks." By the time I graduated from law school in 1967, each Supreme Court justice was entitled to two law clerks—three for the chief justice— and each lower federal court judge received one. (The number of law clerks per judge has continued to grow, and with it the number and, many think, the length of the average judicial opinion. Supreme Court justices now have four clerks, federal appellate judges three, and federal district judges two.)[1]

From the beginning it has been the general practice for law clerks to serve for only a year or at the most two, though some judges, particularly in recent years, have tired of the turnover and hired more or less permanent clerks. The constant turnover of the clerks is seen in most chambers, however, as having value: it both prevents the buildup of power and interest in the clerk that a more permanent arrangement might entail and ensures a flow of fresh, new ideas brought to the courts by the brightest graduates of the best law schools.

Naturally, law clerk positions are highly sought after, both for the prestige they bring to the young law school graduate and for the heady experience of participating in the crafting of judicial decisions at a very early stage in one's career. The most highly sought-after clerkships are at the Supreme Court of the United States.

I was fortunate that my law school grades and my service on the law review put me in a position to have a serious chance at a high-level clerkship, perhaps even at the Supreme Court. As I contemplated the possibility of clerking, I made what seems to me in retrospect a very foolish, even arrogant, decision, for which, as luck would have it, I was not punished. Feeling old—I was twenty-six when I graduated, a year or two older than many of my classmates—tired of hopping careers, and very responsible as an about-to-be father, I decided it was time to get on with my life. I would take my shot at the Supreme Court, but if I did not obtain a clerkship there, I would forego the experience and head straight for the practice of law.

My dream clerkship would be with Chief Justice Earl Warren. I had to be one of only a tiny minority of southern white boys who grew up in the years after *Brown v. Board of Education* greatly admiring Chief Justice Warren. I firmly believed that *Brown* was a long-overdue call to justice and equality, and I also admired the chief justice's leadership in enforcing the simple promises of the Bill of Rights in many other contexts. But I could not afford to apply only to him. I applied to seven of the nine sitting justices and one retired justice, Stanley Reed. I wound up with a very interesting clerkship. I was technically Justice Reed's clerk, but in fact worked almost entirely for the chief justice.

Shortly after Justice Reed retired in 1957, Chief Justice Warren asked if he could use the Reed law clerk any time he was not working for Reed. The chief justice was in need of extra clerking assistance, as in those days his clerks prepared memoranda for all nine members of the Court on some 3,000 petitions a year on the *in forma pauperis* docket. Virtually all of the Supreme Court's jurisdiction is—and was then—discretionary. Parties who lose in lower courts file petitions to have the Supreme Court hear their cases. Most of these are called petitions for *certiorari* after the old common-law writ the Court had borrowed for this purpose. It takes the votes of four justices to grant the writ of *certiorari* and bring the case before the full Court for decision on the merits. Much of the work of law clerks at the Supreme Court has always had to do with the *certiorari* (or *cert* for short) petitions. Parties who can afford to do so are required to pay a filing fee in the Supreme Court and to have their petitions (and briefs, if the Court takes the case) printed. Parties who demonstrate that they cannot afford the fee or the printing cost—mostly, though not entirely, prisoners appealing their criminal convictions—are allowed to file "*in forma pauperis*," meaning that the Court waives the fee and the printing of the petition. (If an *in forma pauperis cert* petition is granted, the Court appoints a lawyer, often a former law clerk, to represent the petitioner, and it pays for the printing of the briefs.) Though the way petitions are processed has changed since then, in the 1960s the chambers of each justice handled all the fee-paying, printed petitions on its own. Usually one of the clerks would write a memo to the justice about each case. In addition to their work for the chief justice on these cases, the Warren clerks did all the work on the *in forma pauperis* petitions, writing a memo on each one that went to the entire Court. This was an enormous amount of work, and the one extra clerk granted to the Chief was simply not enough. When Justice Reed first retired, he spent a lot of time sitting by designation of the chief justice on lower federal courts (a retired Supreme Court justice is eligible to sit on any federal court other than the Supreme Court), but as he grew older and sat less, the Reed clerk had come to work almost exclusively for the Chief.

Justice Reed was from Maysville, Kentucky, a tiny town on the Ohio River not far from Cincinnati, and had been a lawyer for tobacco interests and agricultural cooperatives in the 1920s. He took a job with the Federal Farm Board in 1929, arriving in Washington just after the Wall Street crash that set off the Great Depression. Less than six years later, he found himself in the position of solicitor general of the United States—the official in charge of the government's business before the Supreme Court. He earned President Roosevelt's gratitude for his stalwart defense of the administration and its legislative program, the New Deal, before an often hostile Supreme Court, and in 1938 was appointed an associate justice on that Court. Justice Reed, who was about 80 when I met him, related all this to me in the most modest and self-effacing terms at our initial meeting, as if he still could not believe his good fortune. He served on the Court for nineteen years, retiring in 1957, and he had the genuine affection and respect of the chief justice for his courage as a southerner in signing on to the *Brown* decision. He was the last justice to serve on the Supreme Court without a law degree, though he studied law at both Columbia and the University of Virginia.

Justice Reed mentioned that the chief justice had recommended me to his attention, and he made me an offer the day of my interview with him. I did almost no work for Justice Reed during my year at the Court. He sat only one day, on a panel at the U.S. Court of Claims. The panel heard only two cases, and Justice Reed was assigned no opinion to write. The chief justice and everyone in his chambers treated me as one of his own clerks, but my office was in Justice Reed's chambers, and thus I had the opportunity to get to know him, his secretary Helen Gaylord, and his messenger Gerald Ross. Despite his age and his virtually complete retirement, Justice Reed came into the Court every day, largely, we suspected, to get away from his wife, a formidable lady who accepted far more social invitations in Washington than the justice would have on his own. Justice Reed was a genuinely nice, humble gentleman, with whom I had many pleasant chats. At one point

during his service on the Court, Justice Reed had been significantly over-
weight and suffered from serious hypertension. He had devoted one entire
summer recess to the Duke University Medical Center's famous rice diet
and had lost some 60 pounds. Many years later, his daily lunch still consisted of a plate of rice and an apple, served to him in chambers by Gerald
Ross. I will have more to say about Gerald later, but he was one of the true
characters of the Supreme Court. And Helen Gaylord was a delightful person who, on the occasions when the work seemed overwhelming, made my
life much more cheerful.

❖ ❖ ❖

I arrived at the Court some time around Labor Day and dug into the
work that had piled up over the summer recess. The Supreme Court con-
venes for its annual term the first Monday in October, and it adjourns usually the last Monday in the following June. While the justices hear no cases,
except in rare emergencies, between the end of June and the beginning of
October, the *cert* petitions continue to pile up, and the briefs are filed in
cases where the Court has granted *cert*. Thus my new co-clerks and I had a
lot to do before the term began. The chief justice wanted a memorandum
for his use on each *cert* petition on the paid or "appellate" docket and a
"bench memo"—a much more detailed examination of the issues and arguments—in each case that the Court was going to hear. And then there were
the *in forma pauperis* petitions.

My co-clerks were an interesting and pleasant group, and we all got
along very well throughout the year. One was designated the chief clerk,
whom the chief justice held responsible for the mechanics of processing
the work of the chambers. This was Charlie Wilson, a tall, taciturn man
from Massachusetts, who had just graduated from Boalt Hall, the law
school at the University of California at Berkeley. Charlie, I soon learned,
had by coincidence spent the two or three years before law school working
for UPI in San Francisco. He and I later practiced law together for several
years. Tyrone ("Ty") Brown, a graduate of Cornell Law School, was only the
second African American to serve as a Supreme Court law clerk. Almost
twenty years earlier Justice Felix Frankfurter had hired Bill Coleman, later
Secretary of Transportation in the Ford administration, as his clerk. It had
taken a long time for a second African American to be given this opportunity. Ty was an extraordinarily able and pleasant person, with whom I stayed
vaguely in touch for many years, and who went on to a distinguished career

in private practice. Larry Simon had graduated from Yale Law School, and he was the only one of us to have clerked at a lower court before joining the chief justice's staff. (It was only then becoming common for justices to choose clerks who had a year of "seasoning" at a lower court, though that practice swiftly became universal. In my term fewer than half the clerks in all the chambers had clerked elsewhere first.) Larry had clerked for Judge Irving Kaufman on the Second Circuit Court of Appeals in New York. Kaufman was notorious for his blatantly pro-prosecution, red-baiting performance as the presiding judge in the trial of Soviet spies Julius and Ethel Rosenberg, and Larry had detested him. Larry later became a law professor at the University of Southern California. Rounding out the chambers was Larry Nichols, who was Justice Tom Clark's clerk. Justice Clark had announced his retirement over the summer to remove potential conflicts arising from the appointment of his son Ramsey as attorney general. He was replaced by Thurgood Marshall, the great African-American lawyer who had led the campaign to overthrow legally enforced segregation and had argued *Brown v. Board of Education*. After retiring, Justice Clark had made it clear to the chief justice that, unlike Justice Reed, he did not want to sit on lower federal courts in retirement. Thus he had no use for a law clerk. The chief justice leapt at this chance for more help, and Larry, like me, was essentially an extra Warren clerk. Larry was from Oklahoma and had gone to Michigan Law School. He became my best friend among the clerks and my golfing companion.

The work of the chambers was essentially distributed at random. When we arrived there was an enormous pile of unprocessed *cert* petitions that were ready for action by the Court. (A petition was considered ready, and hence was distributed by the Clerk's Office to the justices, when the opposing party's time for responding to the petition had run.) Each of us would go up to the pile and grab a handful of petitions off the top, as many as we thought we could process in a day or two. If the Court granted *cert* in a case, that case stayed with the clerk who had worked on the petition. Thus it was a matter of the luck of the draw how many of one's cases were ultimately decided on the merits by the Court and how interesting those cases were. There was, however, a payback. The more of one's cases the Court decided to hear, the more work one had to do. It was a fair tradeoff.

A *cert* memo was generally a fairly short document, though in a complicated case it could take a fair amount of time to prepare. Our first responsibility was to make sure that the Court had jurisdiction over the case and that all the procedural formalities prerequisite to its consideration of the case had been met. Then we would state the salient facts as briefly as possible and outline the issues that the petitioner sought to present for resolution by the Supreme Court. We would discuss those issues briefly—whether, for example, they were firmly settled by existing precedent, or whether there were conflicting decisions on them in the lower courts. In the final paragraph of the memo, the chief justice encouraged us to make a recommendation to him as to how he should vote on the petition and why. By contrast, in a *cert* memo in an *in forma pauperis* case, our recommendation paragraph appeared only on the chief justice's copy. We said nothing to the other justices about what we thought should be done with the case.

A bench memo in a case where *cert* had been granted was a much more elaborate affair. We would outline the parties' arguments in considerable detail and offer our own analysis of those arguments and of the Court's precedents in the area. It was harder here to separate our legal analysis from our opinions, but we tried to confine the latter to a section at the end, longer than the final section of a *cert* memo, where we would spell out our views in somewhat greater detail.

Although some have argued that law clerks often exert great influence over their justices,[2] I was never sure that the chief justice actually read the recommendations we made in either our *cert* memos or our bench memos. He had been on the Court for almost fifteen years, and he was pretty confident of his own mind on most matters. If he looked to others for guidance, it was, I believe, to his colleagues—and in particular to Justice Brennan, to whom he was very close—and not to his callow law clerks. I thought the recommendation sections of the memos were basically sops to our young egos, though we all took the responsibility to try to formulate a proposed course of action very seriously.

❖ ❖ ❖

Chief Justice Warren arrived from California a few days before the term was scheduled to begin. I have never forgotten our first meeting with him. Earl Warren had been, and remained for all of his life, the golden California politician. He had begun his career as deputy city attorney of Oakland and then as an assistant district attorney in Alameda County. After a few years he was appointed district attorney, was elected to the office three times, and wound up putting a large number of the county's political bigshots in jail for corruption. He went on to statewide elective office as attorney general and was then elected governor. He was so popular that when he ran for reelection as governor, he won both the Republican and the Democratic primaries, though he had always been registered as a Republican. He was nominated at the Republican Convention in 1948 to serve as Tom Dewey's vice-presidential running mate, and he harbored serious ambitions to be the Republican nominee for president in 1952. He secured the unanimous backing of the California delegation as a "favorite son" candidate. His only hope was that the convention would reach an impasse between the supporters of General Dwight Eisenhower, the victorious leader of the Allies in Europe in World War II, and those of Senator Robert Taft of Ohio, the grandson of President William Howard Taft. At every stop on the way from Los Angeles to the convention site, Chicago, the junior senator from California, Richard Nixon, one of the slimiest self-promoters in American history, would get off the special train and tell the local press, "There is a lot of Eisenhower sentiment in the delegation." This helped force Governor Warren's hand and undermined his strategy of awaiting a possible deadlock. He ultimately supported General Eisenhower for the nomination and was rewarded with a promise of the first vacancy on the Supreme Court. That came sooner than anyone had anticipated, when Chief Justice Fred Vinson, a Truman appointee, died suddenly in the summer of 1953. Nixon, of course, was also rewarded—with the vice-presidential nomination. Warren never forgave "Tricky Dick" for this self-aggrandizing display of disloyalty.

When Earl Warren entered a room, he lit it up. Not because he was a noisy, self-promoting glad-hander. He wasn't. He was instead quiet and dignified, someone people instinctively liked and respected and to whom they looked for leadership. He had the knack of all great politicians of making the person he was talking to at the moment feel like the most important person on earth. Whenever he called me into his office to discuss a matter of Court business, he began with unhurried inquiries about me and my family, and he gave the impression that he really cared and seemed to listen to my responses. He was a great person to work for. In my experience, especially in the political world, there are two kinds of bosses: those who make their staff members feel useful and those who make them feel used. Earl Warren was supremely one of the former. Of all the public figures and officials I have met, he was the one with the least difference between his public and his private personas. He was the one really great man, in my estimation, that I have ever known. He would have made a formidable president, much better than the one we got in 1952. But maybe he was needed more where he went.

The chief justice welcomed us in that first meeting warmly, inquired of us individually about ourselves, and told us what he expected of us in our work. We were, he said, his lawyers, and our work for him was, in his view, covered by the attorney-client privilege. That meant that we were to maintain the confidentiality of our dealings with him. We were not to talk about cases to anyone outside the Court. He acknowledged that we would inevitably discuss the Court's work with clerks from other chambers, but even here, he cautioned, what was said in chambers was to stay there. He told us that the Court was a friendly and collegial place, and that was borne out by the obvious affection and respect in which all his colleagues held the Chief.

❖ ❖ ❖

Presiding over the chief justice's chambers was his secretary, Margaret McHugh, known universally among the law clerks as "Mrs. Chief Justice McHugh." She had been Chief Justice Vinson's secretary, and she stayed on to guide the new chief justice through the labyrinth of the Court, where the tiny staff and the traditions of secrecy and independence bore no resemblance to the governor's office in California. She viewed it as one of her tasks to keep the law clerks in a state of sufficient intimidation that they would give no trouble. She had a gruff demeanor when she needed it, but underneath it was a real fondness for us and a twinkle in her eye. She and I always got along very well. A few months after I left the Court, when I was interviewing for a job in his law firm, the famous lawyer Edward Bennett Williams, who was close to the chief justice, asked me if I would mind his calling the Chief for a reference. I said not at all. An amused smile then flickered across his face, and he said, "Would you mind if I called Peggy McHugh? You know that's a different question, don't you?" I acknowledged that it was indeed a very different question and said I had no qualms about his calling Mrs. McHugh. She must not have knocked me, for I got the job.

❖ ❖ ❖

I soon began to get to know the clerks from the other chambers. They were a powerful and interesting group, who went on to have very distinguished careers. Justice Potter Stewart's clerk Larry Tribe became perhaps the leading constitutional law scholar of his generation. Lance Liebman from Justice Byron White's chambers was later dean of the Columbia School of Law. Ray Fisher from Justice William Brennan's staff became a judge on the

U.S. Court of Appeals for the Ninth Circuit. Justice Hugo Black had hired Steve Shulhofer, first in his class at Harvard, and Justice Abe Fortas had the editors-in-chief of both the *Harvard Law Review* and the *Yale Law Journal*, David Rosenblum and Peter Zimroth. And so on. Our gathering time was lunch, and we had a special dining room set aside for us, just off the Court's public cafeteria, so that we could talk in confidence without fear of being overheard. The discussions, occasionally turning into heated arguments, about pending cases and other legal and political issues were an intellectual feast. We in the Chief's chambers took his injunction about confidentiality pretty seriously, but some clerks would occasionally vent their frustrations with their justices before the whole group.

❖ ❖ ❖

Most chambers at the Court consisted of a suite of three large rooms. There was a central room, where the justice's secretary sat, which served also as a reception room for those waiting to meet with the justice. On one side was the justice's spacious and comfortable office, with a small law library, containing the reports of all Supreme Court decisions and most published opinions of lower federal courts, and fitted out with a working fireplace. On the other side of the secretary's office were the law clerks in a generous room of their own containing a similar array of law books.

The chief justice's arrangement was different. His reception room was larger, and it contained the desks of Mrs. McHugh and two or three others, who provided typing assistance and help with the chief justice's many administrative duties, which included overseeing the operation of the Supreme Court building, the Clerk's Office, the Marshal's Office and the Supreme Court police; leading the Judicial Conference of the United States and its standing committees, which considered and recommended procedural and other reforms; and serving as chancellor of the Smithsonian Institution, the federal government's major museum system in Washington. The Chief's own office was larger than those of the other justices, and his suite also contained the Court's conference room, where the justices met in secret to discuss and vote on argued cases, and its robing room, where the justices gathered each day the Court was sitting to don their robes before taking the bench. The Chief's suite of offices was directly across the hall from the back wall of the courtroom itself, so the justices could walk directly from the robing room to the courtroom as they were impressively ushered in by the Marshal's call to order.

Lacking in the chief justice's suite was any separate room for law clerks, so his clerks were housed in a large suite of offices on the second floor of the building. This had two major consequences. First, his clerks had less direct personal contact with him than the clerks for other justices had with their bosses. If an associate justice wanted to ask his clerk a question, or just sit and chat, he could walk to an almost adjoining room and sit down, or call the clerk into his office within the same suite. For the chief justice to confer with one of his clerks was much more of a project, which involved the clerk hiking for several minutes from the upstairs office. The second consequence, however, was that Larry Nichols and I did not feel deprived of contact with the chief justice by virtue of the fact that our offices were in the chambers of our retired justices. Indeed, Justice Reed's chambers were on the first floor, so I was physically closer to the Chief's chambers than his own clerks were. All of us saw the Chief on business only when summoned to his office by Mrs. McHugh and then usually to discuss something specific, such as an opinion that one of us was working on.

❖ ❖ ❖

The location of our offices did not mean that we had no relaxed time with the chief justice, however. Whenever he was in town, he took us to lunch on Saturdays. We regularly worked Saturday mornings, and sometime after noon we would get a call from Mrs. McHugh telling us to meet the chief justice down in the Court's underground garage, where we would all pile into his Court limousine and head off for lunch, often at the University Club or the Federal City Club. These were wonderful sessions that we clerks cherished. The chief justice liked to relax with a drink or two before lunch on Saturday (vodka gimlets on the rocks), and he was very open and freewheeling with us. He loved sports, and in the fall lunch would usually extend to at least halftime of whatever college football game was on ABC (the only network then broadcasting college football) that week. As the term wore on and we became more comfortable around him, we asked more pointed and interesting questions about his life experience and his views on a variety of topics, and the chief justice responded with candor and relish.

One Saturday over lunch the chief justice told an amusing story about Justice Charles Whittaker, who replaced Justice Reed on the Court in 1957. Though he had sat on both the district court and the Eighth Circuit Court of Appeals, Justice Whittaker was simply not up to the job of being a Supreme Court justice. He had difficulty making up his mind, and it was widely reported that he suffered a nervous breakdown that led to his resignation from the Court after only four terms. One day, the Chief said, Whittaker came to him and said he had a question about the traditions of the Court. He said his best friend's daughter was about to get married, and the family had asked him to perform the ceremony in his chambers. He had agreed to do so, he said, subject to checking with the chief justice to make sure it did not violate any Court tradition. The Chief told Whittaker, "I don't know about any traditions of the Court, but do you have the authority to marry anyone?" Whittaker responded that he was a judge, and thus he obviously had the authority. Warren said, "I'm not so sure," so the two of them began rummaging through the D.C. Code without benefit of law clerk. They identified the correct legal issue. One section of the code authorized all magistrates of the District of Columbia to perform marriages. The question was whether a Supreme Court justice was a magistrate of the District of Columbia. They found a provision that made federal district judges on the D.C. court magistrates and another conferring such status on judges of the D.C. Circuit Court of Appeals, but none making Supreme Court justices magistrates of the District. "See," the Chief said to Whittaker, "you don't have the authority." Whittaker began wringing his hands and said, "What am I going to do? The family is counting on me." After a few minutes, according to the Chief, Whittaker set his jaw and said, "Maybe I'll just go ahead and do it, and no one will ever question it." "Well, Charlie," the chief justice replied, "if you want to be responsible for a bunch of little bastards, you go right ahead."

❖ ❖ ❖

Being a law clerk has never been a nine-to-five sort of job. Clerks are always on call when their judges need—or want—their assistance. We were not permitted to leave the building in the evening until the chief justice had gone home, and there was much more work to be done than could be accomplished in an ordinary work day. Fortunately for us, the chief justice kept very regular hours. We could expect a call from the guards in the garage around 6:30 p.m. telling us that the Chief had departed. And a lot of the work—reading petitions and briefs, for example—could easily be done at home. So virtually every night during my clerkship I went home to the apartment Louise and I had rented in Falls Church, Virginia, in time for dinner, taking with me a briefcase full of reading material. This gave me some time to talk to Louise and play with Will for a while before his bedtime. After dinner I would unload the briefcase and read until around

10 p.m. Saturday mornings were spent at work, and Saturday lunches generally with the chief justice and my co-clerks. Sundays I usually managed to take all or most of the day off. It was a demanding work schedule, but nothing compared to the hours I had put in on the managing board of the law review.

❖ ❖ ❖

The Supreme Court of the United States, of all places, harbored in the late 1960s one of the last obvious vestiges of slavery in the entire country. Each justice, including the retired ones, had a messenger who was to all intents and purposes a manservant. In the days before the construction of the Supreme Court building in the mid-1930s, the government did not even supply justices with office space, so they worked out of their homes, and the messengers served an important official function, circulating opinion drafts and memoranda among the justices. I am sure they performed more personal tasks for the justices as well. By 1967 the Court had occupied its marble palace for more than thirty years, and the messengers were mostly personal gofers, driving the justices (or their wives) around and performing personal errands. All the messengers were black, and most, if not all, were elderly or the next thing to it. Most displayed some degree of the self-effacing obsequiousness that generations of slavery had imprinted on black people and that persisted among many, especially southern blacks, well into the 20th century. Worse, it was the tradition of the Court to call these men by their unadorned last names. Justice Reed and Helen Gaylord never referred to his messenger, Gerald Ross, by any other name than "Ross."

Things were a little better, I think, in the chief justice's chambers. His messenger, Alvin Wright, was called by his first name, and I don't believe Alvin was ever called on to do anything but drive the chief justice to and from work and to official functions in his Court-supplied limousine—the only government car that any justice had. There was a widely told story about Chief Justice Warren giving a speech or attending a conference in a southern city during his first term and discovering to his horror but too late—the next morning—that poor Alvin had slept in the car because there was no hotel in the rigidly segregated town that would take him. Sadly, Alvin was pressed into service by Warren Burger, Chief Justice Warren's pompous successor, as a kind of personal crier. The famous book about the Burger Court, *The Brethren*, contains a scene in which Burger was piped into his first meeting with a new set of law clerks by Alvin intoning, "Gentlemen, the chief justice of the United States."[3]

Along with several other clerks, I found the practice of calling these men by their last names demeaning. But finding an alternative was hard. In context, calling them "Mr. So-and-So"—the solution adopted by Justice Stewart's clerks—seemed stilted and distant and only called attention to the unhappy general practice. Though it went against the grain of my polite southern upbringing to call someone so many years my senior by his first name, I thought it was the warmer, friendlier option, so I began calling Gerald Ross "Gerald."

Gerald Ross was from Maysville, Kentucky, Justice Reed's home town. Though I am not sure of this, I believe he had worked for the Reed family in some capacity before the justice left for Washington in 1929. When Stanley Reed was appointed to the Court, Gerald followed him to the capital and served as his messenger. By the time I came to the Court, Gerald was largely in charge of catering to the rather imperious demands of Mrs. Reed, taking her to the grocery store and the beauty parlor and running household errands for her. Gerald was perfectly capable of putting on the air of a long-time family retainer, calling the justice "the Boss" and speaking with an exaggerated air of deference. When he served Justice Reed's daily lunch of rice and apple quarters, Gerald donned a white waiter's jacket.

But things are not always as they seem. One day Gerald walked into my office with an air of nonchalance and pulled from behind his back a paperback book, which he handed to me, saying, "I thought you might want to read this." It was *The Autobiography of Malcolm X*, the firebrand Black Muslim who raised fear and outrage among whites by his fervent attacks on white racism, and who was assassinated after he broke with Elijah Muhammad, the founder and leader of the Black Muslims. It was a powerful book, in which Malcolm X detailed the outrages perpetrated on him and his family by whites when he was young and his struggle to come to terms with the racial divide in America as an adult. I read it and discussed it with Gerald. It was the first of many long conversations I had with this very interesting man.

Gerald was very bright, but he had been handicapped all his life by the relatively poor education the South offered to its black citizens and by the absolute cap it put on their aspirations. Nonetheless, he had read a lot, and he was a close observer of the institution where he worked. He would occasionally slip into the courtroom to listen to an argument, and he had a list of his least favorite decisions of the Supreme Court. At the top of this list was the grisly case of *Louisiana ex rel. Francis v. Resweber*.[4] It involved the question whether it was a violation of the Constitution to electrocute a man twice. The state of Louisiana had tried to execute the defendant, a black man convicted of murder, and had sent vast currents of electricity surging through his body. The state had botched the job, however, and the defendant lived and recovered. After he was well, the state wanted to do it all over again. The Supreme Court held, five-to-four, that there was no denial of due process of law in this. Though the case was decided twenty years earlier, and the prevailing opinion was written by Justice Reed, it still outraged Gerald in 1967, and he became agitated when he talked about it.

Gerald Ross was a big—and very pleasant—part of my education during my year at the Court. He was also, I learned, an entrepreneur. In his spare time, he catered parties. He was an excellent cook (he worked generally alone) and an impeccable server. In 1970, when my sister was married in our apartment, Gerald catered the wedding. It was wonderful. Gerald had very high standards, and Louise still recalls that he politely pointed out to her that the salt and pepper shakers needed washing.

Gerald's catering business gave rise to at least one very amusing story. John Pickering, a consummate and well-known Washington lawyer and a senior partner in the firm of Wilmer, Cutler & Pickering, had clerked for Justice Frank Murphy in the 1940s. He had met Justice Reed at the time, and the two became good acquaintances over the years, seeing each other with some frequency at cocktail parties. One day after the justice retired, John called the Reed chambers looking for Gerald Ross to ask him to cater a party at the Pickerings' house. On about the third ring the phone was answered by a gravelly voice saying, "Justice Reed's chambers." It was the justice, who sometimes answered his own phone when both Helen and Gerald were out somewhere. (I had the same experience when I called to arrange an interview with Justice Reed.) John identified himself and the two exchanged pleasantries for a while. Finally, Justice Reed asked the purpose of John's call, and somewhat abashed, John said, "Well, actually Mr. Justice, I am trying to reach Gerald Ross." The justice meekly took a message for his in-demand messenger.

❖ ❖ ❖

Cert memos and bench memos are all well and good, and some are interesting and challenging, but a law clerk lives for working on opinions. It is by far the most exciting part of the job. At its best it offers an opportunity to express, perhaps even to help shape, the thinking of the judge or the court on an issue, and it holds out the hope of a little bit of immortality, or at least what passes for immortality in the rather narrow world of the law—having one's own words printed in the official publication of the court's opinions.

Just how much and what kind of work a law clerk gets to do on opinions is a function of the work habits of the judge and of the degree of trust the judge reposes in the judgment and writing skill of the individual clerk. At the Supreme Court in 1967, for example, Justices Hugo Black and William O. Douglas, both of whom had served roughly thirty years on the Court and were men of strong opinions and forceful expression, did almost all their own writing. Their clerks principally checked the citations in the justices' drafts to make sure there were no mistakes, found precedents to support positions the justices wanted to take, offered suggestions on various points, and got to draft an odd footnote here or there. Some justices asked their clerks for extensive, detailed memos on particular aspects of a proposed opinion, parts of which they might incorporate in the opinion itself. Some let the clerks write the statement of facts at the beginning of the opinion, but reserved the legal analysis to themselves. Others split the writing with their clerks, with the justice doing the first draft of some opinions and the clerks drafting others.

Chief Justice Warren, at least by the time I clerked for him, did none of the original drafting of opinions. I never asked him why, but none of his prior jobs had involved much writing, and I had the sense that he was not comfortable with the process of putting words on paper. His success as a politician was not dependent on memorable rhetoric, but on performance. He outworked everyone else and did a first-rate job. The fact that he did not put the words on paper, however, did not mean that the opinions were not ultimately his product. Before a law clerk began work on an opinion draft, the chief justice would have a lengthy conversation with the clerk, in which he made clear what he wanted the opinion to say and what arguments he found persuasive. Once the law clerk had produced a draft with which he was happy and that had passed the inspection of the other clerks in chambers, it would be submitted to the chief justice. After he had read it carefully, the Chief would call the law clerk into his office and go over the opinion literally word by word, reading it aloud to the clerk, including the footnotes. This could be an excruciating, and excruciatingly long, process. If the chief justice encountered an argument he did not like, or a citation he thought did not support the assertion for which it was offered, or found a word or phrase that offended his sensibilities, he would stop, discuss the issue with the clerk, and tell him how to revise the draft. Once the dodgy parts had been rewritten to the Chief's satisfaction, he would send the draft to the printer for typesetting and circulation. Thus the final product was something he controlled intimately and carefully. The words might be mostly the words of the clerk, but the opinion was that of the chief justice.

❖ ❖ ❖

One of the prerogatives of being chief justice is that you get to choose which opinions you write for the Court. The Court usually hears oral arguments in two-week sessions. At the end of each argument week, the Court meets in conference, where the justices discuss and vote on the argued cases. The conferences are secret, attended only by the justices—no clerks or secretaries. At the end of each conference, the chief justice would call us into his office along with the clerk of the court, to whom he would communicate the Court's rulings for publication. After the clerk left, he would tell us about the votes in argued cases and answer any questions we had about what had gone on. The votes at conference are tentative; a justice is free to change his or her vote until the moment the decision and opinion are announced in the courtroom. Based on the tentative votes in conference, the chief justice circulates the following week a list of opinion assignments. The power to assign opinions and to preside at Court sessions and conferences are the only powers the chief justice has that the associate justices do not. Moreover, the chief justice assigns opinions only when he is in the majority. Where his tentative vote is a dissent, the opinion is assigned by the senior associate justice in the majority. (Chief Justice Warren Burger, Earl Warren's successor, deeply annoyed his colleagues with his practice of voting at conference with the majority so that he could control the opinion assignment, and then "switching" his vote to the dissent he had all along planned.[5])

Chief Justice Warren never discussed opinion assignments with us clerks, but it was easy to see that he made in the first instance a scrupulous effort to spread the work of the Court evenly among the justices. He also tried, I think, to spread around the more interesting and important majority opinions, but this is a tricky business. If a justice finds himself or herself in disagreement with the chief justice on most issues of constitutional law, he or she can hardly complain that the plums always go elsewhere. And in difficult or important cases, there is undoubtedly a temptation for the chief justice to keep the case or assign it to a close ally on whom he can count to write an opinion with which he will be comfortable. Despite Chief Justice

Warren's best efforts, I recall Justice Stewart at some point complaining that he got too many "dogs" to write, especially tax cases.

Once a proposed majority opinion is circulated, the real fun begins. A justice who is satisfied with the draft opinion sends a memo to its author, with a copy to all the other justices, saying "join me." A justice will sometimes send a memo to, or go to see, the author suggesting changes in the draft opinion, and will on occasion make those changes the price of his joining the opinion. Not until five justices have signed on to some version of a draft does an opinion really become "the opinion of the Court." Meanwhile, all the justices are free to circulate their own opinions dissenting from the decision, or concurring on the basis of some difference from the majority in reasoning. Sometimes the author of a circulated opinion will take issue with something said in another opinion, circulating a new draft of his own, and this process occasionally goes through several exchanges of fire. In rare instances what began life as a proposed majority opinion will not garner enough votes, and the tentative result in the case will change. Once the shouting has died down and every justice has made his or her position clear (only four times in the history of the Court has a justice declared himself *dubitante* on one or more of the issues in a case[6]), the decision is scheduled for public announcement at a future sitting of the Court, usually by tradition on a Monday.

❖ ❖ ❖

In the remainder of this chapter I will be writing in some detail about my efforts in connection with the preparation of opinions in several cases, which naturally raises the question whether that is consistent with the chief justice's emphasis on confidentiality. This is a good and important question, and to answer it, I must leap forward some thirty years. One of the cases I worked on, *Terry v. Ohio*,[7] (about which more later) became very famous and was often cited and much discussed. In 1998 a professor at St. John's Law School in New York named John Barrett undertook to organize a conference of legal scholars to celebrate the case's thirtieth anniversary and to debate various aspects of the decision and its effects. He learned that I had been the Chief's law clerk on *Terry*, and he called and invited me to talk about the Court's decision-making process in the case. I initially declined, citing the Chief's strong feelings about confidentiality and saying that I had never spoken in public or even in any detail in private about my work for him. John thanked me and said he hoped I would at least attend the conference. A couple of months later he called me back and said that he had been researching in the Court's archives at the Library of Congress, which contained Chief Justice Warren's papers, and that he had copies of all my memos to the Chief, all the opinion drafts in the cases, and memos sent to the Chief by other justices. He was, he said, preparing a detailed article on the Court's inner deliberations in *Terry* for publication in connection with the conference and that it would be based to no small degree on my writings.[8] In fact, he sent me copies of all the material I had written in connection with the case. I figured that the attorney-client privilege had been pretty solidly waived, and I agreed to speak at the conference.[9]

❖ ❖ ❖

My first opinion-drafting assignment, in the case of *Will v. United States*,[10] involved a narrow and technical point of federal law, on which the Supreme Court was in unanimous agreement. The Seventh Circuit Court of Appeals in Chicago had employed the old common-law writ of *mandamus* to reverse before trial an otherwise unappealable order of a federal district judge requiring the government to disclose some aspects of its evidence to the defendant in a criminal case in advance of trial. The court of appeals had the undoubted power under a federal statute to issue a *mandamus*, but the Supreme Court took a very narrow view of the scope of the writ. It was not, the Court held, to be employed to expand the jurisdiction of the appellate court in contravention of the general rule that only "final judgments" could be appealed. The function of the writ of *mandamus* in this context was only to confine the lower court to legitimate exercises of its own jurisdiction. Here the district judge might have been wrong to order the disclosure, but he was clearly within the scope of his jurisdiction. There were a couple of Supreme Court precedents that arguably supported the court of appeals' decision, which had to be distinguished, but essentially the case was uncontroversial.

The chief justice and I went through his elaborate editorial process without too much difficulty, and the opinion draft garnered general acceptance. Only Justice Black added a very brief concurring opinion. It was a good warm-up exercise, as my later efforts proved much more difficult and controversial.

❖ ❖ ❖

My second, and most important, opinion-drafting adventure involved one of the two or three most controversial decisions of the term, and the one most cited by far in subsequent years. It grew out of three separate cases that the Court had consolidated for argument and consideration—*Terry v. Ohio*,[11] *Sibron v. New York*, and *Peters v. New York*.[12] All three dealt with the controversial police practice known as "stop and frisk," which the Supreme Court had never before considered.

The 1960s were a tumultuous and violent time, marked by sometimes feisty political demonstrations in favor of civil rights and against the Vietnam War, by political assassinations and race riots, the latter venting the pent-up frustration of the black community with the slow pace of legal and social change, and by a rise in the general rate of violent crime. In this overheated and often dangerous context, police officers asserted the authority to stop people they suspected of engaging in or planning criminal activity and to frisk them by patting down their clothing to see if they were carrying weapons. The police argued, with some force, that they needed this authority to protect themselves and others from possible injury or death.

The criminal defense bar and civil rights lawyers argued that the practice violated the Fourth Amendment to the federal constitution, which provides in part that "The right of the people to be secure in their persons, houses, papers, and effects against unreasonable searches and seizures shall not be violated ...." The Fourth Amendment's second clause provides that no search or arrest warrants can be issued by magistrates "but upon probable cause, supported by oath or affirmation." The term "probable cause" had been interpreted by the Court to mean that the magistrate—or the police officer acting without a warrant—must be possessed of sufficient evidence "to warrant a man of reasonable caution in the belief that an offense has been or is being committed" before a person could be arrested or a search of his person, house, papers, or effects could be undertaken.[13] The standard was a significant bar to police action. Essentially the officer had to demonstrate that the evidence in his possession made it more likely than not (*"probable* cause") that criminal activity was afoot and that the individual seized or searched was engaged in it.

The facts in *Terry* illustrated the problem clearly. Martin McFadden, an experienced plainclothes detective on patrol in downtown Cleveland, observed Terry and two other men pacing up and down the same block and alternately peering intensely into a store window and conferring with one another. This went on for some time. McFadden believed that the men were "casing" the store for a possible robbery or burglary. He went up to the men, identified himself as a police officer, and asked their names. When one of them "mumbled something" in response, McFadden grabbed Terry, placed him between himself and the other two, and frisked him, finding a revolver in his overcoat pocket. Terry was prosecuted for illegal possession of a concealed firearm, and his lawyer objected to the introduction of the weapon in evidence on the ground that the prosecution's possession of it was the result of an unconstitutional search and seizure. It was clear that McFadden did not possess "probable cause" to arrest Terry or his companions for any crime before he found the gun. But as the finding of the revolver underscored, it was difficult to say that McFadden was wrong in suspecting that the men were armed and dangerous and up to no good. (One of the other men was also found to possess a gun.)

The initial question in the cases was whether the Fourth Amendment applied at all, whether a "stop" was a "seizure" of the person and whether a "frisk" was a "search." The police took the position that the Fourth Amendment did not come into play until a person was arrested and taken to the police station, at which point they concededly needed "probable cause." The lesser intrusion represented by a "stop and frisk," they urged, could be undertaken on a less demanding evidentiary showing. The other side argued, with the force of considerable logic, that when a policeman grabs a person forcibly, spins him around, and pats him down for weapons, he has undoubtedly physically "seized" the person and conducted a "search," acts for which the officer needs "probable cause," which, they asserted, was often lacking when the police acted quickly on the basis of their "hunches" about suspicious-looking persons. Civil rights advocates made the additional troubling point that this kind of police conduct was most often directed at members of minority groups who frequently lived in "ghettos" in major cities and were targeted by police sometimes without rational basis. (McFadden was white. Terry and his friends were black.)

These were very hard questions, and they arose in the context of the bitterly contested 1968 presidential campaign, in which the Chief's old nemesis, Richard Nixon, was leading an attack on the Court as siding too often with "the criminal forces" against "the peace forces" in its decisions holding police and prosecutors to the strictures of the Bill of Rights. In this context, some have argued, the Court blinked and pulled back from the confrontation.[14] Its initial vote at the conference after argument in the *Terry* cases was a unanimous one to uphold the "stop and frisk" practices.

The chief justice assigned the opinions in all three cases to himself, and as I had been the clerk who did the *cert* and bench memos, the drafting fell to me.

The Court's initial unanimity in *Terry*, as I soon learned, masked an almost complete lack of consensus about how to justify the police conduct under the Fourth Amendment. The chief justice told me that the opinion should say that stop and frisk practices were indeed searches and seizures subject to the constraints of the Fourth Amendment, and that the appropriate standard was "probable cause," but that in the context of potentially dangerous street encounters with suspicious persons, "probable cause to frisk" demanded less evidence than the traditional "probable cause" to make an arrest or a full-body search. I drafted an opinion along these lines, and the chief justice seemed pleased with it. We circulated it, and it sank like a stone to the bottom of a pool of water. No one joined it. The problem was that, while it might well be that Officer McFadden had acted reasonably in the circumstances, it was difficult to argue with a straight face that he had "probable cause" to do anything.

After several weeks of deafening silence, Justice Douglas gave the chief justice a memorandum with a suggested rewrite of portions of the opinion. The Chief was unimpressed and rejected the Douglas draft. Then Justice Brennan, the Chief's closest ally on the Court, offered his own suggested revisions of parts of the opinion. The essence of the Brennan suggestion was to uncouple the two clauses of the Fourth Amendment. The Court had said in the past that the only standard for a "reasonable" search under the first clause was "probable cause," for the simple and persuasive reason that a police officer should not have the authority to do something on his own that a magistrate could not authorize him to do if he applied for a warrant.[15] This made sense, Brennan argued, in situations where applying for a warrant was at least theoretically possible; however, in rapidly unfolding street encounters between police and citizens, where getting a warrant was completely out of the question, the standard for defining an "unreasonable search" could be separated from the "probable cause" standard of the Warrant Clause. Standing on its own, "reasonableness" could permit a sliding-scale approach that weighed the information possessed by the police officer against the risk involved in the situation and the intrusiveness of his actions. Measured against this standard, McFadden's patdown of Terry was, according to Justice Brennan, reasonable.

It was an ingenious and typically Brennanesque move, and the chief justice decided to adopt it. He told me to prepare a new draft incorporating

the Brennan suggestions. In the process of doing so, I had numerous conversations with Justice Brennan's clerk on the cases, Ray Fisher, with whom
I was friendly and who also spoke at John Barrett's conference thirty years
later. The move led, however, to the defection of Justice Douglas, who
adhered to the view that the clauses should be read *in pari materia* and
thus that McFadden's actions could be justified only if he had "probable
cause" of some sort.[16]

There then developed a sticking point that led to my scariest experience
as a law clerk. Chief Justice Warren's instinct had been from the start to
uncouple the "stop" and the "frisk" and to give the Court's explicit approval
only to the latter, as a necessary protective device. He was much more troubled by the power to "stop," to detain a person possibly for investigative
purposes on less than probable cause. He thought it was potentially subject
to great abuse and could lead to what amounted to arrests in many cases
on mere suspicion. Thus the initial draft of the opinion had said that, since
McFadden had done nothing that could be construed as a "seizure" before he
grabbed Terry and patted him down, the Court need not reach the issue of
investigative stops at all. Justice Brennan suggested, however, that the Court
reach and decide the "stop" issue in favor of the police. I was very concerned
and wrote the chief justice a long memo urging him not to accept this part
of the Brennan position. Somewhat to my surprise, the chief justice shared
my memo with Justice Brennan. He called me into his office one morning
and said that Justice Brennan did not share my concerns and had assured
him that there was no problem in reaching the "stop" issue. When I stuck
to my guns in our conversation, the chief justice buzzed Mrs. McHugh and
asked her to find out if Justice Brennan was in his office. When she buzzed
back a couple of minutes later and said the justice was in, the chief justice
stood up and said, "Come on." I was to say the least shell-shocked. Mrs.
McHugh didn't help. As we passed her desk, she said under her breath so
that only I could hear, in a little singsong, "He's gonna be sur*prised.*" As we
entered Justice Brennan's office, Chief Justice Warren was in the lead. When
Justice Brennan saw him, his face broke into a huge grin. When he saw me,
it froze. The chief justice was obviously troubled and was, I think, looking
to have a debate between Justice Brennan and me over the "stop" issue. I
soon learned to my great relief that there was one person in the room who
wanted such a debate even less than I did. Justice Brennan seized the floor
and began telling jokes non-stop, as only a delightful Irishman could. After
about five minutes, the chief justice got the point and we left.

In the end, Chief Justice Warren stuck with his own initial instinct and

avoided the "stop" issue.[17] This led to concurring opinions from Justices
John Harlan and Byron White urging that logic required the Court to
reach the "stop" question.[18] But the chief justice's opinion with the Brennan
modification, and without any approval of investigative stops, garnered a
solid majority of six. And I like to think that it may have led the Court to
approach the "stop" issue in future cases with great caution and to place
serious limitations on the power to detain for investigation on less than
probable cause.[19]

❖ ❖ ❖

Late in the term, in May 1968, my co-clerks and I attended our first
reunion of the chief justice's law clerks. It was an annual gala event. Former
clerks came from around the country to pay their respects to the Chief and
to renew acquaintances or friendships with each other. I spent a pleasant
time chatting with Peter Low, my old Criminal Law teacher, and his wife. It
was a weekend-long affair. The former clerks wandered in and out of chambers on Friday afternoon, chatting with Mrs. McHugh and the others. On
Saturday night there was a black-tie dinner for the chief justice and the
clerks, and on Sunday morning the Chief and Mrs. Warren hosted a brunch
for the clerks and their wives and significant others. It was a very pleasant
ritual that went on until the chief justice died in 1974.

In 1968 one of Chief Justice Warren's former clerks, Jim Gaither, was
working as an aide to President Lyndon Johnson. It was the Chief's fifteenth
anniversary on the Court, and Jim arranged for President Johnson to come
to the Saturday evening dinner as a surprise to the Chief. It was the height
of the Vietnam War and only two months after deep opposition to the war
in the Democratic Party had led Johnson to withdraw from the presidential race. When the president entered the room during the cocktail hour,
a hushed silence fell over the crowd. It was very odd. I sensed no hostility
to Johnson, despite the fact that many of us strongly opposed his handling
of the war. We all thought it was a very nice gesture on his part to come to
honor the Chief. It was just, I think, that we had no idea what to say at a
cocktail party to the president of the United States—this despite the fact
that the group was full of sophisticated lawyers, many of them already well-
launched on what would be very distinguished careers, who had been chatting away quite comfortably with the highest judicial officer in the land. The
president slid over to the bar, took pains to shake hands with the wait staff,
ordered a Scotch, and chug-a-lugged it. After about fifteen minutes of really

awkward small talk, he said some very nice things about the chief justice, handed him a gift-wrapped present, and departed. We learned from Jim Gaither that Johnson had originally planned to stay for dinner but decided to leave when things seemed so uncomfortable. In retrospect, I felt sorry for President Johnson. He must have been very lonely. The chief justice did not open his gift from the president while the latter was still there. There was a tradition of the clerks' collectively giving the Chief a gift, and he did not open that until after-dinner remarks were under way, so the president's gift was set aside and opened after dinner as well. When the Chief opened the president's gift, it turned out to be a bronze bust of President Johnson himself. The Chief said, a bit ruefully, "I guess I should have opened that while the president was here."

❖ ❖ ❖

My final opinion-drafting exercise involved another case of great public interest and controversy, *Powell v. Texas*,[20] and my work on the case was truly an eye-opening experience. *Powell* raised the question whether it constituted "cruel and unusual punishment," prohibited by the Eighth Amendment, to convict a chronic alcoholic of the crime of being drunk in public. To understand this issue requires a little background. The state of California had in the 1950s made it a crime to be addicted to narcotics. In 1962, in the case of *Robinson v. California*,[21] the Supreme Court had struck down this law under the Eighth Amendment, holding that to penalize under the criminal law a "status"—being an addict—over which one might have no control—as opposed to an act, which one presumably undertook voluntarily, violated basic norms of a free society and constituted "cruel and unusual punishment." In the wake of *Robinson*, defense lawyers around the country had sought to extend its reach to chronic alcoholics and to their punishment for public drunkenness. The argument was that being an alcoholic was a status, like being a narcotics addict, and that an alcoholic could not control his state of inebriation in a public place. It was thus, the argument ran, essentially the punishment of a mere status.

Some lower courts, most notably the federal court of appeals for the District of Columbia Circuit, had bought the argument and reversed the convictions of alcoholics for public drunkenness. Others had rejected it. The topic was hotly debated in the law reviews and among lawyers generally.

Leroy Powell, a Texan with a long history of arrests and convictions for public drunkenness, was arrested once again in public in a state of inebriation. His lawyer put on expert testimony that Powell was an alcoholic and that a chronic alcoholic, at least once he takes the first drink, has no power to control his further consumption of alcohol. Powell took the stand in his defense, and on cross-examination the prosecutor took a shot in the dark. He asked Powell if he had had anything to drink that morning before the trial. The bolt went home. Powell admitted that he had taken one drink that someone had given him, presumably to steady his nerves. The prosecutor pressed his advantage, getting Powell to admit that he had been able to stop at one drink that day because of the importance of his trial. Even in the face of this admission, the trial court found that Powell was a chronic alcoholic and that as an alcoholic he had no power to stop drinking once he had started, but ruled that this was no defense to the charge. The Texas Court of Criminal Appeals denied its version of *cert*, and the U.S. Supreme Court granted Powell's petition.

The stock liberal position favored Powell's argument. Lawyers for him and for people like him contended that the Constitution should be used to break the "revolving-door" cycle of arrest, conviction, brief incarceration, release, and re-arrest that these unhappy people faced and force the states to replace it with some form of humane treatment. In my bench memo, I urged the chief justice to adopt this position.

The Chief was clearly troubled by the case, and at our Saturday lunch the weekend before the argument, he took the unique step (our term at least) of asking the assembled clerks for their views of what he should do. He went around the table, and all five of us in turn expressed our support for Powell's position. The Chief chuckled and said, "Well, that's very interesting, because I think I am going to vote the other way." He explained that, while psychiatrists now generally agreed that alcoholism was a disease, there was no real consensus about what that meant; that there was no agreed-upon course of treatment for alcoholics; and that even if there had been, there weren't enough psychiatrists in the country to treat all the alcoholics, even if the latter could all afford treatment and the doctors dropped their treatment of all other patients. He went on to say that no city would tolerate large numbers of unruly and often unsanitary drunks on its streets, and that the inevitable result of decriminalizing public drunkenness by alcoholics would be involuntary "civil commitment." The latter would carry with it indefinite incarceration until the patient was "cured," which in most cases would simply never happen, both because of the intractability of the condition and of the lack of resources to try to treat it. At least under the present system, despite its obviously ugly features, the chronic alcoholic convicted of public drunkenness got a few days in jail to sober up, some solid food, and most important of all, his liberty back once he had served his brief sentence.

It was a powerful argument, and it was vintage Earl Warren. It cut through, if indeed it did not ignore, nuances of constitutional theory and focused on the practical impact of legal rules on human beings. The chief justice was deeply schooled in the craft of government, and he had spent a lot of time thinking about how the actions of government actually affect people. And the argument was at bottom intensely empathetic and humane.

At the conference after the argument, the Court voted five-to-four to reverse Leroy Powell's conviction. The split defied conventional liberal-conservative distinctions. The majority consisted of Justices Douglas, Brennan, Stewart, White, and Fortas. Stewart and White were on many issues among the more conservative members of the Court. The dissenters were the chief justice and Justices Black, Harlan, and Marshall. Warren, Black, and Marshall were thought of as stalwart liberals. Justice Douglas, as the senior justice in the majority, assigned the opinion to Justice Fortas. The chief justice made it known that he was contemplating writing a dissent.

Once the proposed majority opinion by Justice Fortas had circulated, the chief justice called me in and instructed me to prepare a dissent. Its outline was to be essentially the argument he had presented to his clerks over lunch several weeks earlier. I got to work, and I found as my research delved more deeply into alcoholism and its treatment that the chief justice had spoken from solid knowledge throughout. I also made use of Powell's admission on cross-examination that he could limit himself to one drink if the incentive were powerful enough, in an effort to undercut the defense bar's implicit assertion that the "disease concept" of alcoholism had a clear meaning. While I was still working on the draft, Justice White switched his vote, circulating a brief statement saying only that *Robinson* was distinguishable because it involved punishment of a mere status, while in this case the acts of getting drunk and going into public were the crux of the offense. Thus the status of the chief justice's emerging draft opinion was unclear, but on his instructions I continued to cast it as a dissent from the Fortas draft.

The Chief seemed pleased with my draft, and after a few revisions it was ready to circulate. Or so I thought. At the end of our last meeting he said, with an apparently musing air, "I think I'll show this to Thurgood." I assumed he meant that he would try to get Justice Marshall to sign on before he circulated the draft, in order to show that it already had some purchase among the erstwhile dissenters. As I learned, however, he was up to something deeper. I soon began to get a lot of phone calls about the draft from Peter Lockwood, one of Justice Marshall's clerks, that seemed to go into more detail than would have been required to decide whether to sign onto a proposed dissent. Then one day, to my complete surprise, I received a printed version of the draft headed, "Mr. Justice Marshall, with whom the Chief Justice joins, dissenting." Peter and his justice had made a few modifications, but it was for the most part the draft I had given the chief justice. Justices Black and Harlan also signed on, though Justice White stuck to his brief concurrence,[22] so the opinion ultimately spoke for a plurality of the Court. Peter Lockwood and I had a good laugh, and he proclaimed me an honorary Marshall law clerk.

I never took the opportunity to ask the chief justice why he had done what he did, but if I had studied his career on the Court with a little more care, I might have seen it coming. Chief Justice Warren disagreed from time to time with the majority of the Court, as all justices do. He joined dissenting opinions. But he relatively rarely wrote them himself. I think I know why. A dissenting opinion inevitably is a frontal attack on the work of a colleague, and while most judges develop fairly thick skins, they are not immune to the sting of criticism. I believe the chief justice thought that such attacks were divisive and could, if undertaken often enough, undermine his relationships with other justices and his ability to build consensus in the large run of cases, as he believed it was his responsibility as the Chief to do. So he put Justice Marshall out front, at one and the same time avoiding the need to take on Justice Fortas directly and giving the spotlight in a major case to a newly minted justice.

I learned a tremendous amount from the chief justice in the *Powell* case, both about the sometimes tenuous relationship between legal argument and the practicalities of decision-making, and about leadership in a group of equals. It was a bravura performance.

❖ ❖ ❖

Sometime in the middle of my term at the Court I received a call from my hero-become-friend Army Boothe, who invited me to lunch. When we met, he made me an offer that was the most flattering I had ever received and over which I agonized considerably. He offered me a job with his law firm at a salary of $10,000 a year and said that he would try to help me get established in politics, perhaps by backing me to run for the legislature. He said that he did not have the authorization of his partners for the salary figure (entry-level lawyers in the major Richmond firms were then being paid $6,600 a year) but that if they balked at the number, he would make up the difference out of his own pocket. I told him that I was deeply honored and that I would think very hard about it.

This offer opened a vista that resonated deeply with my reasons for going to law school in the first place and my choice of Virginia in particular. I had always been interested in public affairs and harbored a hankering to run for public office. It would also give me a chance to deepen my relationship with Mr. Boothe, whom I admired greatly, and his family. His political mentorship would mean a great deal. He was known all over the state and was the most revered figure among those who lined up on the correct side of the racial issues that defined southern politics at that point in time. And I was deeply touched by his personal commitment to sweeten the pot with a salary that was fifty percent more than the state's biggest firms were then offering, although money was not then and has never been something that strongly motivates me. It was a very tempting prospect.

On the other side of the ledger were two major considerations. Having spent a summer in the Boothe firm in Alexandria and then two summers in major urban law firms, I was conscious of a significant difference in the quality of the law practice. Alexandria was only across the river from Washington, but it seemed a long way away. In the 1960s it remained a small southern town, with a law practice that was, at least in my view, much less sophisticated and challenging intellectually than what I had experienced at Gibson, Dunn and at Covington. I had found in law school something I had really not expected to find, an intellectual home, a sense of excitement and ferment in the law itself that drew me powerfully. This had been only reinforced by my year at the Supreme Court. I was afraid, perhaps wrongly but nonetheless genuinely, that if politics didn't work out I would be bored practicing in Alexandria, and I knew that even if I had some success in politics, my bread and butter would still always be purchased as a lawyer. Equally important, I was coming to believe that I simply was not cut out for politics in Virginia. My views on almost all issues were substantially more liberal than those of the vast majority of Virginians. This was especially the case with respect to race—and gender issues, for that matter. These seemed to me such fundamental questions of fairness and equal opportunity that I was not prepared to compromise or temporize, the only tactics that promised any long-range hope of success in Virginia. I thought there was a substantial possibility that I would crash and burn on the political launching pad.

I worried long and hard over these issues, talking about them a lot with Louise. As decision-making time approached, I decided to turn down Mr. Boothe's offer and opt instead for practice in Washington. It was perhaps the most difficult decision I ever made about my career, and of all the turns in my career the one at which I have most often looked back and wondered "what if."

I took a job with Wilmer, Cutler & Pickering, a very well-connected Washington firm with a great practice and very pleasant people. The firm had begun life as the Washington office of Cravath, Swaine & Moore, one of New York's largest and most prestigious firms, and it still had a close connection to Cravath and did a lot of Washington work for Cravath clients. "Washington work" meant interface with federal government departments and administrative agencies, a highly specialized practice located for the most part in Washington. It would satisfy, I thought, my desires for involvement in public policy and an intellectually challenging practice.

❖ ❖ ❖

As the Supreme Court term wore down toward its end, Chief Justice Warren continued his kindly interest in us and our families. He insisted that we pick out a morning when Louise and Will could come to the Court to see him. He had met Louise at the reunion festivities, but he wanted to chat with her more personally and to see Will. He had a poli-

Will, at age one, with Chief Justice Warren.

tician's gusto for babies. We still have the picture of Will, roughly a year old, in the Chief's arms. The following year on Valentine's Day, Will, perhaps remembering the Chief's kindly manner, sent him a valentine card. The chief justice wrote back a thoughtful thank-you note, complimenting Will on how well he made his letters.

Our last day at the Court was both a pleasant and a bittersweet one. The chief justice called us all into his office, gave us autographed pictures of himself, and told us what a pleasure it had been working with us. He also told us that he had sent his retirement letter to President Johnson that morning. The news came as a shock to us law clerks. None of us could really remember a chief justice before him, and we all admired him enormously. We knew that he deserved retirement—he was almost eighty and had been in public service all his adult life—and that he had some health issues. But we also knew that his leadership would be sorely missed. The world of the Court was about to change, and not, I thought, for the better.

As it turned out, Chief Justice Warren served another term when President Johnson's choice as his successor, Justice Fortas, withdrew his name after a bruising confirmation fight in the Senate. To the Chief's dismay, I am sure, his successor was ultimately appointed by Richard Nixon.

❖ ❖ ❖

Nixon's election as president, of course, still lay in the future on that day in late June 1968 when we said our goodbyes to the chief justice. I had decided to postpone my entry into law practice for a few months. I could not in good conscience sit idly by and watch this man I despised so much become the president of my country. I signed on to the campaign of Vice-President Hubert Humphrey, who was then seeking the Democratic nomination for president. When I told the chief justice that I planned to do this, I think he was pleased.

Notes

[1] For a history of the institution of the judicial clerk at the Supreme Court level, see Todd C. Peppers, *Courtiers of the Marble Palace: The Rise and Influence of the Supreme Court Law Clerk* (2006), written by one of my former students.

[2] See Todd C. Peppers & Christopher J. Zorn, *Law Clerk Influence on Supreme Court Decision Making* (June 14, 2007), available at SSRN http://ssrn.com/abstract=925705.

[3] See Bob Woodward & Scott Armstrong, *The Brethren: Inside the Supreme Court* 183 (Simon & Shuster paperback ed. 2005).

[4] 329 U.S. 459 (1947).

[5] See Woodward & Armstrong 204-17, 507, 514, 530.

[6] See Jason J. Czarnezki, *The* Dubitante *Opinion*, 39 Akron L. Rev. 1, 3 (2006).

[7] 392 U.S. 1 (1968).

[8] See John Q. Barrett, *Deciding the Stop and Frisk Cases: A Look Inside the Supreme Court's Conference*, 72 St. John's L. Rev. 749, 793-830 (1998).

[9] My talk was published in the *St. John's Law Review* under the title Terry v. Ohio, *the Warren Court, and Fourth Amendment: A Law Clerk's Perspective*, 72 St. John's L. Rev. 891 (1998).

[10] 389 U.S. 90 (1967).

[11] 392 U.S. 1 (1968).

[12] The latter two cases were decided together in a separate set of opinions under the title *Sibron v. New York*, 392 U.S. 40 (1968).

[13] Brinegar v. United States, 338 U.S. 160, 175-76 (1949).
[14] For an argument that the Warren Court's reputation for innovation and courage in the sphere of constitutional criminal procedure is overrated, not only in *Terry*, but more broadly, see the article of my former student, Corinna Barrett Lain, *Countermajoritarian Hero or Zero? Rethinking the Warren Court's Role in the Criminal Procedure Revolution*, 152 U. Pa. L. Rev. 1361 (2004).
[15] See, e.g., Wong Sun v. United States, 371 U.S. 471, 479 (1963).
[16] See *Terry*, 392 U.S. at 35 (Douglas, J., dissenting).
[17] See *id* at 19 n.16.
[18] *Id.* at 31 (Harlan, J. concurring); 34 (White, J., concurring).
[19] See Dudley, *A Law Clerk's Perspective* at 895-98.
[20] 392 U.S. 514 (1968).
[21] 370 U.S. 660 (1962).
[22] 392 U.S. at 548 (White, J., concurring).

CHAPTER NINE

Presidential Politics and Personal Loss
1968

1968 was the worst year of my life. The Vietnam War was tearing the nation, and more specifically the Democratic Party, apart. Like the majority of educated people of my generation, I thought the war was a tragic mistake. It was the child of the theory of "containment" of communism around the globe—a policy with longstanding bipartisan support—but unlike World War II or even the situation in Korea in 1950, it was not a war between nations, with boundaries and relatively measurable outcomes. It was an effort to prop up a corrupt and undemocratic regime against a popular insurgency that wouldn't quit and that had behind it the moral force of anti-colonialism. The war was taking many thousands of American—not to mention Vietnamese—lives, it was diverting resources and political will desperately needed to fight poverty and racism in this country, and its fighting force was the product of a grossly inequitable draft system that laid the burden of sacrifice squarely on the poor and the minorities.

Although the war had its roots in efforts by the Eisenhower administration to defend the government of South Vietnam, a relic of French colonialism in Southeast Asia, against efforts to overthrow it that were inspired and supplied by the communist government of North Vietnam, the major buildup and commitment of American forces had come under the Democratic administrations of Presidents Kennedy and Johnson. Under Kennedy, American involvement had increased significantly, but the Johnson administration had dramatically raised the stakes in 1964 in response to purported attacks on American naval vessels in the Gulf of Tonkin. The Democratically controlled Congress had swiftly passed a resolution authorizing a huge military buildup and response. At first, the American people had accepted the need for this military commitment, but as casualties mounted and the war dragged on with little if any observable progress and with a daily diet of gory scenes on television (Vietnam was the first war in history with saturation coverage on TV) this began to change. And when the Gulf of Tonkin incident was exposed as little more than a fraud and the Viet Cong sprung its surprise Tet offensive in early 1968, things started to come apart.

All this took place in the context of the already angry and tumultuous decade of the 1960s. In the early part of the decade black leaders, frustrated with the snail's pace of legal and social progress, had taken the case of the Civil Rights Movement from the courts to the streets, beginning with the lunch-counter sit-ins in 1960 that my Amherst friends and I had supported. They were met with vicious resistance on the part of many southern whites, who dominated the political power structures in their states. Television news coverage was filled with ugly scenes of pro-civil-rights demonstrators in the deep South being beaten by police, doused with powerful fire hoses, and set upon by police dogs. Southern governors refused to enforce or follow court orders to integrate public schools and state universities. Then came the assassination of President Kennedy, which plunged the country into gloom. Race riots in Los Angeles, Detroit, and Newark marked the summers of the middle years of the decade, as blacks vented their pent-up anger.

Things came to an ugly head in 1968. Early in the year, with anti-war demonstrations becoming more frequent and being met with a police reaction often as violent as those marking civil-rights demonstrations, major figures in the Democratic Party began deserting the Johnson administration over the war. First Minnesota Senator Eugene McCarthy and then President Kennedy's brother Robert, now himself a senator from New York, declared their candidacies for president, based on their opposition to the war. Unable to command much support in his own party, President Johnson withdrew from the race in late March. In early April civil rights leader Rev. Dr. Martin Luther King, Jr., was gunned down in Memphis, Tennessee. Many American cities, including Washington, DC, erupted in rioting and looting that went on for days. In early June, on the night of his victory in the California primary that probably would have made him the front-runner for the Democratic nomination, Senator Kennedy was shot in a Los Angeles hotel. As he clung to life for most of a day, the nation held its breath—and then mourned again.

The Republicans, led by Richard Nixon, who had been out of office since 1961, took major advantage of this general breakdown in order, though ironically, they were the principal supporters of the war the Democrats had started and now desperately wanted to stop. Nixon campaigned against the Warren Court, which he sought to blame for the "permissiveness" that he claimed underlay the demonstrations and riots that frightened many Americans. As the spring wore on into summer, it became increasingly likely that Nixon would win the Republican nomination for the second time.

My reaction to all of this was horror and dismay. I too opposed the war, but felt that the singular focus of so many Democrats on the war threatened to sidetrack the hard-won progress of recent years in civil rights and efforts to provide real equal opportunity to poor folks of all races in the country. In the wake of President Kennedy's assassination, President Johnson, the former Senate majority leader, had managed to put through an avalanche of long-overdue (in my view) legislation, including the Civil Rights Act of 1964, the Voting Rights Act of 1965, and a series of laws aimed at creating genuine economic opportunity for all Americans, which went under the collective heading of the War on Poverty. Johnson himself had betrayed the latter initiative with the military expenditures in Vietnam, despite his claim that the country could afford both "guns" and "butter." The wild deficit spending of his administration set the stage for dramatic and crippling inflation in the 1970s.

In conversations with my friends I argued against the impetus of many liberals to punish the Democratic Party for Vietnam. Tearing the party apart, I urged, would spell disaster, not only for civil rights enforcement and the War on Poverty, but ironically, for the effort to end the Vietnam War itself, as only a Democratic president would make that a major objective. On more than one occasion in that dreadful year, guests at dinner parties at our apartment, usually happy and convivial gatherings, were reduced to tears by the passion with which opposing convictions were held by normally like-minded people.

I had favored the effort to change presidents and was glad that President Johnson had seen the handwriting on the wall and had withdrawn. However, I never particularly cottoned to Eugene McCarthy, who struck me as a bit smug and superior. Instead, I believed that Bobby Kennedy would make a serious effort to unite the party, that he had the best chance of doing so, and that he, of all the candidates, was least likely to overlook the other priorities I held so dear. Thus his assassination deeply depressed me. The prospect that Richard Nixon, whose career was born in the red-baiting muck of the 1940s and 1950s, and whose utter lack of political principle was made transparent by the number of times he reinvented himself into a "new Nixon," designed to appeal to what he saw as some emerging political consensus, would become president made my depression complete.

Within days of Robert Kennedy's death during the first week in June, I had decided that I would get involved in the campaign and do my best to avoid the multifaceted disaster that I thought a Republican victory—and especially a Nixon victory—would bring.

❖   ❖   ❖

I saw no alternative but to support the candidacy of Vice-President Hubert Humphrey. I had no doubt that Humphrey's heart was in the right place. He had been a leader on civil rights issues since the 1948 Democratic Convention, where, as the young mayor of Minneapolis, he gave a floor speech supporting civil rights that helped to spark the defection of the pro-segregation "Dixiecrats," who walked out, held their own convention, and put forward segregationist diehard Strom Thurmond of South Carolina as a third-party candidate. As one of the leading liberals in the Senate in the late 1950s and early 1960s, Humphrey had also championed the economic agenda that had been a major focus of the early efforts of the Johnson administration.

The problem was that as Johnson's hand-picked vice-president, Humphrey was in no position to oppose the president publicly on the issue of the war. Like many who supported him, I believed that Humphrey personally opposed the war. Any other stance would have been inconsistent with his lifetime of liberal leadership. But his voice was stilled by his position in the administration. To the many liberals who wanted to punish Humphrey for his silence and hence, they claimed, his tacit support of the war, I argued that the alternative, Nixon, was simply, in Bobby Kennedy's word, "unacceptable." Nixon would cut the rug from under the Democrats' civil-rights and economic programs, and he was an unabashed supporter of the war. Even if Humphrey were to stay with Johnson's war policy, which I thought inconceivable, his administration would at least continue the good fight on the two other significant fronts. Without great enthusiasm, but with firm resolve, I decided to seek a place on Humphrey's campaign staff.

❖   ❖   ❖

In June of 1968, hiring for the Humphrey staff was being done by Secretary of Labor Willard Wirtz, a long-time Humphrey ally in Democratic Party affairs. With the help of my friend Evan Kemp, whose uncle by marriage was the well-connected nationally syndicated columnist Drew Pearson, I obtained an interview with Secretary Wirtz. By sheer happenstance, Wirtz was the father of my Amherst classmate Dick Wirtz, with whom I had been friendly, but not close, in college. The Secretary had noted the connection on my resume, as he made it clear in our interview that he had called his son and inquired about me. During the interview he said to me, "All the young people today seem so disaffected. Why aren't you disaffected?" I replied, "I *am* disaffected. I hate this war. But I don't want to see every good thing the Democrats have done go down the tubes."

❖ ❖ ❖

I was hired to work in the "issues" section of the campaign. From the beginning it was a dispiriting experience. Humphrey's staff, most of whom had moved over from his vice-presidential office and who would make up the core of his White House staff if he won, were not particularly impressive. Things were disorganized, there seemed to be little discipline, and morale was not high. Worse, as I began reading the transcripts of Humphrey's campaign speeches in an effort to get a feel for how he thought and talked, I began to suspect that the lack of discipline and organization were a reflection of his own weaknesses. The speeches were long and rambling. They lacked both intellectual focus and rhetorical punch. The vice president had a serious case of verbal diarrhea. He thought out loud, a very bad trait in a politician. Moreover, the speeches themselves bore very little relation to the texts from which he was supposed to talk.

Later in the campaign, Humphrey's chief speechwriter, John Stewart, asked me to research and write a speech on issues affecting the elderly that the vice-president was to deliver at a major retirement complex somewhere in the West. I asked how long Humphrey planned to talk. Stewart said about forty-five minutes. Knowing the candidate's proclivities, I gave Stewart a draft that was five typed pages long, triple-spaced, with large margins, on letter-sized paper. It could be read aloud by anyone in six or seven minutes. A couple of hours later, Stewart came to my desk and said, "This is great. The substance is exactly right, and I like the tone. There is only one problem: it's much too long. If you give Humphrey this much copy, he'll talk for two and a half hours."

I began to worry seriously that, however good a senator Humphrey had been, he would not make a very good president. Having his heart in the right place was not enough. Being a senator is largely a matter of positioning oneself on the issues, and I admired the way Humphrey had done that. But being a good president demands focus, discipline, organization, administrative skill—all the things that I was coming to believe Humphrey lacked. Nonetheless, he was the best hope we had.

❖ ❖ ❖

My sense of despondency during the campaign gave rise to one amusing story, the punchline of which I learned only years later. On the street after lunch one day I ran into Lloyd Cutler, the senior partner of Wilmer, Cutler & Pickering, where I was committed to begin practice after the campaign was over. I had of course obtained the firm's agreement to the postponement of my arrival, and I assumed that Cutler was aware of it. He asked me how things were going, and I let my hair down and told him that it was one of the most difficult and dispiriting experiences I had ever encountered. Cutler thought I was talking about practicing at the firm. As I learned in the 1980s from Roger Wollenberg, another senior member of the firm, Cutler, who could be imperious when he wanted to, stormed back to the office and immediately convened a meeting of the firm's executive committee. He proceeded to recount what I had said to him and to demand to know why the firm was not seeing to it that its young lawyers had a positive experience. Wollenberg and the others, aware that I was not yet at the firm, looked from one to another wondering, "Who is going to tell him?"

❖ ❖ ❖

The Democrats gathered in August for their convention in Chicago. As low man on the totem pole of the issues section, I was left behind in Washington to man the files and pull any information that the higher-ups on the campaign staff might decide they needed. Initially, I was very disappointed not to be able to attend the convention. I had little or nothing to do at Washington headquarters. At least as I now recall, there were no requests for information to fill. Thus I simply watched aghast as the convention unfolded—came unglued—on national television. There were massive anti-war demonstrations in the streets of Chicago, which were met with wholly unnecessary brutality by the Chicago police, acting on the orders of the longtime Democratic boss of the city, Mayor Richard Daley. Because by the time of the convention there was no doubt that Humphrey would win the nomination, the anger of the demonstrators and their supporters around the country was aimed squarely at Humphrey, who had no control over Daley and his police, but who was the visible symbol of the administration's wildly unpopular policies. I was glad in retrospect to have missed being at the convention.

The Democratic Party staggered out of Chicago even more divided and disorganized than it had been before the convention. And broke. There was no money to pay the campaign staff, which was now to be transferred to the payroll of the Democratic National Committee. Humphrey's senatorial successor from Minnesota, Walter Mondale, was made chairman of the DNC, and he called me and many other Humphrey campaign staffers in, one by one, to tell us we were being let go because of a lack of funds. Some sources of funding were quickly found, and we were all rehired in only a few days, but the lack of money continued to plague the DNC until late in the campaign. For example, it never paid its share of the health insurance premiums for the staff, with the result that our daughter Susan, with whom Louise became pregnant in the fall, was born uninsured. She was born a month prematurely, required considerable medical attention, and remained in the hospital for a couple of weeks. The lack of health insurance put a major crimp in our personal finances for more than a year.

❖ ❖ ❖

The post-convention campaign was a bruising affair. The country was in an ugly mood. The Democrats were savaging each other. Nixon was in his fear-mongering element. And to add to the ugliness, George Wallace, the segregationist governor of Alabama, mounted a third-party campaign, attempting to capitalize on a white backlash to the increasingly strident demands of African Americans for some justice at long last. It was difficult to figure what Wallace's impact on the election would be. Nixon's "southern strategy"—his barely concealed racist appeal to the segregationist rump in the South—represented the final abandonment of the Republican Party's legacy as the party of Abraham Lincoln, the historic friend of oppressed black people. Nixon and Wallace were essentially competing for the same segment of the population, the disgruntled, mostly lower-income whites who felt threatened economically and socially by the emergence of a politically stronger black constituency. On the one hand, these people were socially very conservative and unlikely to vote for Humphrey. On the other, they had historically been part of the FDR coalition that had elected Democratic presidents and Congresses like clockwork since the beginning of the New Deal in 1932. Just how they would split between Nixon and Wallace was the big unknown.

My principal assignment was to compile the "black book" on Nixon, essentially an encyclopedia of his public life and utterances, for use in responding to things he might say in the campaign. It was a job I undertook with some relish. Nothing I found in my weeks of intense research diminished in the least my longstanding distaste for this vile man. I could find no act in his entire career that seemed to be based on any principle that transcended his determination to exploit whatever the general public might be afraid of at the moment.

Humphrey's campaign lurched on through the rest of August, all of September, and early October with no momentum, no optimism, and haunted at every turn by the terrible image of the confrontation between demonstrators and police in Chicago. We were trailing by huge margins in the polls. Then around Columbus Day the vice president made a nationally televised speech from a studio in Salt Lake City. For once he stuck to the script, and it was a carefully crafted and well-delivered speech. Without ever quite repudiating President Johnson's conduct of the war, Humphrey made it clear that his administration would design and implement its own policies in Vietnam, and that those would be based on a clear-eyed assessment of what had gone wrong. He also sounded the traditional Democratic themes of racial, social, and economic justice.

The Salt Lake City speech was a watershed. It convinced people that Humphrey could indeed be his own man, independent of Lyndon Johnson. It finally united and energized Democrats and appealed strongly to independents who were skeptical of Nixon's hawkish position on the war. Overnight the campaign took on real life. Money began to pour in. Nixon's lead in the polls and Wallace's share of the poor white Democratic vote began to shrink dramatically, almost daily.

At the end, Humphrey almost won. He lost the popular vote by a margin even smaller than the one by which Nixon had lost to John Kennedy in 1960. A switch of a few precincts here and there around the country would have given him the election. I have always wondered whether, had the Salt Lake City speech been given even a day or two earlier, we would have pulled it out.

❖ ❖ ❖

After the campaign, exhausted physically and emotionally, I came down with a very nasty throat infection. I have been subject to such infections all my life, but this one was memorably unpleasant. I could barely talk or eat for days. When I was finally on the mend, Louise, Will, and I embarked on a trip to see some of our friends in New York and New England, many of whom we had not seen for several years. Our last stop was in Williamstown, Massachusetts, to visit Peter Berek and his wife Ellen. Peter had just joined the English faculty at Williams College. As we drove through the Berkshires, it began to snow hard. It was late afternoon and already quite dark, and there did not seem to be any establishments of any kind that were open. Will, who at eighteen months had just achieved a surprising level of competence in potty training, announced that he had to poop. The driving conditions were terrible, I was fearful for my wife and baby, and there was no place to stop. To his great consternation, we told the poor little guy to do it in his pants. Thus he made his first entry into Williamstown, where he was to spend many happy years later in life, with a pair of very muddy diapers.

❖ ❖ ❖

We returned from our trip in mid-November, and I began my practice at Wilmer, Cutler & Pickering, who had been quite happy for me to take part in the presidential campaign. Very shortly after I started work at the firm, my mother became seriously ill. Always a heavy smoker, she contracted some kind of upper respiratory infection that she could not shake. She seemed to grow quite weak. Liz was away at college, and though Mom's sister Monk and her husband Vic were nearby and she had kind and friendly neighbors, she was alone much of the time and very sick. After Thanksgiving Louise and Will went down to Hampton to be with her and help all they could. I think it very much cheered Mother to have her only grandchild there. Her condition seemed to stabilize somewhat, and Louise, who was four months pregnant and had a young child to care for, thought it was best to come home. I was very glad to see them, but also still quite worried about Mother.

We had been planning to go down to Hampton to spend Christmas with Mother and Liz. On December 20, we received a call from Liz that Mother had been taken to the hospital. We decided to pack up and leave that afternoon, two or three days earlier than we had planned. We got to Hampton late in the evening, after hospital visiting hours were over. We had some supper, chatted with Liz, and went to bed. After we were all asleep, there was a knock on the door. It was Mom's close friends and neighbors, Gordon and Helen Poole, whom the hospital had called to say that Mother had died, thinking that Liz was probably home alone and not wanting to give her the bad news over the phone.

The doctors told us that Mother's health had just generally worn down, that her heart and lungs were in terrible shape, and that she couldn't fight a fast-developing pneumonia. I am sure that the years of malnutrition and deprivation during the war were a major factor. She was only 63.

We had a sad little service in Hampton and then drove north to bury her next to Dad in Great Falls. Laura Sanders, our wonderful neighbor when we lived there, gave a very sweet and lovely reception for old friends after the burial service. It was Christmas Eve, and it was cold.

So we celebrated Christmas at our little apartment in Falls Church. It was just Louise, Will, Liz, and I. The three adults were all grateful that there was a tree to be trimmed, food to be cooked, and toys to put together for Will, as it gave us something to do and took our minds off our sadness.

New Year's Eve we went to a party at the apartment of Rick and Gail Lowery, not far from where we lived. I told them that I had never been so happy to see something end as 1968. The next year, I said, could not help but be better. Thank goodness, it was.

CHAPTER TEN

Law Practice

1969–1975

I did not last long at Wilmer, Cutler & Pickering, although I was treated very well. The people at the firm were uniformly very bright and very pleasant, and I number some of them among my friends today. Most of the lawyers were Democrats. Senior partner Lloyd Cutler would serve as White House counsel to two Democratic presidents, Carter and Clinton. A younger lawyer in the firm, David Anderson, had served as the campaign chief-of-staff to Hubert Humphrey's vice-presidential running mate, Senator Edmund Muskie of Maine.

There were two problems. The firm's practice was, as advertised, a blue-chip corporate "Washington" practice. That meant, though unaccountably I don't seem to have understood it before signing on, that we were representing interests to which I was not necessarily hostile, but whose welfare was not what I really wanted to spend my life promoting. Most of the young, liberal lawyers in the firm seemed to me, at least, to wring their hands and tell themselves constantly that their professional lives were justified because they were somehow making corporate America "better," whatever that meant. I didn't buy it.

The second problem was that the firm was doing almost no litigation (though that certainly changed later), and I was at the end of a longish queue to do what little there was. I discovered in my brief time at Wilmer, Cutler that, while I had found an intellectual home in the law, my competitive instincts were strong enough that I could not be satisfied with a behind-the-scenes practice designed to improve a corporate client's position before some government regulatory agency. I was bored. I craved action. What had seemed fascinating intellectual projects as a summer associate seemed excruciatingly dull as a long-term prospect—the law-firm equivalent of a desk job at UPI. I found a fellow in misery, another ex-Warren clerk named Dennis Flannery, with whom I swiftly became close. We were both restless, and we talked a lot about what to do.

❖ ❖ ❖

Not everything about early 1969 was dull and unhappy. Louise was due to give birth in mid-May, almost exactly two years after Will was born. When I came home from work on Friday, April 18, Louise announced that she had had a "twinge" a little earlier, something that she described as not a full-fledged contraction. She seemed to think it was nothing to be concerned about. I insisted—thank goodness—that we call the doctor and have it checked out. Our apartment was only a few blocks from the new Fairfax Hospital, and we located her obstetrician there. He said to bring her in and he would examine her. We deposited Will with some neighbors, and I drove Louise to the hospital. The people at the check-in desk told me to go get something to eat because it would be a while before the doctor saw her. I grabbed some fast food and returned to the hospital. They told me to wait in the fathers' waiting room. I settled in to watch the seventh game of the NBA finals between the Boston Celtics and the Los Angeles Lakers, which was on the television in the lounge. In those days I was a big Celtics fan. With less than five seconds left in the game, the Celtics were one point down and had the ball out of bounds. The game was on commercial break. Naturally, that was the moment when I was paged over the loudspeaker and told to report to some room in the maternity ward. I left without finding out how the game came out, which I have always claimed as a mark of my devotion as a husband and father. (The Celtics, as I learned later, won.)

As I walked down the corridor toward the room I was seeking, I saw a woman lying on a gurney with a flat stomach. Not until I was next to her did I realize it was Louise. It was barely two hours, if that, since I had checked her in, and she had already been delivered of a baby girl, whom we named Susan Hall in honor of my mother. (Louise wouldn't go near Susie as a name, and I didn't really blame her.) Louise seemed in excellent shape. It had obviously not been a long and difficult labor.

I soon learned, however, that all was not well. A doctor took me aside and, out of Louise's hearing, told me that the baby was doing poorly. She was a month premature, she was not breathing on her own, and they had put her on a respirator. Also, her liver was not functioning properly, she was jaundiced, and her bilirubin count was very high. He said they might have to do a blood exchange if things did not improve rapidly. He was not alarmist, but he said that there were no guarantees and that the next twenty-four to forty-eight hours would be very important.

Within a day, fortunately, Susan was breathing well and was off the respirator. They did have to do a blood exchange, but her bilirubin count went down immediately. After the first day or so, it was mostly a question of getting her big and healthy enough to leave the hospital. She weighed five pounds when she was born and then, typically, lost weight. Not until she was over five pounds could we bring her home. She initially had some difficulty learning how to eat, but soon she was on the right road. It was two weeks, however, before she was big enough to leave the neonate ward and live on her own at home.

Susan has always been tough, in the very best sense of that word—like her grandparents. Louise and I have attributed that trait in part to her successful battle to live in her first two weeks. We were very happy to get her home where we could hug her and love her up close.

❖ ❖ ❖

At the Warren clerks' reunion in May I poured out my professional unhappiness to Charlie Wilson, the chief clerk during my term at the Court. Charlie had joined Williams & Connolly, which was the fastest-rising litigation firm in the city and probably the country. It was headed by Edward Bennett Williams, who was still in his late forties and was perhaps the best-known trial and appellate lawyer in the nation. He had had a string of very high-profile clients, ranging from mob boss Frank Costello to Teamsters' Union president Jimmy Hoffa to Lyndon Johnson's one-time right-hand-man Bobby Baker. When I told Charlie that I thought I might leave law practice before I wanted to if I did not have the opportunity to try litigation, he said, "Why don't you come talk to us? We've lost a couple of people lately and are looking for someone."

I swiftly sent my resume to Charlie and had a series of interviews at Williams & Connolly, whose offices were diagonally across the street from Wilmer, Cutler's, both on Farragut Square in downtown Washington. By the end of June I had accepted an offer to cross the street. I finished my stint at Wilmer in early August. Louise, Will, Susan, and I then took that long-postponed vacation. We stayed for three weeks at Aunt Louise and Uncle George's beach cottage in Avalon. It took me half the time to unwind enough to be ready for a vacation. We returned, rested and refreshed, right after Labor Day, and I eagerly reported for work at Williams & Connolly.

❖ ❖ ❖

From the very beginning, I reveled in my new professional setting. The firm did nothing *but* litigation. Yet the practice was full of really interesting and important issues, and the firm tackled them at the highest intellectual level. It was less than half the size of Wilmer, Cutler—I was the eighteenth lawyer—which was a major plus as far as I was concerned. It had no defining clientele but represented many very unpopular people accused of significant wrongdoing. The place was full of extremely bright, tough, aggressive lawyers who had no qualms about what they were doing and who were great fun to be with. The small size permitted one to have lunch with every other lawyer in the place at least once every couple of weeks, and we all kept track of each other's cases and rooted hard for each other. Each victory was savored over drinks and lunch, each defeat mourned. The atmosphere was electric and bracing. The firm was run as a benevolent dictatorship. All the major decisions were made by Ed Williams and Paul Connolly—most, I suspect, in reality by Ed Williams—but that did not bother any of us. We were paid more than our contemporaries in other firms, and we were given lots of interesting work to do and the freedom to do it. There were no bean counters keeping track of how many hours each associate billed. Indeed, hourly billing of clients was not at the outset the norm at the firm. We all did our work with enthusiasm, and we stayed as long as it took to do it and went home without guilt when we were through.

The place was sports-mad, which was not surprising given the intensely competitive character of what we did and who we were. One of the lawyers, David Povich, was the son of Shirley Povich, the legendary sportswriter and columnist for the *Washington Post*. More important, Ed Williams was then president of the Washington Redskins, and on Saturday mornings of weekends when the Redskins were scheduled to play at home, he would almost always call around to the young lawyers in the firm and offer each of them two tickets to the Sunday game. (This was also a good way to make sure that we worked on Saturdays, which we almost always did.) On Saturday afternoons in the fall most of us, including Ed, would be out playing touch football. (It was Ed's ball, and he was always the quarterback of one of the teams.) In the spring and summer, we would play slow-pitch softball, sometimes among ourselves, and sometimes against other firms or groups. Often our coffee breaks turned into sports trivia games.

Two of Ed Williams' many strengths were that, while he was a very smart man, he was not afraid to surround himself with equally smart—indeed, on rare occasions, smarter—people, and that he instinctively sought out people who would confront and challenge him. One Saturday morning I found myself in the library with two or three other young lawyers when Ed walked in, sat down, and put his feet up. He was in an expansive mood and wanted to chat. The conversation eventually wended its way around to the case he was preparing to try three weeks from the coming Monday. It involved a challenge under the Establishment of Religion Clause of the First Amendment to federal grants to Catholic institutions of higher education.[1] Ed was a very serious and active member of the Catholic Church, and the firm did a lot of work for church-related institutions. The senior lawyers in the firm were all Irish Catholics. Indeed, coming as I did from a WASP background, I was in a distinct minority in the firm. I guess I was feeling my oats that morning, for I said to him, "You know, you ought to lose that case. Your position is wrong." He was not offended, and we argued about the general constitutional principles for a while, and then the conversation moved on. I thought nothing more of it until Monday morning, when at about 9:30 my phone rang. It was Williams. "Do you find this argument persuasive?" he asked. We talked for a while and hung up. Less than an hour later, the phone rang again. "What if I was able to prove this fact?" And so it went for the next three weeks. I was not working on the case, but he had found a point of resistance (the firm's Irish mafia was cheering him along) and he went for it like a moth seeks a flame. The value of the lesson was not lost on me. You don't learn a lot talking to people who agree with you, and as an advocate you need to learn as much as possible about the other side's views.

❖   ❖   ❖

"It's dark as a dungeon way down in the mines"

At about 10 o'clock on my first morning at the firm, after introductions to the people I hadn't met in the interviewing process, Paul Connolly walked into my office and asked, "Do you have some time?" Glancing at my bare desk, I allowed as how I did. Thus began my involvement in the affairs of the United Mine Workers of America, which would last for several years and put me on the front lines of fascinating litigation and dramatic turns of events.

Paul was preparing for a preliminary injunction hearing scheduled for 10 the next morning in federal district court in Washington in a case challenging aspects of the union's process for its upcoming election of international officers. He needed some quick legal research and a memorandum of law supporting the union's position to be filed before the hearing began. I was at the office until 1 a.m. writing the memorandum, and then accompanied Paul to the hotly contested hearing the next day. Some history is necessary to understand the setting of the case.

Efforts by American working people to organize themselves into labor unions to provide a counterweight to the dominant economic force of capitalism, which imposed often barbaric working conditions, including widespread child labor, had been frustrated throughout the 19th and early 20th centuries by a two-pronged strategy. Big employers—mining, manufacturing, and transportation interests—had enlisted the complaisant federal courts in an effort to break unions with injunctions against collective efforts to improve wages and working conditions, on the theory that such efforts constituted conspiracies in restraint of trade, in violation first of the common law and later of the federal antitrust laws. Thus union members charged with activities that were already crimes, often violent ones, were denied jury trials by courts exercising their contempt powers under these injunctions, where juries were traditionally not used. When that tactic didn't work, the employers resorted to violence and thugism of the worst sort. Unions retaliated in kind, and the decades from the 1890s to the 1920s were marked by repeated episodes of labor-management violence. The economic collapse of the Great Depression swept away many years of Republican dominance in American politics and ushered in the massive Democratic majorities that gave rise to the New Deal. The Wagner Act of 1935 and the Norris-LaGuardia Act of 1936 legitimized union activity and took the federal courts out of the labor-injunction business.

In the ensuing decades of Democratic party dominance, the 1930s and 1940s, however, some labor unions became fat and corrupt. The Republicans hammered away at the unions as bastions of communism, and congressional hearings revealed major abuses and criminal activity in the longshoremen's and teamsters' unions, among others. The mid-1950s saw congressional exposés of union corruption led by the unions' friends, the Democrats. The chief counsel to the Senate Labor Committee, chaired by John McClellan of Arkansas, was Robert Kennedy, younger brother of committee member John Kennedy of Massachusetts. Robert Kennedy became in particular the *bete noire* of the Teamsters' Union and its corrupt bosses, Dave Beck and Jimmy Hoffa. The result of these extended hearings was the Labor-Management Reporting and Disclosure Act of 1959 (LMRDA), known as the Landrum-Griffin Act. It sought to impose on union leaders a significant degree of accountability for the use of union funds and for internal democratic processes.

John Llewellyn Lewis was one of the lions of the labor movement in the 1920s through the 1950s. President of the United Mine Workers of America, Lewis led one of the largest, toughest, and economically most powerful unions in the country. Most of American industry fired its plants with coal, and until after World War II a significant percentage of Americans heated their houses with coal. Relations between coal operators and workers were often tense and sometimes violent. Lewis was a charismatic Welshman who was unafraid to take on even the Democratic president, Franklin Delano Roosevelt. Within the union itself, Lewis was an imperious presence who brooked no opposition. I have no reason to believe that Lewis was personally corrupt, but he viewed the coffers of the union as his private preserve, to be spent as he saw fit. He did not see any reason to account for the use of those funds in any detail to his membership. The union had only the most rudimentary system of keeping track of how its members' dues money was spent. Although it was not a target in the McClellan hearings, the UMWA was, in short, a paradigm case for reform under the Landrum-Griffin Act.

The statute was passed in 1959, and in the ensuing decade, no real reform had come to the Mine Workers. Lewis had retired as president of the union in 1960, and was succeeded by his vice-president, Thomas Kennedy, who died in 1963. Kennedy's successor was W.A. "Tony" Boyle, whom Lewis had groomed for the presidency. Boyle was not a good choice for a union facing great challenges in a time of conversion from coal to oil, natural gas, and electricity as energy sources for home heating and in many industries. Boyle was from Montana and was not really plugged into the coal-mining constituencies of the Appalachian chain, which represented the bulk of the union's membership. Boyle was every bit as high-handed as Lewis, but he was not nearly as smart or as charismatic.

In 1969 Boyle was running for reelection as president of the UMWA and expected no real challenge. He was therefore surprised and angered when Joseph A. "Jock" Yablonski, from the coal fields of western Pennsylvania, whom he considered one of his loyal lieutenants, declared his candidacy in the spring. Yablonski raised the banner of reform, campaigned on the alleged corruption of the Boyle regime, and enlisted the support of liberals in the labor movement. His legal advisor, and the architect of his brilliant, if partly twisted, use of the Landrum-Griffin Act in the campaign, was Joe Rauh, longtime friend and legal advisor to Walter Reuther, president of the United Auto Workers, viewed as one of the cleanest unions in the nation. Rauh mapped out a strategy to use the labor reform statute as a tool to put—and keep—Boyle on the defensive. Rauh's first salvo was a lawsuit seeking an injunction requiring the union to adhere to a number of the LMRDA's internal democracy procedures, which Lewis and Boyle had essentially ignored. The union's general counsel, longtime Washington lawyer Ed Carey, turned to his old friends Ed Williams and Paul Connolly to represent the union. The hearing to which I accompanied Paul Connolly that morning in early September was on Rauh's motion for a preliminary injunction in that first lawsuit.

I had heard of Joe Rauh. He was a player in Democratic politics, one of the leaders of the liberal but ferociously anticommunist Americans for Democratic Action. My impression of him from afar was favorable. I soon learned that he was not only a formidable foe, but an unrelentingly rude and bitter opponent, whose approach to litigation had one note—all-out attack, thumb-in-the-eye and knee-in-the-groin style—and that he was not careful with the truth. He won his preliminary injunction that week, as he should have, given the union's pattern of ignoring the commands of the LMRDA, but the hearing was unnecessarily antagonistic and set the tone for what was to follow.

A master manipulator of the media, Rauh trumpeted his victory to the press. It was but the prelude to his second highly publicized lawsuit, one based on the classic "big lie" that has just enough truth in it to be tough to combat. Section 501 of the LMRDA permitted union members to bring lawsuits, analogous to shareholders' "derivative" actions in the corporate world, to recover on behalf of the union membership funds that had allegedly been diverted by union leaders in breach of their fiduciary duties to the members. Rauh brought suit under section 501 in Yablonski's name against Boyle and the other top international officials of the union, claiming that they had "looted" the union treasury of several million dollars. In support of his charge, he pointed to the fact that the assets listed on the union's balance sheet had declined precipitously since Boyle took office. The latter part was undeniably true, but as Rauh knew full well, it was the result, not of corruption on Boyle's part, but of perhaps the most significant act of fiscal and political courage and responsibility Boyle had undertaken in his years in office.

While the UMWA was very strong in the coal fields of Pennsylvania, Ohio, and West Virginia, organizing in the southern states, where unions were much less popular, even among working-class people, was always difficult. The collieries of Kentucky and Tennessee had been hotbeds of industrial violence for years. Desperate to organize a major southern coal operation, John L. Lewis in the late 1940s cut a deal with the industrialist Cyrus Eaton, who was trying to purchase the very large, non-union West Kentucky Coal Co. The union, which then had a lot of cash, loaned Eaton several million dollars toward the purchase of the company, with the understanding that Eaton would immediately recognize the union and sign its national collective bargaining agreement. The deal was an unconscionable act on Lewis's part. Not only did it put the union in bed with a major coal operator, it put the union's funds at unacceptable risk. The note Eaton signed bore no interest. It was a demand note that provided that, if and when the union called the loan, Eaton had the option either to repay it or to tender to the union his shares of stock in West Kentucky Coal Co. Thus from Eaton's perspective it was a heads-I-win-tails-you-lose proposition. If the company prospered, Eaton would pay off the note. If it floundered and the value of its stock plummeted, Eaton had no repayment obligation beyond the value of his stock. Eaton signed the union contract, but his stewardship of the company was a disaster. By the early 1960s the company's stock was worthless. Nonetheless, Lewis and Tom Kennedy continued to carry the loan at face value as an asset on the union's financial statements, thus grossly overstating the union's net worth.

Shortly after Tony Boyle succeeded to the presidency he did the responsible thing—he told Eaton that the charade was over and called the loan. Eaton handed over his worthless West Kentucky stock and went his merry way, having effectively plundered the union's treasury. Rauh used Boyle's honest and courageous act that reduced—and corrected—the union's public statement of its assets as the basis of his allegation that Boyle had himself looted the union's coffers. It was a wildly irresponsible allegation, but Rauh knew that, given the pace of litigation, there was no way it could be exposed in court in the brief time before the union's international election in early December.

The election campaign among the union's membership was a roiling, angry affair. Yablonski, a dark, brooding, bitter-sounding man, had no more charisma than Boyle. Despite Rauh's successful legal strategy, Boyle won by a substantial majority when the votes were counted. Rauh complained of what he claimed was widespread misconduct on the part of Boyle's partisans, who controlled most locals, in the administration of the balloting process. The Department of Labor commenced an investigation under other provisions of the LMRDA, which gave the Secretary of Labor the power to bring a lawsuit to set aside the results of a union election and order a new one under the Secretary's supervision.

Then came the most appalling turn of events. On New Year's Eve 1969 Jock Yablonski, his wife, and his daughter were shot to death in their home in Washington, Pennsylvania. Our hearts went out to his son Joseph "Chip" Yablonski, a young lawyer who had joined Joe Rauh's legal team and who was the most decent and likeable member of their crew. A major criminal investigation traced the murders to members of the UMWA's District 19 in the violent coal fields of Kentucky. A series of plea bargains uncovered a conspiracy directed by one of the principal officials of District 19, a man with the wonderfully symbolic name of Bill Turnblazer. Charged with conspiracy to murder, Turnblazer gave the investigators what they had been seeking all along—a case against Tony Boyle. In return for lenient sentencing treatment, Turnblazer pleaded guilty and testified at Boyle's trial that at a session of the union's International Executive Board in Washington shortly after Yablonski announced his candidacy, Boyle said to him words to the effect of "We've got to kill this guy Yablonski." Taking this as a directive from the boss, Turnblazer said, he organized and carried out the murders. Including Yablonski's wife and daughter was apparently the idea of the killers.

Turnblazer's testimony was deeply suspect, not only because of his cozy plea bargain, but because it made little sense to anyone familiar with the layout of the union's headquarters and with Boyle's typically flamboyant speech. The "order" was supposedly given just after the board meeting broke up, in the large vestibule between the board room and the elevator on the fifth floor of the union's headquarters building. It was about as public a private space as can be imagined, hardly a place one would choose to initiate a conspiracy to murder. Even if other board members were not within earshot, milling about after the meeting, there was always at least one staff member on duty at a desk in the vestibule. The chances of being overheard—and I never heard Tony Boyle whisper—were enormous. Moreover, Boyle habitually spoke in the hard-boiled hyperbole that the movies often portrayed as typical of tough union leaders of the mid-20th century. Boyle was still reeling from Yablonski's unexpected—and unexpectedly harsh and personal—announcement of his candidacy. He was trying to organize an energetic election campaign that he had not expected to need to mount. If he said the words, and if he said them in the setting to which Turnblazer testified, the most natural meaning of the words was not "go out and murder the guy," but "let's smash him in the campaign." Nor did it make a lot of sense that Boyle would give an order to kill a rival for union power in the spring and then wait idly and quietly for his order to be carried out weeks after he had soundly trounced the rival in the international election.

Boyle consistently protested his innocence, but by the time of his trial, his mental faculties had noticeably deteriorated. As the months wore on, my colleagues at the law firm and I found him increasingly incoherent in conversation and began to suspect that he might have suffered a series of minor strokes. Thus he was no match for a prosecutor's searching cross-examination. I do not think Boyle was well defended. (Williams & Connolly was not involved in his defense.) Despite the weakness of Turnblazer's testimony, the jury found Boyle guilty. I shall always believe it was a miscarriage of justice. Tony Boyle was in many respects a lousy labor leader, but he was not in my judgment a murderer.

After the election, Rauh continued to press his derivative action against Boyle and the other international officers of the union. In an embarrassment for Williams & Connolly, Rauh moved to disqualify the firm from representing the organization on the ground that it had represented the officers as well as the union in the election-related case and, for a brief period of time, in the derivative action itself. The role of union counsel in a derivative action is to represent the interests of the union itself, which may well diverge from those of the officers accused of breaching their fiduciary duties to the membership. Although the district judge denied Rauh's motion, he took an appeal, and the court of appeals reversed, disqualifying the firm.[2] Thus I was suddenly out of the coal-mining business.

My absence was only temporary, however. After conducting an extensive investigation, the Department of Labor brought a lawsuit to set aside the results of the 1969 election. The union decided to defend the case through a member of its in-house legal staff. The government took almost three months to put on its case, and right before the government was ready to close, the union's lawyer died of a sudden massive heart attack. General Counsel Ed Carey once again turned to Williams & Connolly for help. Both Ed Williams and Paul Connolly were tied up in lengthy trials of their own, so the case was assigned to Jerry Collins, a senior member of the firm who had known Carey for many years. Jerry was a good friend and mentor to me, and, knowing that I had been involved in the earlier litigation for the union, he asked if I could work on the case with him. At first I had to turn him down, as I was committed on another big case, but that one was suddenly resolved, and I swiftly joined the trial team.

The judge in the case was William Bryant, a former Assistant United

States Attorney in Washington, and the first African American appointed to the federal bench in the nation's capital. He was a fair and decent judge, one whom I came to know well and grew to admire. However, he wanted to move the UMWA election case along, and so he gave the union only a month after the death of its lawyer to get new counsel and bring them up to speed. The trial was a bench trial with no jury, but it was clogging up his docket, and the judge insisted on moving rapidly ahead. This made the trial experience perhaps the most hectic of my entire career. We had barely enough time to read the transcript of the proceedings up to that point before the trial resumed, and we never did read much of the discovery record.

The details of the trial are for the most part not worth relating, but it was a wonderful opportunity for me. I was in court every day for more than two months, and Jerry Collins very generously gave me a major role in the examination of witnesses and the argument of legal points to the court. Actually, it may not have been so much generosity as desperation on Jerry's part. Against our advice, the union insisted on mounting an extensive local-by-local defense to the government's case, which all too often resulted in merely confirming the government's allegations of indefensibly sloppy, if not actually unfair, balloting practices. With the judge laying the lash to our backs, we moved at breakneck pace, putting on an average of twenty witnesses a day. In the evenings we would repair to the hotel where the union was housing its witnesses to meet and interview the ones who would testify the following day. We had no role in selecting the witnesses and no time to prepare them adequately, let alone to formulate and implement a coherent trial strategy.

We had a third lawyer with us, an older African American named Belford Lawson. Belford was a graduate of Howard University Law School, where most of the great lawyers for the NAACP in the desegregation struggle had trained under the legendary Charles Houston. While he had eventually established his own practice, Belford had argued a number of important cases for the NAACP. The union had hired Belford in the belief that having a black lawyer in the case would help curry favor with Judge Byrant—a dubious proposition to start with—but then had given him nothing whatever to do in court. Jerry and I thought this was demeaning to Belford and almost certainly insulting to the judge, so we asked Belford to take a real role in the trial. Besides, with all the witnesses we were putting on, we needed another body.

The three-ring circus we were orchestrating did lead to some amusing moments. One day Belford was examining a witness, and it became clear that something was wrong. Belford was asking the witness a series of questions for which the latter was totally unprepared and to which he gave confused and garbled answers. Suddenly I realized what was wrong. I whispered to Jerry, "This guy isn't Belford's witness. He didn't interview him last night." Jerry replied, "Whose witness is he?" "Yours," I said. "He was on the list that you interviewed." "Ohmigod, you're right." As casually as I could, I approached Belford, who was at the podium. "Belford," I whispered, "this isn't one of your guys." "I didn't think he looked familiar," he replied. Aloud he announced to the judge, "No further questions, your honor."

Despite our valiant effort, we really had no chance from the beginning. The union's disregard of the requirements of the statute regarding the conduct of elections was overwhelming. Judge Bryant had no trouble ruling against us and ordering a new election under the supervision of the Secretary of Labor.[3]

Nonetheless, I came away from the trial with newfound confidence born of constant and repeated efforts on my feet in the courtroom, with a couple of small triumphs, and with real friendship and admiration for both Jerry Collins and Belford Lawson. I also gained great admiration and affection for the men who risk their lives daily in one of the most dangerous occupations known to man. I met many coal miners and found them to be uniformly hardy, gruff, direct, and largely honest and endearing.

Notwithstanding the picture frequently painted in fiction and film, it is rare in real life for a cross-examiner to destroy completely the utility of a witness called by the other side. This trial offered me the first of the tiny handful of such moments in my career, and in a most unlikely setting. When Jerry and I entered the case, the government still had a few witnesses to call. Among them was a statistician who had analyzed the election results in all the local unions and testified to what he claimed was the measurable impact of the different kinds of electoral violations—lack of secrecy in the voting process, the presence of printed sample ballots for the Boyle ticket inside the polling places, confusion in the roles of "tellers" (impartial vote-counters) and "watchers" (candidate supporters trying to ensure fairness for their ticket), etc.—on the final outcome. He employed a standard statistical analysis known as chi square. We hired a statistician of our own, who read the government witness's report, listened to his testimony, and explained that the premises of the government's analysis were deeply flawed. The government statistician testified in the morning, and over the lunch break Jerry, our statistician, and I worked on the cross-examination. I had never taken a course in statistics; indeed, my mathematical education in college had ended with freshman calculus. Also, it was early in our participation in the trial, and I was very inexperienced. But I could see that Jerry felt even more uncomfortable on this terrain than I did. I felt I understood the flaws in the government's approach pretty well after being coached by our statistician. So with some trepidation, I said to Jerry, "I understand why you may feel this is a cross that you should do, but I would like to try this one if it is okay with you." Obviously relieved, he said, "Be my guest." The statistician's evidence was the only aspect of the government's presentation on which Judge Bryant placed no reliance in his opinion ruling against us.

My other small triumph came in the post-trial argument about the ground rules for the new election. Rauh, who had been permitted to intervene in the case on behalf of the remaining candidates on the Yablonski ticket, and the government's lead lawyer, both of whom were in their sixties, argued, among other things, that the challengers should be given one-half of the space in the union's newspaper during the campaign, with the result that the union would have to publish sentiments with which it disagreed and would have to pay with union dues money for the challengers' campaign publications. It was our position that this would be a blatant violation of the First Amendment's guarantee of freedom of speech to the union and its members. Rauh was at his most unctuous and obnoxious in the argument, referring several times to civil rights cases he had argued that had no bearing on the issue before the court. When I got up to argue the other side, I decided to take a calculated risk. I had gotten along well throughout the trial with Judge Bryant, who I thought liked me. "Sometimes, your honor," I said, "I feel the disabilities of youth very keenly." The judge looked at me kindly and said, "What do you mean?" I said, "I respect my elders, but I think I have listened to more arrogant nonsense in the last hour than I can ever recall hearing." I was certain that behind me at counsel table Jerry Collins was having a heart attack, which he later confirmed was the case. The judge was so mad that if he could have reached me, I am sure he would have swatted me with his gavel. But my sally had its desired effect. The judge attempted to argue the First Amendment point with me, and I was fairly confident that I had the better side of that argument. After about half an hour, the judge essentially gave in. When we left the courtroom, I was back in his good graces, and the only aspect of the government's proposed ground rules that he did not accept was the handing over of half the newspaper to Rauh's clients.

Finally, getting to know Belford Lawson was one of the great delights of the trial. Belford, Jerry, and I shared many a late-evening dinner after interviewing the next day's boatload of witnesses. It was a pleasure and an inspiration to listen to this man who had lived through so much and who had worked with the legal giants of the Civil Rights Movement, including Thurgood Marshall, Bill Hastie, and Spottswood Robinson. He had many stories to tell, and not all of them about the law. Belford had been an outstanding college football player, a starting halfback on the University of Michigan's team in the 1920s. He told the story of playing a home game against the University of Alabama. He said he was kicked and punched and gouged and called vile names all afternoon by the white boys from the deep South. Then, he said, some thirty years later a man he had never met showed up at his law office. The man introduced himself, saying that he had played on that Alabama team and that he wanted to apologize for the unjustified and illegal beating they had given Belford on that long ago day.

I learned a lot working down in the mines.

❖ ❖ ❖

Babies, Blood and the Book of Deuteronomy

One evening during my first year at the firm, I was working away at my desk around 7 p.m. when the phone rang. It was after regular business hours, and the secretary in charge of answering the phones said that I was the first lawyer she had been able to locate. There was a doctor on the line from Georgetown University Medical Center who said he urgently needed legal assistance. Williams & Connolly was full of Georgetown law graduates, and the firm represented both the university and its excellent hospital. When I took the call, the doctor said that he was with the neonatology unit, that he had a premature infant who needed a blood transfusion, and that the baby's parents, who were Jehovah's Witnesses, were refusing to give their consent to the procedure. He wanted a lawyer to obtain a court order authorizing the transfusion.

I asked the doctor why the baby needed the transfusion. He explained that the infant was quite premature and tiny, that its lungs were immature, and that it needed oxygen to survive. With a baby that small on oxygen, it was necessary to monitor the oxygen content of its blood. If it received too little oxygen, there was a strong risk of permanent brain damage. If it received too much, there was an equally strong risk of permanent blindness. The only way to monitor the oxygen content of the baby's blood was to remove some blood periodically. This baby was so small and had so little blood that they could not continue the monitoring without putting some more blood in. I asked how long they could continue removing blood before they had to stop, and he said no later than noon the following day. I told him I would get to work on the problem and call him back.

As soon as I hung up the phone I made a tour of the firm's suite of offices in search of someone with more experience than I to help me cope with the problem. It was one of those rare evenings when very few people were working late, and I could find no one who knew any more than I did. I was on my own. I had no idea how to convene an emergency hearing to consider an application for such an order.

I had at that point met only one judge in the city, federal district judge Gerhard Gesell, a former Covington & Burling partner who had led a seminar in Antitrust Practice at Virginia that I had taken my third year in law school. I had also spent a fair amount of time talking to him at a reception the firm gave for members of the seminar after it was over. President Johnson had thereafter elevated him to the federal bench. I thought there was a decent chance he would remember me.

I called Judge Gesell's chambers. I was in luck. He was still at work, and he took my call. He said he did remember me. I explained my problem to him, said that I had looked unsuccessfully for a more experienced lawyer, that I was unsure how to proceed, and that I would appreciate any suggestions he might give me. He told me that I should enlist another lawyer whom I trusted, not from Williams & Connolly or Covington, that the two of us should go to the hospital and interview all the participants, and that we should then come to his home. He would appoint the other lawyer as guardian *ad litem* for the child, would receive a report and recommendation from him, and would hear any argument I wanted to make. I thanked him, said that I would do as he suggested, and that I would see him later in the evening.

I then called my good friend Bob Hacker from Wilmer, Cutler and asked if he was up for an adventure that evening. He asked what I had in mind, and when I explained, he said he would be glad to help, that whatever he was working on that evening could wait. So Bob and I piled into my car and headed for Georgetown Hospital.

When we arrived, we met the father of the infant. The mother was still bedridden following delivery of the baby. I explained to the father that I represented the hospital, that the doctor had told me that his baby needed a transfusion, and that I was investigating the possibility of applying for a court order authorizing one. I introduced Bob Hacker and explained his role. I told the father that he was entitled to participate in the process and that he was free to contact a lawyer if he chose. He said he had no access to a lawyer—the family was obviously of very modest means—but that he wanted to be kept informed. He made it clear that he and the baby's mother were unalterably opposed to the transfusion.

There are several passages in the Bible that forbid the eating or drinking of blood, principal among them Deuteronomy 12:23, which reads in the King James translation: "Only be sure that you eat not the blood: for the blood is the life; and you may not eat the life with the flesh." To some modern readers this might seem an injunction against drinking raw blood or eating raw or rare meat, a wise if perhaps outdated sanitary precaution laid down in times when nothing was understood about the dangers of bacterial infection. Jehovah's Witnesses, however, read the passage differently. Though the doctrine has developed unevenly over time and there is some dissent within the sect, most Jehovah's Witnesses read this and other passages very literally as forbidding the consumption of blood in any way, including as part of any medical procedure. Some, the majority I believe, take the view that the introduction of blood into the body damns a person's soul for eternity. A minority believe that if there is compulsion, such as a court order, the person is not damned. This baby's parents took the former view.

The situation presented an exquisite dilemma. I believe strongly in religious liberty, which is guaranteed by the First Amendment to the Constitution. For the most part, we all take the view, not only that each person is entitled to worship—or not to worship—as his or her conscience dictates, but also that parents should be permitted to raise their children in accordance with the tenets of their faith. On the other hand, little is so precious as the welfare of a child, and infants in particular are wholly at the mercy of others for nurture and protection. The refusal of this baby's parents to accept what to the vast majority of people is a routine medical procedure, and one that was undeniably vital to the well-being of the baby, created a clash of two supremely important values. My role was to advocate on behalf of the care-givers, the hospital and medical staff, and I found the particular belief system of the parents unattractive and primitive, but I empathized with the agony the parents must have been going through.

Bob and I got to work and interviewed the doctor, the nurses, and the father. The situation was exactly as the doctor had told me over the phone. Bob and I then conferred, and he said that he thought that a transfusion was the only course consistent with the baby's best interests. I explained to the father that we were on our way to the judge's home to seek an order and that he was welcome to come with us. He said he would like to and asked if his pastor, who was present in the hospital, could come too. I said I had no objection, and the four of us headed for Judge Gesell's house in my car.

It had taken longer to accomplish things at the hospital than we had anticipated, and it was getting on toward midnight when we arrived at the judge's Georgetown home. He greeted us in his shirtsleeves and bedroom slippers and ushered us into his study. He formally appointed Bob as the baby's guardian for the purpose of the proceeding and listened carefully as Bob outlined what he had done and the evidence he had gathered and recommended that the court enter an order authorizing a transfusion. I addressed the issue of religious freedom, arguing that, while a mentally competent adult might have the right to refuse treatment for him or herself on religious grounds, the medical welfare of a helpless infant was paramount and should override considerations of the parents' religious beliefs.

The family's minister then asked leave to speak, and Judge Gesell listened to him. He proceeded to talk for at least fifteen or twenty minutes on the biblical foundations of the opposition of Jehovah's Witnesses to blood transfusions. As the minister droned on, I distinctly recall thinking that if anyone had suggested to me that morning as I was leaving for work that sometime after midnight I would be sitting in Gerhard Gesell's study listening to a preacher expound the Book of Deuteronomy, I would have thought he or she was certifiably loony.

When the minister finished, the judge turned to me and said, "Mr. Dudley, I am going to deny your application. You have not demonstrated enough of an emergency." Not enough of an emergency?! There was no dispute that the sword would fall at noon the next day, less than twelve hours from then, and that without a transfusion at or before that time the baby would be at unacceptable risk for either brain damage or blindness. My mind was racing at warp speed. Did I have to try to knock up some appellate judge at this very late hour to try to get Judge Gesell reversed? I recalled that Judge Skelly Wright of the D.C. Circuit had recently authorized a transfusion for an unconscious adult Jehovah's Witness. Was there enough time if I waited until the morning? But then another thought dawned on me. Perhaps what the judge was saying was that he was not prepared to trample upon the obviously sincerely held beliefs of this poor and ill-educated parent, with him and his pastor present in the judge's elegant study late at night. I decided to test this thought. "In the event things become more exigent in the morning," which of course he and I both knew they would, "would your honor entertain a renewed application?" The twinkle in Gesell's eye told me I had read him correctly. "I would always entertain a renewed application based on changed circumstances," he replied. I thanked him for hearing us and apologized for intruding upon him so late at night, and we left.

I drove the father and the minister back to the hospital and told the father that I thought it very likely that I would approach the judge again in the morning. I said if I did, I would notify him so that he could be present. I thought he had the right to be there. I then drove Bob Hacker back to his office and went home, getting to bed around 2 a.m.

Between 9:30 and 10 the same morning, after checking with the doctor to make sure that nothing had changed, I called Judge Gesell's chambers and asked if I could bring a renewed application before him. He told me to come on down and he would sign the order. I told him I had promised the father that if I approached the court again, I would notify him and let him be there. The judge said quite firmly, "I don't think that's necessary. I heard what they had to say last night." It was not a suggestion. So I broke my promise to the father, took a cab to the courthouse, and entered the judge's chambers alone. He signed the order, and we had a brief, pleasant chat. I had a copy of the order immediately delivered to the hospital and then called the father and told him what had transpired. He was understandably furious and threatened to sue me. Though I sympathized with his frustration at being excluded from the morning's doings, I smiled at the thought of being sued for wrongful life.

A couple of years later a very similar situation arose. Having done the earlier case, I was of course known as the firm's expert in this field, so the call was routed to me. It came fairly early in the business day. By this time I knew my way around the court system a great deal better, and the provisions of the D.C. Court Reform Act of 1970 were in full effect. I knew that D.C. Superior Court was now the appropriate court. I took the matter before the Superior Court's emergency motions judge, John Doyle, who heard me in the latter part of the afternoon. On this occasion, the father and the mother were of differing views. When I interviewed the father, he said to me, "I cannot as a matter of religious conscience consent to the transfusion. But this baby's welfare is my principal concern. If you obtain a court order, so be it." The mother, however, was strenuously opposed to the idea of a transfusion and hired a lawyer, an elderly gentleman named Ezor Keagle, himself a Jehovah's Witness, to oppose my application.

Mr. Keagle was not a litigator, and his principal argument before Judge Doyle was that hospitals should be condemned for seeking out trumped-up occasions on which to violate the religious freedom of members of the sect. Judge Doyle kept a straight face but swiftly signed an order authorizing a transfusion.

As we left the judge's chambers at a little after 5 p.m., Mr. Keagle expressed the intention to take an emergency appeal. He had not, however, the vaguest clue as to how to do it. So in an amusing role reversal, I, the now-grizzled veteran of the court system in my early thirties, took the septuagenarian neophyte by the hand, walked him to the Clerk's Office, and helped him convene an emergency three-judge panel of the District of Columbia Court of Appeals, which would hear argument at 8 o'clock that evening. At the argument Mr. Keagle repeated his attack on the good faith of the hospital, adding that its defalcation was symptomatic of so many degrading developments in American culture, such as women's liberation, an argument that sent the eyes of Judge Katherine Kelly in search of the ceiling. Within twenty minutes of the end of the argument, the panel announced that Judge Doyle's order was affirmed.

I had brought a close friend from the firm, David Webster, along for the ride that evening, and after getting a copy of the court's order to the hospital, David and I repaired to Duke Zeibert's restaurant, a firm hangout, for a late supper. There we encountered the three appellate judges, who were savoring some food, wine, and the evening's proceedings.

❖ ❖ ❖

The "Elvis Bandit"

In 1951 Allen Carroll Pruitt, then fifteen years old, pleaded guilty to burglary, robbery, and second-degree murder in connection with the stabbing death of an elderly newsdealer in Norfolk, Virginia, who died in the hovel behind his kiosk, where he lived. Pruitt was from Spartanburg, South Carolina, and he was living at the time of the crime with relatives in Norfolk. Nineteen years later his two sisters and their husbands mortgaged their houses to raise $10,000 to hire a lawyer to try to free their brother. They approached Edward Bennett Williams, the best-known criminal defense lawyer in the country. Even in 1970, $10,000 was not a fee that roused Williams' interest. He told Pruitt's family, however, that one of the younger lawyers in the firm might help them, and he referred them to Bill McDaniels, a third-year associate who had spent a year as an assistant public defender in Philadelphia before joining Williams & Connolly. Bill agreed to take the case and asked if I wanted to work on it with him. Thus began an incredible odyssey in criminal law, procedure, injustice, and man's inhumanity to man.

The robbery and murder took place in November 1951. The Norfolk police suspected Pruitt and traced him to his parents' home in Spartanburg. On their request, the authorities in Spartanburg arrested Pruitt, literally dragging him away from the Thanksgiving dinner table. Over the next two and a half days, Pruitt was held incommunicado and interrogated by relays of police officers. His parents' efforts to see him and to provide him with a lawyer were rebuffed. He was deprived of sleep. He was given a polygraph examination and was told, possibly falsely, that he had failed it. After protesting his innocence for more than 50 hours, Pruitt finally confessed to the crime. Without any extradition proceedings or notification to his family, he was handed over to the Norfolk police, who drove him back to Virginia. The next day he was taken to juvenile court with no counsel appointed and no notice to his family at home or his kinfolk in Norfolk. There the juvenile court waived jurisdiction over him and sent him on to be tried as an adult, which among other things made him eligible for the death penalty. In the Circuit Court he was charged with first-degree murder, burglary, and robbery. The court appointed a lawyer to represent him, an older gentleman of a type that then existed in every city and town in the country. His job was not really to defend Pruitt, but to convince him to plead guilty to lesser crimes to avoid a conviction for first-degree murder, which then carried an almost automatic death sentence. Pruitt took the deal. He received three life sentences, to be served consecutively.

Pruitt was sent to the maximum-security prison in Richmond, known simply in the criminal law community by its location, "Spring Street." A grim, forbidding fortress whose core dated from the time of Thomas Jefferson, Spring Street was a hell-hole. After several years Pruitt managed to escape, one of the tiny handful who ever did. He headed for Georgia, where he went on a spree robbing convenience stores. His slick, black hair, combed back in a ducktail cut, together with his swarthy, good-looking features, earned him the sobriquet of "the Elvis Bandit." It was not long before he was caught and found himself on a chain gang in sweltering rural Georgia. When Georgia authorities learned that he was under three consecutive life sentences in Virginia, they decided to let the taxpayers of the Old Dominion pay for his upkeep and returned him to Spring Street. It was not a happy homecoming.

Allen Carroll Pruitt was not a nice young man, but by the mid-1960s he had become in the insufferable conditions of Spring Street something he had never been before—a drug addict. The guards at Spring Street, like many prison guards elsewhere, had a nice little racket going. They supplemented their meager incomes by selling drugs to the prisoners, who paid with the pittances that their families were able to give them, supposedly for extra food and cigarettes. One day, Pruitt shot up something very bad—who knows what concoctions the guards were selling—and got hold of a big knife. He went berserk, and before the guards could subdue him, he had killed the prison doctor—whom no one seems to have mourned—and the prison industrial program director—his only friend in Spring Street—and carved up a prison guard.

The prosecutors charged Pruitt with a specific crime under the Virginia Code—murder by a life prisoner—which then carried a mandatory death sentence. The court again appointed counsel to defend Pruitt, but this time his lawyers took their responsibilities seriously. They pleaded Pruitt not guilty by reason of temporary insanity, and they put the prison system on trial. They proved the prevalence of drug sales by the guards and demonstrated that Pruitt had been mentally out of control during the killings and the wounding of the guard. Then the prosecution made a major mistake. Many crimes have what are known as "lesser included offenses," which means offenses involving fewer than all the elements of the main offense. Murder and manslaughter afford an example. Murder requires a showing of deliberate intent to kill, while manslaughter, for which the penalty is less, does not. Offered a chance to have the jury instructed on one or more lesser included offenses, such as second-degree murder or manslaughter, the prosecution decided to roll the dice and seek the mandatory death sentence or nothing. Knowing that Pruitt was still subject to three consecutive life sentences for the 1951 Norfolk killing, and having heard of the repulsive behavior of the guards, the jury chose life. It found Pruitt not guilty by reason of temporary insanity.

So Pruitt returned yet again to Spring Street, which exacted its fierce revenge. Pruitt spent the next three and a half years in solitary confinement. If Spring Street was a hell-hole for the general prison population, it was treble that for those in "solitary." Solitary confinement consisted of an unheated cell, roughly eight feet by ten feet, with a thin mattress on the floor for a bed and an open hole in the middle of the floor for a toilet. The prisoner was given two meals a day, one of which, as the system so delicately put it, had "some meat content." The prisoner was allowed out of this tiny cell once a week to shower, shave, and brush his teeth and one additional hour for exercise. Bill McDaniels and I first met Carroll Pruitt when he was near the end of this fearful time in triple hell. By then he was as close to being simply an animal as any human being I have ever seen.

I have gotten a little ahead of the story. A couple of years after his acquittal for the prison killings, Pruitt's family had retained F. Lee Bailey, a nationally known criminal defense lawyer from Boston. Bailey and his associates at first did a good job. They petitioned the Virginia Supreme Court for a writ of *habeas corpus* on the ground that the 1951 convictions were invalid because the waiver of juvenile-court jurisdiction was defective and thus that the Circuit Court never properly acquired jurisdiction to try Pruitt. Somewhat surprisingly, the Virginia Supreme Court, not generally known for its tender mercy toward convicted felons, agreed.[4] It held that the failure either to appoint counsel for Pruitt in the juvenile court or to notify his family that the juvenile court was going to consider waiving jurisdiction was serious error and thus that he was not properly tried as an adult. On this basis it reversed Pruitt's convictions for burglary, robbery, and murder.

Suddenly the Commonwealth had no legal basis for holding its most notorious multiple killer. The Commonwealth Attorney for Norfolk immediately announced that he would retry Pruitt for the 1951 crime, and he swiftly obtained a new indictment for first-degree murder. Thus the death penalty was once again in play. With Pruitt's 1951 confession hanging in the air, the best strategy seemed to be to try to stop the retrial. The argument for doing so was that, since Pruitt was a juvenile at the time of the crime and the adult court never properly obtained jurisdiction over him, it could not cure the problem and take jurisdiction eighteen years later. The very decision that made him eligible for the vastly increased penalties of the adult system had been wrong. Not perhaps the strongest of arguments, but one well worth pursuing, given the stakes.

At this point Bailey and company made an elementary procedural mistake. They filed an action seeking a federal-court injunction against retrying Pruitt in state court. They filed it in the Norfolk division of the federal district court for the Eastern District of Virginia, the federal jurisdiction within which the proposed retrial would take place. But they overlooked a basic federal statute that deprives the federal courts of the power to issue injunctions in such circumstances to stop state judicial proceedings. It was known as the Anti-Injunction Act. They also overlooked the fact that the judges of the Norfolk division were notoriously pro-prosecution. The action was dismissed almost as soon as it was filed. Bailey's people filed an appeal to the federal court of appeals for the Fourth Circuit, which has jurisdiction over Virginia federal trial courts. The appeal was hopeless.

Perhaps worst of all, Bailey's firm overlooked the fact that only one federal judge in the entire country had ruled that a retrial in similar circumstances, where the original trial court had not acquired proper adult jurisdiction because of a defective waiver of juvenile jurisdiction, was forbidden by the Constitution. That judge was Robert Merhige of the Richmond division of the Eastern District of Virginia, and Pruitt was still being held in Richmond. The proper mode of proceeding would have been an application for a federal writ of *habeas corpus*, which would come before Judge Merhige, who was then the only federal district judge in Richmond. It may seem highly technical, but the writ of *habeas corpus* would challenge the constitutionality of Pruitt's confinement by the state (in Richmond), which the state could justify only on the basis of its intention to retry Pruitt, which Merhige had already held was unconstitutional, while the injunction action sought to bar the proposed criminal proceeding itself (in Norfolk), which federal law prohibited.

Perhaps because of this procedural screw-up, or perhaps for other reasons, Pruitt's family lost faith in F. Lee Bailey's firm and discharged them. It was at this point that Bill and I entered the case. Though we viewed the effort to forestall the retrial as a long shot with little hope of success, we determined to pursue it as far as we could. When the appeal from the dismissal of the Norfolk injunction action was argued in the Fourth Circuit, I stood up and admitted that the lower court had been correct to dismiss the action, but asked the court of appeals to make it clear that a decision affirming that dismissal would not prevent us from pursuing the proper remedy of *habeas corpus*. The court of appeals obliged, and we swiftly filed an application for the writ in front of Judge Merhige. When we argued the matter before him, Judge Merhige acknowledged that he had previously held such retrials unlawful, and announced that he would entertain a renewed *habeas* application in the event Pruitt was again convicted, but said that he had no intention of stopping the trial. Bill and I felt that we had retrieved the Bailey firm's mistake and teed the matter up as best we could, and so we turned our attention to getting ready for the retrial.

The state had never had much of a case against Pruitt except for his confession, and it was plain that the retrial would come down to a battle over its admissibility in evidence. The Supreme Court of the United States had long held that it was a denial of a defendant's right to due process of law to introduce in evidence against him a confession that was not the voluntary product of his free will.[5] The Court had adhered to and elaborated upon this principle in a long series of cases coming from state courts that often blatantly ignored the law. I read and analyzed every single confession case in the history of the Supreme Court. The Court had identified numerous factors that were powerful indicia of involuntariness. They included incommunicado detention, denial of access to family and counsel, extended interrogation, deprivation of sleep, and trickery—all of them part of the process by which Pruitt had been induced to confess. The Court also said on several occasions that these factors had to be analyzed in light of the vulnerability of the defendant, focusing on such elements as youth and mental incompetence. Pruitt was not mentally incompetent, but he had been only fifteen when subjected to the state's coercive interrogation tactics. I prepared an extensive memorandum citing and analyzing the Supreme Court's confession jurisprudence. I admit to the bias of an advocate, but it was impossible to read the case law fairly without concluding that Pruitt's confession was inadmissible.

Similarly, any careful reading of the confession cases in the Supreme Court showed local judges, often holding elective office, succumbing repeatedly to community pressure to secure the convictions of confessed criminals without regard to the strictures of the Constitution. A major difficulty in controlling this urge was that an appellate court is not supposed to substitute its judgment on questions of fact for that of the trial judge who hears the evidence. Appellate courts sit, in theory, to correct mistakes of law, leaving factual issues to the trial courts and the juries, if any, except in cases of egregious error. The Supreme Court had become so frustrated with the transparent refusals of state trial courts to find even the most obviously coerced confessions inadmissible (the first confession case coming from a state court had involved beating the defendant repeatedly with chains; the state courts found the confession voluntary[6]), that it had developed a special doctrine of appellate review in these cases. The Court held that it was bound by the findings of the state trial courts on initial questions of fact— was the defendant beaten, or starved, or whatever—but not by its ultimate conclusion on the question whether the confession was voluntary.[7]

The Norfolk City Circuit Judge before whom the Pruitt case was retried was W. Moultrie Guerry. Judge Guerry announced at the outset of the trial that he was not going to operate the way California courts did—Pruitt's retrial followed shortly on the heels of the notorious trial of Charles Manson in California for multiple murders, in which jury selection alone took several weeks—and that we would have "a jury in the box this morning." Thus he brushed aside our request for careful individual *voir dire* examination of potential jurors. Our request was based on two considerations. First, the extensive publicity surrounding Pruitt's earlier trial for the prison killings, the reversal of his 1951 conviction by the Virginia Supreme Court, and his reindictment on the earlier murder charge raised serious concerns about whether potential jurors had already formed an opinion that he was guilty. So intense and continuing was the publicity that every time Bill and I visited Norfolk to prepare our defense, it was front-page news in the major Norfolk newspaper, the *Virginian-Pilot*, usually with a headline such as "Mad-Dog Killer's Lawyers Come to Town." Here again there was solid and recent Supreme Court precedent about the need to protect defendants from prejudicial pretrial publicity, which we cited to the court.[8] Second, the Commonwealth was seeking the death penalty, and the Supreme Court had held that juror attitudes toward the supreme sanction were a proper subject of inquiry on *voir dire*.[9] Nonetheless, Judge Guerry conducted only the most perfunctory examination of the members of the *venire*, posing a few simple questions to the entire assembled group. He did ask if any of them had seen any publicity surrounding the case. Bill and I gasped when not one of the fifty or so members of the *venire* admitted to having done so. Either these people never read a newspaper, or they were lying. Within an hour we had a (purportedly) death-qualified jury in the box.

As soon as the jury was selected and sworn, it was sent home. The first and most important question in the case was the admissibility of Pruitt's confession, a question to be determined by the judge, and the hearing on this question had to be conducted outside the presence of the jury, so that theoretically they would never know there had been a confession if it was ultimately excluded from evidence. Of course, the jurors knew exactly what was going on in the courtroom. I sympathized with the jurors to a degree, as they must have been very frustrated. The trial lasted exactly a week, but they were present for less than half a day of testimony.

From Monday afternoon through Thursday afternoon, the judge took evidence and heard argument on the voluntariness of Pruitt's confession. There was remarkably little factual dispute about the events leading up to it. About the only disagreement involved the interpretation of the results of the polygraph test administered to Pruitt during the interrogation. The Commonwealth claimed it showed he was lying. Our expert said it did not, at least not with any degree of certainty. For the rest, the police did not dispute that Pruitt had been held incommunicado, interrogated for hours at a time in relays, deprived of sleep, and generally hassled unceasingly for more than two full days before confessing. There was even a moment of rapport between the judge and Pruitt, who took the stand to testify to the ordeal he had undergone twenty years earlier. Judge Guerry took over the questioning of the defendant, and the two seemed to hit it off quite well. After more than two days of testimony, the judge heard argument for more than two hours. At the end he simply announced that he found the confession voluntary and admissible. It was the end of the day on Thursday. The court ordered that the jury be brought back the next morning to hear the actual case.

Perhaps moved by his observations of Pruitt, who was by this time quite presentable, and by their interaction the previous day, Judge Guerry surprised us Friday morning by announcing that he had decided to take the death penalty issue away from the jury. This was an enormous relief to all of us in the defense camp.

The actual testimony before the jury was quite brief. It consisted almost entirely of Pruitt's confession. The evidence and the closing arguments were over before lunch, and the case went to the jury early in the afternoon. The jury was out for little over an hour, and it returned the only verdict possible on the evidence, guilty of first-degree murder. In Virginia the jury sentences in felony cases, and the jurors gave us another pleasant surprise—they sentenced Carroll Pruitt to the minimum for first-degree murder, twenty years in prison. This meant that he was entitled to his immediate release, as he had already served eighteen years for the crime, and, despite his troubles in Spring Street, he had accumulated more than two years of statutory "good time," and thus had fully served his sentence. After some negotiating with the state Attorney General's Office, we arranged for his release that evening, on the explicit promise that he would not spend the night in Virginia. For technical reasons, he had to check in at Spring Street and be released from there, so Bill and I rode to Richmond with Pruitt and a state trooper. Shortly after he entered Spring Street for the last time, Carroll Pruitt emerged a free man, to the jubilation of his family members, who hugged their son and brother for the first time in twenty years and, true to our bargain with the Attorney General's Office, immediately headed home to South Carolina.

Right after the jury rendered its verdict, Judge Guerry called the lawyers into his chambers for a final chat. He seemed content, if not actually pleased, with the result, and he handed out compliments all around. To Bill and me he said, "You guys did a helluva job on that confession, but I figured it was those seven old men in Richmond [the Virginia Supreme Court] who let him go the first time, and if anybody was going to let him go again, it was going to be them." So much for the integrity of judicial fact-finding in hot-button cases.

❖   ❖   ❖

Among the reasons that I enjoyed criminal defense work so much was that I got to know my clients well and that the impact of the proceedings was so immediate. Usually their liberty, and sometimes their lives, were on the line, and it was my responsibility to give them my very best shot. The Carroll Pruitt who emerged in the course of our representation of him was a complex and in some ways very intelligent man, a far cry from the broken piece of humanity we met after his years in solitary confinement. (However, when he asked to take our son Will, then four years old, home with him for a weekend, Louise and I politely demurred.) Pruitt had certainly led an interesting life, and he was good at recounting his experiences. We listened for hours to his stories. He expressed some pride in the "Elvis Bandit" nickname. In addition, he had written a substantial amount of poetry in Spring Street. He had limited education, and from a literary standpoint the poetry was not very good. But it expressed the profound feelings of a young man without any real hope, and a collection of the poems was published after his release, under the title *Poetry Behind Prison Bars*.

Pruitt returned to his family's home in Spartanburg. He went to work for his father, who was a house painter. Having had nothing to read in solitary confinement save the Bible, he became an ordained minister. The second Christmas after he got out, he organized a campaign to give every inmate in the South Carolina prison system a Christmas gift. He raised the money, purchased the gifts, and delivered them to the prisons. He stayed in touch with Bill and me. He married. Things finally seemed to be going well for him.

Sadly, it didn't last. On New Year's Day the very week after his Christmas present project came to fruition, I received a phone call from a very agitated lawyer in Spartanburg. He said he had just been appointed to represent Carroll Pruitt on a murder charge, and that Pruitt had said that Bill (with whom Louise and I had just celebrated New Year's Eve) and I were his real lawyers. There had been a dust-up after a poker game late one night, and Pruitt had shot and killed a man. Bill and I did go down to Spartanburg to try to help, but representing him again was out of the question. Even at our then very modest hourly rates, our representation of Pruitt had cost the firm vastly more than the $10,000 retainer, which was all the family had.

The firm was not prepared to foot the bill for another murder defense. We did find him a lawyer in South Carolina, who kept us generally abreast of developments, but we had seen enough while we were down there to know that things were pretty hopeless. Pruitt was convicted of first-degree murder and sentenced to life in prison yet again.

❖ ❖ ❖

During these post-clerkship years, I continued to have occasional and very warm contact with Chief Justice Warren. Of course, I attended the annual law clerks' reunions. I have mentioned that the Chief was a big sports fan and personally close to Ed Williams. He was a regular guest in the Redskins' president's box at RFK Stadium when the 'Skins were playing at home. At halftime the team served food and drinks to the guests, and members of the law firm were welcomed. I often had a chance to chat briefly with the Chief while warming up between halves. My friend Dennis Flannery from Wilmer, Cutler and I one day took the Chief out for a memorable lunch at a fancy downtown restaurant.

On another occasion, in March 1971, I attended a luncheon given by some Washington organization and found myself at the chief justice's table. It was the day after the death of Thomas E. Dewey, the former New York governor and the Republican presidential candidate in 1944 and 1948. Warren had, of course, been Dewey's running mate in the latter year. The Chief was in an expansive mood and reminisced candidly about the 1948 campaign. He said that Dewey was quite rigid, that the campaign and all its major speeches had been meticulously planned even before the convention, that the plan was never modified, and that as the vice-presidential candidate, he was kept under a very tight rein. The Chief had little personal contact with Dewey and did not seem to have warmed to him. President Truman's comeback win in the election was quite remarkable. His popularity had been very low earlier in the year, and the Republicans' lead in the polls was so large that no one gave the president a chance. So overconfident was the Dewey team that, on their orders, the campaign's California operation was shut down a full week before the election. The chief justice said that the only person to see what was coming was his wife Nina. A few days before the voting, she said to him, "Earl, I hope you don't have your heart set on this thing, because you are going to lose." Perhaps President Truman's happiest moment came on the morning after the election, when he held up for view a copy of the early edition of the *Chicago Tribune*, whose banner headline prematurely proclaimed "Dewey Defeats Truman."

I did not see a lot of the chief justice in the six years after my clerkship ended, but I saw enough to realize that despite his cheerful and upbeat demeanor, his health was beginning to fail. The end came on July 9, 1974. It was decided that his body would lie in state in the Great Hall of the Supreme Court. Mrs. McHugh quickly organized an honor guard of former law clerks to stand by the casket. Mostly because we were close at hand, Charlie Wilson and I were among the first group to serve in this capacity. It was taking Mrs. McHugh a while to find a second shift, so we stood for more than two hours, as thousands of people walked by the flag-draped bier in a remarkable outpouring of emotion to pay their respects to this great man. I felt sad but honored to be able to take part in this tribute.

❖ ❖ ❖

Bonnie the Space Monkey

It should be apparent by now that there were many people in America in the early 1970s who had heard of only one great lawyer—"the man to see," in the words of the title of his biography— if you were in real trouble, Edward Bennett Williams.[10] There was a steady stream of pleas for his help. He could command what were then astronomical fees, and he took only a tiny handful of the most important cases. However, not only did he not like to turn people away cold, he was happy to have other lawyers in the firm take some of the cases he did not want, which were often interesting and potentially financially rewarding. Thus Williams usually handed off to others, at least for a preliminary interview, the clients that he declined to represent personally, as he had done in Carroll Pruitt's case. He and his secretary, Lillian Keats, would screen the cases, and Lillian would call some other lawyer and ask that he or she see the potential client. We younger lawyers called this process "the wheel."

It was my turn on the wheel one day. Lillian called and asked if I would speak with a woman from New York named Eleanor Sieling, who said she wanted a lawyer to defend a libel suit. I called Ms. Sieling, who sounded somewhat elderly and not a little flighty. She explained that she was president of an animal rights advocacy group called United Action for Animals, which had been sued in federal court in New York over an article she had published in the organization's newsletter criticizing some NASA scientist. I really had no desire to meet with her, but she insisted on taking the train down from New York to tell me more about her case. We agreed to meet one day the following week.

Something flared up in one of my cases that made it impossible for me to meet with Ms. Sieling at the appointed time, so I asked David Webster if he would see her for me. Webster and I often backed each other up in case of scheduling conflicts. I told David that she sounded like something of a kook and that he should probably devise some strategy to get rid of her.

Eleanor Sieling was in her seventies, and she was, as we learned later, known in her Manhattan neighborhood as the "cat lady," because she took in stray cats. Lots of stray cats. As Webster related when I saw him after their meeting, she looked every inch the "cat lady." She had longish, wispy gray hair that she seldom combed, and her clothing was both dated and a bit frayed. She explained her case to David. The defense to the libel suit would involve an invocation of the First Amendment right to free speech. Still pursuing a strategy to get rid of her, Webster told me that he decided he would quote her a fee that was clearly out of her range. "I tried to guess her choking price," he said, "and I figured because of her appearance and the nature of her group that it was probably around $5,000. Just to be on the safe side, I multiplied it by ten." Webster told Ms. Sieling that because of the very important constitutional issues involved, he would not think of undertaking the case unless he could do it right all the way. To do that, he said, he would need a retainer of $50,000. Ms. Sieling did not bat an eye. "I don't think that's a problem," she said. "I can give you a check for $30,000 now. I will have to go to my board for the other $20,000, but I am sure they will authorize it. I will let you know by Monday."

So much for reading books by their covers. The board of UAA swiftly approved the fee, and Webster and I were off for an adventure in space.

In the mid-1960s, when space flight was still in its infancy and little was known about the effects of long-term weightlessness and exposure to other space conditions, NASA decided to explore these issues by putting a monkey into orbit for a month, which at that time was much longer than any human had been in space. The agency contracted the design of the project out to an eminent research physician at UCLA by the name of W. Ross Adey. Adey designed an elaborate experiment, and in 1968 "Bonnie the Space Monkey" (so named even though Bonnie was a boy) was launched in a tiny space capsule to the accompaniment of a fanfare of publicity. There were twenty-some measuring devices attached to or implanted in Bonnie's body. Sadly, Bonnie became quite seriously ill within a day or two, and the mission had to be aborted. The space capsule was recovered from the ocean, but Bonnie soon died.

Outraged, Eleanor Sieling and United Action for Animals went on the attack. Eleanor wrote and published in the organization's little journal a piece railing about the cruelty of the experiment to the monkey. She then turned her attention to Dr. Adey, who, she said, among other unflattering things, "has a long history of cruelty to animals."

Despite the fact that the UAA journal was a mere four- or eight-page newsletter with little if any circulation outside the world of committed animal-rights activists, Dr. Adey decided to bring suit for libel. He obtained the financial backing of a group called the National Society for Medical Research, whose highfalootin' name masked the fact that it was the trade organization for the breeders who supplied animals to research laboratories. Or maybe the NSMR felt threatened and urged Adey to bring the suit. Regardless, the organization underwrote Adey's legal fees and expenses.

The suit was brought in the federal district court for Southern New York—Manhattan—where Eleanor lived and the organization was headquartered. It was assigned to Edward Weinfeld, one of the most distinguished federal judges in the country. For reasons I never understood, the lawyers for Adey, who was entitled to a jury trial under the Seventh Amendment to the Constitution, agreed to a bench trial before Judge Weinfeld. Our defense was relatively legalistic and would surely be better understood by a judge than a jury.

Beginning in 1964 the Supreme Court had begun to rein in defamation suits under the First Amendment to the Constitution. The first case in the line was *New York Times Co. v. Sullivan*.[11] An Alabama jury had awarded very large damages against the *Times* for a full-page ad it had run in which a civil rights group had attacked the brutal behavior of the mayor and police chief of Birmingham toward African Americans and their supporters. The Court held for the first time that the First Amendment's guarantee of freedom of speech imposed limits on the states' ability to award damages for libel and slander. The Court said that the First Amendment was intended to promote "open, robust, uninhibited" discussion of issues of public importance and thus that a public official complaining of defamation on a matter concerning his or her performance in public office had to prove that the defamatory statements were false and that they were said or published by the defendant with knowledge that they were false, or at least with "reckless disregard for the truth." Before this case, truth was a defense to a defamation suit, but the defendant had the burden of proving it. Moreover, to reinforce the protection of speech on public issues, the Court in *Sullivan* held that the defendant's knowledge or recklessness had to proved by "clear and convincing evidence," a higher standard than normal in civil litigation. It had followed up the *Sullivan* case with other decisions extending this same level of constitutional protection to statements made about "public figures."[12]

Dr. Adey was arguably a public official—he worked for a state university, and the statements concerned an experiment he conducted for NASA, an arm of the federal government—but he was at a minimum a public figure in the context of the highly publicized flight of Bonnie the Space Monkey. Thus he had to show by clear and convincing evidence that Eleanor Sieling had known that her statements about him and his experiment were false or that she recklessly disregarded the truth. This question would almost certainly be parsed more carefully and with greater concern for the protection of speech by a judge than by a jury.

The trial was scheduled to begin on a Monday morning, so Webster and I went up to New York over the weekend to finalize our preparation. When we met Eleanor at the federal courthouse on Foley Square in lower Manhattan early Monday morning, she was breathless with excitement. "Did you see Saturday's *Times*?" she asked. We had not. She pulled out a copy. The lady had some impressive connections. Somehow she had persuaded the editors of the *New York Times* to run a story on the case—highly favorable to our side—two days before the trial was to start. Not only that, the story occupied the entire top half of the front page of the second section of the paper, with a substantial runover to an inside page. We read it with general amazement, but almost fell over when we came to a quotation from Eleanor about her lawyers. "I hired the best lawyers in the country, and I paid them $50,000 to defend the case. I am trying to get them to accept more money, but they won't." We just hoped that Ed Williams' perusal of Saturday's *Times* had been no more thorough than ours.

The trial began on schedule, and it went our way from the beginning. The leadoff witness was the plaintiff himself, Ross Adey. He was an impressive figure, and he did well on direct examination, outlining his distinguished career in medical research and detailing the experiment he had designed for NASA.

David proceeded to execute perhaps the best—and certainly the most enjoyable—cross-examination I have ever heard in a courtroom. He established that Bonnie was confined in a tiny space capsule that allowed little room to move, that there were more than twenty measuring devices attached to or surgically implanted in his body, and that he was forced to undergo the trauma of liftoff with its intense increase in gravitational force and the bewilderment of weightlessness. Then he asked, "Dr. Adey, would you not agree with me that someone familiar with your work but with a different point of view from yours could conclude in good faith that your experiments, including this one, involved cruelty to the animals?" This was *the* question, for if Adey agreed, he would be admitting that Eleanor Sieling had not published with reckless disregard for the truth. Adey rose to the bait. "Absolutely not," he shot back, "I care deeply for my animals, and I am never cruel to them."

Webster then turned to a sizable stack of medical journal articles on our table, all written by Adey and his colleagues, describing experiments he had participated in, and all gathered by Eleanor Sieling before she wrote her piece. For the next couple of hours, Webster went through each article with Adey, discussing what was done to the animals in each instance. I have now forgotten all but one of the experiments, but that one gives the general flavor. Adey and his colleagues took several specimens of a small but normally quite aggressive Australian marsupial and surgically excised a portion of each animal's brain hypothesized by them to control or to contribute to aggressive behavior. They then swatted the surgically modified animals about the head and face with sticks to see if they remained as aggressive as they had been before the lobotomies.

After this careful review of Adey's life's work, Webster then said, "So, doctor, I ask you again, could not someone familiar with your work but with a different point of view from yours conclude in good faith that your experiments, including the Bonnie experiment, involved cruelty to the animals?" At this point it did not matter what answer Adey gave. If he said yes, he was essentially conceding our defense. If he said no, he simply made himself out a fool. Ross Adey was no fool, and he was an honest man. There ensued what seemed like more than a minute of total silence in the courtroom. Then he said, "Yes, I guess I could see that." The case was effectively over.

Nonetheless, the trial moved forward. David was several years older than I and had much more trial experience, so he took the lead, but he allowed me a significant role in the proceedings. I did one or two pretty decent cross-examinations of the other side's witnesses, but then I thoroughly embarrassed myself with one cross-examination in which I committed an absolutely classic "one question too many" error. Dr. Adey had brought one of his colleagues from the UCLA medical school to testify to his good character and reputation. The plaintiff's character and reputation are always an issue in a defamation action, as he must show that he had a good reputation that was damaged by the false statements about him. There was evidence in the case that someone had put a copy of Eleanor Sieling's article on a bulletin board in a prominent location at the medical school. The character witness testified that Adey was an outstanding colleague and widely respected in the medical research community. On cross-examination, I asked him, "You saw the article about Dr. Adey and the Bonnie experiment on the bulletin board at the medical school, did you not?" He replied that he had. "And I take it from the fact that you have come here today voluntarily all the way from California to testify to Dr. Adey's fine reputation that you don't think any less of him because of what you read in that article?" "Absolutely not. He is a wonderful man and a great scholar."

It was time to sit down. We did not really contest Adey's good character and reputation, and I had shown that the article had not damaged him in the eyes of this witness at least. Indeed, there was up to that point not a shred of evidence that Adey had suffered *any* injury to his reputation, a showing he had to make in order to succeed. But, being young and feisty, I could not resist another thrust. "And you don't know anyone else who thinks less of Dr. Adey because of what they read in that article, do you?" The witness said, "Yes, I do." In my recollection, at least, the courtroom immediately disintegrated into peals of laughter. Opposing counsel, a Washington lawyer named Walter Bonner, with whom we were friendly, said in a stage whisper, "Why don't you ask him who, Earl?" Mustering what little aplomb and nonchalance I could, I said, "No further questions, your honor."

Realizing, I suspect, that by the end of the trial we were irretrievably ahead on points, David let me do the closing argument. The closing in a case is not only what a trial lawyer dreams of, it is what he or she plans the case around from the beginning. It is the lawyer's opportunity to strut his stuff. Addressing Judge Weinfeld directly, I began, "Your honor, this is the second time that a monkey has played a major role in the development of free speech law in this country." Weinfeld, who was an extremely intelligent, no-nonsense sort of judge, cracked up. "You're a little young to remember the *Scopes* trial, aren't you, Mr. Dudley?" he laughingly asked. "Yes," I replied, "but I have seen *Inherit the Wind*."

I must not have done too badly in the closing, for a few weeks later Judge Weinfeld handed down an elegantly reasoned opinion deciding every contested issue in our favor.[13] Given his very solid opinion and his reputation as an outstanding judicial scholar, an appeal seemed pointless, but Adey's lawyers took one. I drafted our responsive brief and was slated to argue the case in the Second Circuit Court of Appeals. The court listened politely to Adey's lawyer, but then as I rose to speak, it was obvious that the three judges were paying no attention to me. They began whispering among themselves and slipping rubber bands over their briefs. The chief judge leaned forward and said, "Mr. Dudley, we don't need to hear from you. The judgment below is affirmed."[14] Webster and I repaired to an expensive restaurant for a very satisfying celebratory lunch.

❖   ❖   ❖

Presidential Politics in the Courtroom, 1971-1972

I certainly had no desire in 1972 to repeat my disastrous presidential campaign experience of 1968, and besides, the Democrats looked like sure losers again. But I did have the opportunity to litigate a couple of cases raising significant legal issues concerning the Democratic Party's presidential nomination process.

In 1971 Ed Williams had recruited his friend Joe Califano to leave the firm of Arnold & Porter and join Williams & Connolly, which was renamed Williams, Connolly & Califano. It proved in the long term a disastrous move that almost broke up the firm. Califano, who had been President Johnson's lead domestic policy staffer, was a divisive personality, and within months he had poisoned what had been the close-knit, harmonious atmosphere of the firm. But in the short term, he brought with him the Democratic National Committee as a client, and the runup to the 1972 Democratic Convention was a very litigious time.

My first case for the DNC involved essentially a credentials challenge to the Mississippi delegation that was played out in federal court. Throughout the 1960s the Democratic Party, which of course had once owned the "solid South," had been struggling to purge itself and its processes of the ugly heritage of racism that came with being the party of a region that discriminated against African Americans in voting rights as well as on many other fronts. The late 1960s saw a seismic shift in American politics, as the Republicans adopted their "southern strategy," designed to appeal to the white southerners unwilling to accept the Democratic Party's national commitment to racial progress. By contrast, the 1968 Democratic National Convention had adopted a new set of rules designed to open up the party's operations, and in particular its delegate-selection process, to minority participation.

Black civil rights leaders in Mississippi, led by Fannie Lou Hamer and Aaron Henry among others, had formed the "Mississippi Freedom Democratic Party," which was committed to the liberal racial and economic policies of the national Democratic Party. They were locked in a struggle with the "Regulars," the political establishment of the state, for control of the state party. Following a plan developed by a young white Harvard Law School graduate named Wes Watkins, who was from a politically very well-connected Mississippi family, the Freedom Democratic Party had complied with all the new rules adopted in 1968. Under those rules, it, not the Regulars, was recognized by the DNC as "the Democratic Party of the State of Mississippi." Thus when the "call" to the 1972 Democratic National Convention—the invitation to choose a slate of delegates to represent each state—went out in 1971, it was sent to the leaders of the Freedom Democratic Party.

The Regulars, who controlled the Mississippi legislature, had enacted a number of statutes that appropriated to themselves the state political party structure. They brought suit in federal court in Mississippi against the DNC and the leadership of the Freedom Democratic Party, seeking an injunction barring the DNC from recognizing the latter as the Democratic Party of the State of Mississippi. They moved for a preliminary injunction, and given the time constraints of the nomination process, the hearing on that motion would serve as the trial in the case.

The hearing on the preliminary injunction motion began in Jackson. The very decor of the main courtroom in the Jackson federal courthouse had been the subject of heated dispute. The building was built during the Depression, and the WPA had commissioned an artist to paint a large mural behind the bench. In the spirit of the times, the center of the mural depicted a large, white-columned plantation house, in front of which stood a tall, white planter in a frock coat and string tie, with his wife leaning on his arm and his children clutching his legs. To one side was a group of artisans, all white, performing highly skilled tasks. To the other side was a group of African Americans picking cotton and playing banjos and looking thoroughly happy. However it may have struck (white) sensibilities in the 1930s, by the 1960s it was thoroughly offensive. When Elbert Tuttle, a judge in sympathy with the aspirations of African Americans, became chief judge of the Fifth Circuit Court of Appeals, which had jurisdiction over district courts in Mississippi, he ordered the mural covered. The day that Judge Tuttle stepped down as chief judge, the intransigently racist Judge Harold Cox, chief judge of the Southern District of Mississippi, ordered the mural uncovered. So it was there, in all its dated and insensitive glory, as we began the hearing.

The night before the hearing started, I had dinner with the lawyers for the Freedom Democratic Party group, led by Chuck Morgan, a famed Atlanta-based civil rights lawyer. I suggested to them that they file a cross-claim against the DNC. This would have a variety of evidentiary and procedural advantages, and would allow me to appear more neutral before the judge, even though I would be vigorously defending the DNC's action in sending the call to their clients. They liked the idea, and the next day I was served with a cross-claim on my way into the courtroom.

The case was assigned to Judge Dan M. Russell, Jr., a newly appointed district judge, who was from Gulfport in the very southern part of the state and who had never been a litigator. His familiarity with the rules of procedure and evidence was not great. Though he often fumbled, I think he tried to run a fair hearing. It was for him quite a baptism.

The hearing was a truly extraordinary event. Over the course of two weeks, we had virtually every major player in Mississippi Democratic politics on the witness stand, from the governor of the state on down. The testimony ranged over the recent history of party politics in the state and the efforts of both sides to establish their right to the title "Democratic Party of the State of Mississippi." The hearing was covered by major national media, including the *New York Times*. At one point, with Aaron Henry on the stand and under oath in open court, the judge attempted to broker a settlement, probing whether Henry and his group would accept a split delegation. Henry took a pass on the judge's settlement proposal.

During Aaron Henry's testimony, I was cross-examining him—that is, I was using leading questions, which are permitted only on cross-examination—which was one of the advantages I had been seeking when I suggested the cross-claim. One of the Regulars' lawyers objected, saying, "It seems to me Mr. Dudley and Dr. Henry are awful friendly." In my most syrupy acquired Mississippi accent, I said, "Your honor, Dr. Henry's group has sued my client, so he is an adverse party, and besides, I have been friendly to everyone in this courtroom." The judge allowed as how I had indeed been friendly to all, but he thought I was too friendly with Aaron to cross-examine him.

After a week the judge recessed the hearing and moved it to Biloxi, a resort town on the Gulf Coast much closer to his home. Biloxi was a sophisticated town that catered to out-of-state tourists, and it was much more relaxed and tolerant on racial issues than the rest of Mississippi. One night I was working with one of the young African-American party workers, preparing him to testify, and I remarked on this atmosphere. He chuckled, pointed out the window, and said, "Yes, you would never know that Mississippi is only a couple of hundred yards that way."

After two weeks of hearings the judge eventually declined to overturn the DNC's issuance of its convention call to the Freedom Democratic Party. An appeal to the Fifth Circuit left the judge's ruling intact.

Meanwhile, back in Washington, a group of dissident Democrats had sued the DNC, claiming that the 1972 Democratic National Convention's delegates were misallocated among the states. Arguing by analogy from the Supreme Court's then-recent legislative reapportionment cases, with their "one person, one vote" standard,[15] the plaintiffs claimed that the sole appropriate criterion for apportioning delegates to the convention was the proportion of Democratic votes from each state in recent presidential contests, or as they put it, "one Democrat, one vote." The DNC's formula for apportioning delegates took account of voting patterns, but also included other factors, such as electoral college strength, the number of Democratic senators and representatives, and so forth. The plaintiffs were represented by my old friend Joe Rauh. I was assigned to brief and argue the case for the DNC.

There was a substantial question whether the court had the power to hear the case, whether it was "justiciable," to use legalese. The DNC argued that it was not, that the question of how a political party allocated its delegates was a classic "political question" beyond the competence of the federal courts, which were limited by Article III of the Constitution to deciding traditional "cases and controversies." The power of this argument was undercut by the fact that the Supreme Court, after refusing for many years to adjudicate constitutional issues involving legislative apportionment on precisely this ground, had reversed itself in 1962 and entered that very analogous "political thicket" in a big and important way.[16] Legislatures and conventions, the DNC argued, were different animals. I thought that was correct, but it would take some work to convince a court.

On the merits, the DNC had a major historical example on its side. In 1912 the Republican Party was badly split between the supporters of President William Howard Taft, who was running for reelection, and the forces of former President Theodore Roosevelt, who was challenging his one-time protegé for the nomination. The party's delegates were apportioned solely according to the states' votes in the electoral college. This meant that the southern states, which in those days were almost never carried by the Republican candidate, had a power within the convention that was grossly disproportionate to their national voting record. Taft was most popular with the conservative southern wing of the party, and the southern delegates were the deciding factor in giving him the renomination. But they could not deliver in the general election. Roosevelt mounted his third-party "Bullmoose" candidacy, and Taft was crushed by Woodrow Wilson, who carried the traditionally Democratic South. The DNC argued that the example of 1912 meant that parties needed some degree of flexibility to maximize their ability to nominate candidates with realistic chances of winning.

The case was assigned to a relatively senior district judge named June Green. With all respect, Judge Green was not one of the leading intellectual lights of the bench. There was a lot of political interest in the case, and the courtroom was packed for the oral argument. The briefs were voluminous and complex, and the argument was lengthy and intricate. The tension in the atmosphere was heightened by Joe Rauh's typical moralistic posturing.

Given the complexity and significance of the case, we all assumed that Judge Green would take the matter under advisement, mull her options, and write an opinion. To the astonishment of everyone in the courtroom, including Joe Rauh, after more than two hours of argument the judge said simply, "I find the case justiciable and the Democratic National Convention malapportioned. Mr. Rauh, submit an order." It was commonplace for judges in nonjury trials to require both sides to submit proposed findings of fact and conclusions of law, which the court could use or ignore as it pleased. But it was rare—and generally condemned practice—for a court in effect to ask one side to write its opinion for it. Rauh did his best, and the judge signed his proposed opinion without changing a word or a comma. But the court of appeals reversed in a learned opinion by Judge Charles Fahey.[17] The Supreme Court denied *cert*, and the DNC's allocation of delegates for the convention was undisturbed.

❖   ❖   ❖

My own political activities in the early 1970s were essentially limited to taking part in an occasional demonstration against the Vietnam War, which dragged on horribly, though quite predictably, under the Nixon administration. For one thing, I had no time for real political work, as I was putting in tremendous hours in my law practice. My restricted activity did give rise to one memorable family moment, however. One Saturday morning in the late spring of 1970, we were all gathered around the breakfast table, and we began to talk about what we were planning to do that day. I said that I was going into Washington to take part in the demonstration. Will, who was just three, wanted to know what that meant. I explained that a number of people and I were going to tell President Nixon that he shouldn't drop any more bombs on Cambodia. That seemed to satisfy his curiosity, and the conversation passed on to other things. A few days later, Will and I were in the car together, heading for the grocery store or running some other errand. I had the radio on, and the hourly newscast began with an item to the effect that "President Nixon today ordered additional bombing of Cambodia." Will's face fell and his jaw dropped. "But Dad," he said from his little car seat, "I thought you told him not to do that!" So much for parental omnipotence.

❖ ❖ ❖

Before the Deluge

Sometime in late 1972 David Webster received a call from his old friend and law school classmate Clarence Simpson. Simpson was by this time the attorney general of Liberia, and he needed an American law firm to represent the country in a suit filed by an American company. Webster agreed to take the case and asked me to work on it with him.

The West African Republic of Liberia has a fascinating history. It began as a haven of refuge for freed American slaves, who were first relocated there in 1822 by the American Colonization Society. Many, if not most, of those who opposed slavery in the United States in the first half of the 19th century supported a return of freed slaves to Africa, and what became Liberia was the chosen place of colonization. Its capital is Monrovia, named for James Monroe, who was president of the United States in 1822. In 1847 Liberia became a nation with the support of the United States government. The Liberian constitution and government were closely modeled on those of the United States

From very early on, however, there was a deep division in Liberian society between the descendants of former American slaves, the so-called Americo-Liberians, and the descendants of the tribal occupants of the land at the time of its colonization, known as aborigines. The government was established and run by the Americo-Liberians, who also owned most of the property and all of the major wealth-producing assets. The Americo-Liberians tended to be physically large, while the aborigines were mostly quite small. The Americo-Liberians spoke English, which was the official language of the country, and had English names—Clarence Simpson, for example—while the aborigines had local tribal names and learned English as a second language. Many Americo-Liberians sent their children to the United States or to Britain for education. Clarence Simpson had attended both prep school and university in the United States, and he had capped his education at Georgetown University Law Center, where he had met David Webster. Liberia's principal export was rubber, and it was often said that the Liberian rubber plantations were like old-time cotton plantations in Mississippi, except that the owners were black. There was in 1972 an entirely separate part of the Liberian legal code entitled "Aborigine Law."

The government of the country was until 1980 the closely held preserve of the Americo-Liberians, and while it was in form a democratic republic, it tended to be dominated by powerful presidents. William Tubman served as president of Liberia from 1944 to his death in 1971, when he was succeeded by his vice-president, William Tolbert. A small number of families tended to hand prominent office down through the generations. Clarence Simpson's father, for example, had been vice-president, and his grandfather had been chief justice of the Liberian Supreme Court.

The dispute concerning which Clarence Simpson engaged David Webster's services arose from a contract between the Liberian government and a large American firm for the construction of a deep water port at the remote Liberian coastal town of Harper. Harper just happened to be the home town of President Tubman, and the project to create a deep water port there was a dream of Tubman's old age. He died before the project had really got under way, and the new government of President Tolbert made the eminently rational decision that it had no real need for a deep water port in Harper. So it cancelled the contract and was sued by the contractor.

At about this time David and I had several cases going that needed some attention overseas. One of them was the case of Bonnie the Space Monkey, in which we wanted to consult some prominent British antivivisectionists. Another was a major matter for Lloyd's of London on which I was not working directly but on which David sought my help. The third was the case for the government of Liberia, which required us to go to Monrovia and to Belgium to interview the bankers who had agreed to finance the Harper port project. So we put together a bit of a junket in early December 1972. We flew to London with our wives, and in between our business meetings we spent a lovely weekend in the Cotswolds. It was Louise's and my first trip to Europe, and we went a day or two ahead of David and his wife Joan and visited our law school friends Tom and Niki Williams, who were living in Sussex. After our London meetings, it was on to Brussels and Antwerp for meetings with the Belgian bankers. We took the train from Brussels to Paris, where we stayed at the Hotel George V and dined at a three-star restaurant with Louise's Aunt Louise, who just happened to be in France at the same time. From there David and I flew on to Monrovia, while Joan and Louise returned home.

In Monrovia we were greeted by Clarence Simpson and met with most of the important players in the Liberian government, including President Tolbert and his powerful and corrupt brother, Steve Tolbert, who was Secretary of the Treasury. A rising star in the Treasury Department, with whom we dealt over the financial aspects of the lawsuit, was a young woman named Ellen Johnson-Sirleaf, who was obviously very bright and was closely—some said romantically—connected to Steve Tolbert. Thirty-three years later, in 2005, she emerged as President of Liberia after its lengthy and horrendous civil war. She spent much of the time between 1980 and 2005 in exile, and some of it in jail. Our principal contact in the Justice Department was a man named Cheapo, who was the first aborigine to hold a sub-cabinet post in the Liberian government.

There was palpable tension in the air in Monrovia, though it was not clear to us how well attuned to it the leaders of the country were. The aborigines, the low-paid workers of the nation, were restive. While we were there the cab drivers of Monrovia nearly rioted over some economic issue, and President Tolbert convened them all for a stern speech, which David and I attended. It was my impression that the country's leadership and class structure had ossified in the long personal rule of President Tubman, and that the new regime was trying to head off trouble by improving the lot of the aborigines—hence the promotion of men like Cheapo—but that it could not get too far out in front of its very conservative Americo-Liberian political base.

After several days of discussions with government officials and a careful review of the documents involving the Harper port project, David and I concluded that there was not really a viable defense to the contract claim, but that the company's damages were not nearly as extensive as it asserted. Hence we recommended that we negotiate a settlement of the claim without trial. Cheapo, Clarence, and the president agreed, and David and I returned to the States and quietly settled the matter.

It was thus with personal anguish, as well as general sadness, that we watched the horrific events of the revolution and civil war unfold in Liberia seven years later. William Tolbert was personally assassinated by the leader of the *coup d'etat*, an aborigine army sergeant named Samuel Doe, who stabbed the president fifteen times and disembowelled him in his bed. We saw with horror the photographs in *Time* magazine of one of the government consultants with whom we had worked being shot to death piecemeal on a beach outside Monrovia. Clarence Simpson escaped the country, with a big price on his head.

For the next twenty-five years Liberia was torn apart by civil war until finally, exhausted, the country turned to Ellen Johnson-Sirleaf for a restoration of peace and a rebuilding of the government and the economy.

❖ ❖ ❖

Sadly, during the early- to mid-1970s Louise and I went through a very difficult period in our marriage. We were separated on two occasions. The fault lay entirely with me. At some level I know I loved Louise and the children throughout this period, but I was not mature enough to handle the demands of a potentially all-consuming career, parenthood, and marriage. I was unsure what I wanted. I put my family through a lot of turmoil, for which I have blamed myself ever since. Fortunately for me, Louise was constant and was willing to take me back. Ever since that time, my marriage and my family have been the centerpiece of my life. I consider myself lucky far beyond my deserts.

Notes

1. The case was ultimately decided by the Supreme Court in favor of Williams' client. See Tilton v. Richardson, 403 U.S. 672 (1971).
2. Yablonski v. UMWA, 146 U.S. App. D.C. 252, 448 F.2d 1175 (1971).
3. Hodgson v. UMWA, 344 F. Supp. 17 (D.D.C. 1972).
4. Pruitt v. Peyton, 209 Va. 532 (1969).
5. Brown v. Mississippi, 297 U.S. 278 (1936), was the first case in which the Supreme Court invalidated a conviction coming from a state court because the defendant had been coerced into confessing.
6. Brown v. Mississippi, *supra* note 5.
7. Culombe v. Connecticut, 367 U.S. 568, 603-05 (1961) (opinion of Frankfurter, J.).
8. See Sheppard v. Maxwell, 384 U.S. 333 (1966); Irvin v. Dowd, 366 U.S. 717 (1961).
9. Witherspoon v. Illinois, 391 U.S. 510 (1968).
10. See Evan Thomas, *The Man to See: Edward Bennett Williams: Ultimate Insider; Legendary Trial Lawyer* (1991).
11. 376 U.S. 254 (1964).
12. See, e.g., Curtis Publishing Co. v. Butts, 388 U.S. 130 (1967).
13. Adey v. United Action for Animals, 361 F. Supp. 457 (S.D.N.Y. 1973).
14. See Adey v. United Action for Animals, 493 F.2d 1397 (2d Cir. 1974).
15. See, e.g., Reynolds v. Sims, 377 U.S. 533 (1964).
16. Baker v. Carr, 369 U.S. 186 (1962).
17. Bode v. National Democratic Party, 146 U.S. App. D.C. 373, 452 F.2d 1302 (1971).

CHAPTER ELEVEN

Capitol Hill

1975–1977

For the most part I enjoyed my time at Williams & Connolly. The work was fascinating and challenging, and I learned an enormous amount about how to be a lawyer. I sat at the feet of some of the country's best litigators, and I worked with an outstanding group of contemporaries. I made lifelong friends. At the beginning, the atmosphere among the lawyers was, as I have said, entirely collegial and supportive. Ed Williams and Paul Connolly ran the place. There was no real partnership involving any of the other lawyers, but by and large that was not a source of discontent, as the hand of management was extremely light, and we were all satisfied with our work and our level of compensation. All that changed dramatically shortly after the arrival of Joe Califano in 1971. His self-aggrandizing personality soon soured the sense of camaraderie and trust among the lawyers in the firm.

Partly because of my work for the DNC, which was his client, I was thrown more with Califano than were most others at the outset of his tenure at the firm. It did not take me long to become thoroughly disenchanted, and others swiftly concurred. A couple of us went to see Paul Connolly at his home on a Sunday afternoon to tell him of the discontent that was brewing among the younger lawyers. I strongly suspect that Paul had not been consulted by Ed concerning the recruitment of Califano, and that he felt as unhappy and trapped as the rest of us. Be that as it may, he said he hoped nothing would happen to change the firm, which he loved, but he made it clear that he would not, or could not, do anything in response to our concerns.

After a while, I wrote a long memorandum outlining my discontent with the state of affairs at the firm and proposing that a group of us—the best cadre of younger lawyers in the firm, a group that I still think was the finest collection of lawyers of its generation anywhere in the country—leave and set up our own firm. When I circulated this memorandum to the others, it provoked a lot of discussion, and the consensus among the group was that it would be better to remain at the firm for a time at least and to try to force the elders to agree to an actual partnership, in which all members of the firm could have a say on issues of importance. I was deputized to write another memorandum designed to serve as talking points in our discussions with Ed, Paul, and Joe. When we had agreed on the outline of what we would like to see happen, one or two of our number, armed with my second memorandum, approached Ed and told him there was real trouble brewing. They outlined the proposal to convert the firm into a traditional partnership. Ed was not unreceptive, and talks proceeded from there.

At the risk of getting ahead of my story, the firm put a partnership structure in place within about a year and half of our broaching the subject. It didn't really change things much at first. Ed, Paul, and Joe—especially Ed—still pretty much ran the place as they saw fit. Only once before he died did Ed lose a battle within the partnership, and that was a delicious satisfaction. Joe Califano left the firm in 1977 to become President Carter's Secretary of Health, Education, and Welfare. He apparently proved as difficult in the president's cabinet as he had in the firm, and Carter ultimately fired him. When Ed broached the subject of Califano's return to the law firm, he was met with an unyielding wall of opposition. He never put the matter to a vote.

❖ ❖ ❖

One afternoon in very early 1975 I was working away at my desk when the phone rang. It was our good friend, R.W. "Johnny" Apple, then a national political correspondent for the *New York Times*. Johnny had married Louise's close friend from Smith College, Edie Smith, during my last year in law school. They had met in Saigon, where Johnny was covering the Vietnam War and Edie, a Foreign Service officer, was working in the embassy. Edie brought Johnny down to Charlottesville to meet us before the wedding, and we hit it off grandly. After we moved to the Washington area in 1967, we saw a good deal of Edie and Johnny until, sadly, they divorced a few years later. That day in 1975 Johnny asked if I was looking for a new job. Despite my dissatisfaction with recent developments in the firm, I really was not on the market, and I said so. Johnny said, "Would you be willing to talk to Peter Rodino about being his general counsel?" I said, "Are you free for a drink tonight?" He was, and we met.

Peter Rodino, a longtime congressman from New Jersey, was the chairman of the Judiciary Committee of the House of Representatives and had presided with great dignity and aplomb over the committee's debate on articles of impeachment against Richard Nixon. The committee voted on a bipartisan basis to recommend several of the articles to the full House, which led to Nixon's resignation as president in August 1974. Like most Americans, I had been glued to the television set during the committee's proceedings. Its thoughtful deliberation, collegial civility, and genuine seriousness of purpose had done a lot to restore confidence in our system of government after two years of revelations of presidential abuse of office. It was clear from the debates and from the press coverage that Rodino had not only presided well, but that he and his counsel, former Kennedy Justice Department official John Doar, had guided the committee's lengthy and careful study of the issues, and that they had not brought the matter to a vote until the publicly revealed evidence had convinced enough conservative Democrats and Republicans on the committee to vote for impeachment. A gentle consensus-builder, Rodino was the hero of the day to a large part of the American public.

Over drinks that evening Johnny explained that Rodino had had a falling out with the committee's previous general counsel, a man named Jerome Ziefman, who had been upset when Rodino brought in John Doar to head the staff of the impeachment inquiry. Ziefman had afterward done some back-channel maneuvering in an effort to undermine Doar, which annoyed Rodino greatly, and as soon as the impeachment proceedings were done, Rodino had quietly told Ziefman that he needed to find another job. One of Johnny's colleagues at the *Times* had had lunch earlier in the day with Rodino's administrative assistant, Francis O'Brien, who said the chairman was looking for someone with strong legal credentials, ideally a former Supreme Court clerk, on the youngish side, who could provide sound legal analysis and strategic thinking for the enormous backlog of bills that had piled up on the committee's docket during the two years it was preoccupied with the impeachment inquiry. O'Brien asked if this reporter knew anyone who fit the bill. He said that no one came immediately to mind, but that he would inquire around. He buttonholed Johnny that afternoon, and Johnny, flattering me highly, said, "You are describing the resume of a friend of mine." We talked some more, and I said I would think about it.

After discussion with Louise, who was as always supportive of what I might want to do, I told Johnny that I would be willing to explore the matter. He set up a meeting with Francis O'Brien, who then scheduled a meeting with Rodino. As I later laughingly told O'Brien, who became a good friend, Rodino, who was a master of understatement and indirection, never offered me the job; indeed, to my mind he never really interviewed me. We met three times, for about an hour each, and he did virtually all the talking. The only way I figured out that I was hired was by the structure of his sentences. In the first meeting, most sentences began, "The general counsel would ...." The second time, they began, "You would ...." And in the third meeting, the sentences started, "You will ...." Ironically, Rodino told me that I came highly recommended by Joe Califano. I did not tell the chairman that I was sure that was because Califano wanted me gone from the firm.

So in late February or early March 1975, I wandered into a world about as different from litigation as one could imagine. It was a world with very different structure, much looser rules, and land mines hidden everywhere. Everyone had an agenda, one which was not always obvious from the uniform he wore. I was used to knowing where everyone was coming from because of the client he or she represented, and I could anticipate the tactics and strategy of co-counsel, opponents, and judges by thinking long and hard about what they might be up to. Not so on the Hill, where people often concealed their motives and acted by indirection. Someone—a committee member, indeed, a subcommittee chair—who seemed to be on your side could suddenly introduce a bill or an amendment that came out of left field and totally changed the dynamic of the situation. One could not trust everyone on the committee staff, which I was supposed to manage, but the troublemakers were often protected by longstanding relationships with members of the committee. Fortunately, Francis O'Brien took me by the hand at first and promised to watch my back.

❖ ❖ ❖

I soon found myself in conflict with the counsel to the Subcommittee on Monopolies and Commercial Law. Rodino himself was the chair of this subcommittee, as well as chair of the full committee. It was not an area of the law that he was fully comfortable with. During his long period of apprenticeship on the Judiciary Committee, which was chaired for many years by Emmanuel Celler from New York, Rodino had worked on and subsequently chaired the Subcommittee on Immigration, which was a topic of considerable interest to his northern New Jersey constituency. Celler, who was in his eighties, was defeated in the 1972 Democratic primary in Brooklyn by a young woman named Elizabeth Holtzman. This, by the way, proved in my judgment to be Richard Nixon's undoing. Celler was high-handed, brusque, and, frankly, a bit past it. He would never have had Rodino's patience for quiet consensus-building, and I am convinced that under Celler the impeachment proceedings would have gone off half-cocked, and Nixon would have remained in office. When he became chair of the full committee in January 1973, Rodino had decided for some reason that he should take over Celler's old subcommittee, Monopolies and Commercial Law, which dealt primarily with antitrust law issues. I had taken several courses in antitrust in law school and had worked on antitrust issues at both Wilmer, Cutler and Williams & Connolly.

The counsel to the antitrust subcommittee was a relatively new hire named Jim Falco. Rodino had made it clear in our discussions that directing the work of the subcommittee staff would be among my responsibilities as general counsel, and he urged me to get to know and to work with Falco. He also made it clear that it was important to him that Falco was an Italian American. The chairman was proud of his Italian heritage and of the many contributions of Italian Americans to American public life. He often looked for opportunities to promote Italian Americans in public office. From the beginning, however, Jim Falco had a chip on his shoulder. I think he was surprised and disappointed to learn that I had some background in antitrust law and was planning to take an active role in the work of the subcommittee. I have always prided myself on my ability to get along and work well with virtually anyone, but despite my best efforts, Falco seemed deliberately to twist and misunderstand everything I said and to resent my every inquiry about his work.

My working relationship with Falco was important, not just because this was the chairman's own subcommittee, but because the chairman was planning to process a significant piece of antitrust reform legislation, a bill that became known as the Hart-Scott-Rodino Antitrust Improvements Act. In anticipation of this push, and because the subcommittee staff had mostly departed after Celler's defeat, the chairman wanted to hire two or three new lawyers with some antitrust experience. I interviewed a number of candidates and recommended three, Leonard Shambon (an old friend), Alan Ransom, and Tom Runge, all of whom the chairman liked and hired. I deliberately did not say a word to any of them about Jim Falco's strange and prickly personality, thinking that maybe I was the problem. Within a week of starting work, each of them came to me inquiring what Falco's problem was.

The subcommittee held hearings on the proposed antitrust legislation, and the bill proceeded to markup. It was opposed by significant elements of the business community, spearheaded by a lobbying organization called The Business Roundtable, which was represented by Wilmer, Cutler & Pickering. The firm sent its antitrust guru, Arnold Lerman, to testify against portions of the bill before the subcommittee. I had worked fairly closely with Lerman during my nine months at Wilmer, Cutler, and we got along well. Despite that, I strongly supported those portions of the bill that he opposed. Indeed, these portions of the bill were a direct outgrowth of some private antitrust litigation, and I had worked with the plaintiffs in some of the cases in point. Arnie Lerman and I greeted each other in a friendly fashion and chatted for a while after his testimony. I thought nothing more of it until later.

The bill was sent by the subcommittee to the full committee, which marked it up and voted it out. Still trying to work with Jim Falco, I asked him to prepare the draft of the committee's report on the bill to the full House. The committee report is a very important document, for it provides the information and arguments on which members of the House who are not on the committee often base their voting decisions, and it is the source most often cited by courts seeking to determine what Congress intended by particular provisions of the law. It has to be clear, concise, and persuasive.

After a couple of weeks, Falco gave me a draft, which I read with some trepidation, for I had come to believe that he was not only a very defensive personality but a poor and inarticulate lawyer as well. My worst fears were not just realized, they were exceeded. The draft report was garbled to the point of unintelligibility. This was a controversial piece of legislation, and while I am sure Falco did not do it deliberately, he handed me a draft report that would have sunk the bill on the floor of the House. Not wanting to involve the newly hired staffers in what was becoming a serious contretemps between Falco and me, I spent the best part of a week rewriting the report into something that members could use in their deliberations.

Between the time the report was filed and the bill was to come up for debate in the House, syndicated columnist Jack Anderson, who had taken over the "Washington Merry GoRound" column of my friend Evan Kemp's late uncle, Drew Pearson, published a column in the *Washington Post* attacking me by name for cleverly undermining the antitrust bill. Pointing to my past work with Arnold Lerman as a motive, the column accused me of delaying the progress of the bill to the floor and of savagely weakening the original draft of the committee report in an effort to kill the legislation. The brief delay in sending the report on to the full House was the direct result of the incompetence of Jim Falco's work product. And no one who had read Falco's draft and compared it to the final product could possibly have harbored the notion that the latter had weakened the report. Though he denied it, there could have been only one source of the column's false statements—Jim Falco. The Chairman and one of the prominent members of the subcommittee, John Seiberling of Ohio, with whom I had worked closely on the bill, took to the floor of the House to defend me against the column's charges. I discussed the matter with Francis O'Brien, and he and I went together to the chairman to say that Falco's continued presence on the subcommittee staff was intolerable. The problem, we told the chairman, was not merely his poor work and the heavy-handed leak. He could not get along with a single member of the subcommittee staff. The chairman reluctantly agreed and terminated him.

The bill, I am happy to say, sailed through the House. When a slightly different version was passed by the Senate, a conference committee ironed out the differences, and the Hart-Scott-Rodino Antitrust Improvements Act became law.

My conflict with Jim Falco was among the most unpleasant experiences of my life. Never before or since have I tried to get anyone fired from his or her job. I blamed myself and I agonized over what to do to the point that I wound up in a nervous state with a significantly elevated heartbeat that I could not control for quite a while. I learned that with responsibility comes difficulty and that one cannot avoid tackling it head-on.

❖ ❖ ❖

In addition to directing the work of the Monopolies Subcommittee staff, I had two other large areas of responsibility. One was working closely with the counsel to other subcommittees to monitor legislation they were considering, to schedule such legislation for full committee markup when it was ready, and to coordinate the committee's management of the legislation on the floor of the House. In this capacity, I often met with lobbyists whose clients were interested in legislation pending before the committee, sometimes with the chairman, and sometimes alone or with other staffers. My other primary responsibility was speechwriting for the Chairman. After the triumph of the impeachment hearings, Rodino was in great demand as a speaker. Indeed, before I even formally came aboard, he asked me to draft a major speech for him, which I read to him over the telephone on a Saturday. He liked it very much, and he relied on me from the outset to draft his speeches.

It soon became clear that, while it was from the committee's point of view the least important of my responsibilities, writing speeches for the chairman and reviewing them line-by-line with him was taking up the largest chunk of my time. After a few months, I approached Francis O'Brien about this, and we sought a solution to the problem. Francis proposed hiring a newsman named Larry Taylor, who had covered the impeachment proceedings for the *St. Louis Post-Dispatch* and whose writing Francis admired, to do the basic work on the chairman's speeches, with me offering general advice and supervision. I read some of Larry's writing, liked it, interviewed him, and liked him. Francis and I recommended that the chairman hire Larry, and he did. For some inexplicable reason, however, the arrangement never worked. Larry would do a speech draft, and I would review it. I liked Larry's writing very much and at first simply forwarded his drafts on to the chairman with little editing. Rodino, however, always found fault with Larry's work, and I wound up rewriting it, which took as much or more time as I had been spending doing the initial writing. Being a speechwriter for a particular person is difficult. One has to have a feel for the rhythms and habits of the speaker's expression. I thought Larry's work was excellent, but he never seemed to develop the correct "ear" for the chairman's speech that he needed.

Being Rodino's speechwriter was not all a bother, however; it gave me at least one truly memorable experience. In the summer of 1976, a presidential election year, Francis O'Brien insisted that I hire as a summer intern a young law student from Georgetown University named Sally Regal, who had worked on the impeachment staff. I tried to tell Francis that the committee did not have a summer intern program, but he would not take no for an answer. So I hired Sally and assigned her to do some work on pending legislation with one of the subcommittee staffs. Though I didn't know it then, the working relationship between Sally and Francis went back to New York City Mayor John Lindsay's campaign for the Republican presidential nomination in 1972, when Sally was a teenager. A couple of weeks after she came on board, I was meeting with the legal staff of the subcommittee to which I had assigned her, and I asked how Sally Regal was working out. They looked at me blankly and said, "Who?" I headed for Francis's office to find out what was up. I found Sally running a copying machine in the chairman's office and learned that Francis had wanted her all along to work on a little Rodino-for-Vice-President boomlet that he was trying to promote.

Rodino, of course, had not the slightest prospect of being chosen by the ultimate nominee to run for vice-president. For one thing, he had taken no part in the presidential politicking and had no particular connection to any of the candidates. For another, he was 67 years old, which in the days before Ronald Reagan was thought much too old to be a heartbeat away from the presidency. But Francis was having his harmless fun, and I threw up my hands in resignation. Sally Regal never did do any work for the subcommittee.

By the time of the Democratic Convention later in the summer, Governor Jimmy Carter of Georgia had locked up the party's presidential nomination. The chairman was a delegate to the convention, which was held at Madison Square Garden in New York City, and he and Francis had arranged for me to attend it and to stay near them in the Algonquin Hotel. I thought I would have a little fun and watch the proceedings from a ringside seat. Little did I know. Francis had made enough noise with his Rodino-for-Veep campaign that the chairman was among the first people that Carter asked to meet after arriving in New York for the start of the convention. The governor explained how much he admired the chairman's work on the impeachment proceedings, but said that he had other plans for the vice-presidential nomination. This came, I am quite sure, as a great relief to the chairman, and an even greater one to his wife, who was quite shy and who had never even moved from their home in New Jersey to Washington. Governor Carter went on to say, however, that he would be honored if the chairman would make the speech placing his name in nomination at the convention. Rodino agreed, and my work for the next three days was cut out for me.

Somehow Francis found me a typewriter, and I spent the first day roughing out a speech that drew on other speeches the chairman had delivered but focused primarily on Governor Carter's background and the themes of his campaign for the presidency. The next two days were spent with the chairman intermittently coming to my room, going over the speech, critiquing it, and working on his delivery. He would leave from time to time to let me rework the portions of the speech that we thought needed improvement. Ultimately, after much nervous pacing and rehearsing, he was happy with the speech and we gave it to the people who would prepare it for release and put in on the teleprompter.

I had a floor pass for the evening of the nominating speech, and I went anticipating with pleasure listening to the chairman deliver my words. I found a group of members of the Judiciary Committee, who invited me to sit with them. It was one of the most frustrating evenings of my life. I never heard a word of the speech. To begin with, the acoustics in the Garden were terrible. To make matters worse, the delegates and people in the gallery had no interest in what was going on at the podium, which had already become a purely made-for-television event, so the roar of conversation among the crowd was deafening. I left very disappointed.

There was, however, at least one small closing of the circle that evening. As Rodino was delivering the speech, one of his journalist friends tossed Johnny Apple, who was covering the convention, a copy of it, with a note saying, "I thought you might want to know Earl Dudley wrote this."

❖   ❖   ❖

Despite my small, back-room role in the nomination process, I came very close to voting for Governor Carter's opponent, President Gerald Ford, who had succeeded from the vice-presidency upon the resignation of Richard Nixon. I thought then, and I still think, that Ford may have been the only truly sane president we have had since Harry Truman and Dwight Eisenhower. He made solid appointments to high government office, and I thought most of his policy decisions were sound. He seemed direct and honest with the American people. In the end, however, Ford's pardon of Richard Nixon and the strong pull of my lifetime allegiance to the Democratic Party won out. I voted for Jimmy Carter. I am still not convinced I did the right thing.

❖   ❖   ❖

The 94th Congress, elected in 1974 in the wake of the Watergate scandal and Richard Nixon's resignation in disgrace, was the most heavily Democratic Congress in many years, so it seemed a good opportunity to try to enact some gun-control legislation. Jurisdiction over this subject matter was lodged in a subcommittee chaired by John Conyers of Michigan. Conyers, among the most senior African Americans in Congress, was from a safe Democratic district in Detroit, and his longevity in office has been remarkable. In 1975 he was already third or fourth in seniority on the Judiciary Committee, and as I write this in 2008, he is still serving, now as chair of the full Judiciary Committee.

Conyers held hearings on the politically volatile issue at venues around the country. The high crime rates and political violence of the 1960s had given rise to considerable concern about the prevailing easy access to cheap handguns called "Saturday night specials." The hearings focused in large measure on what to do about these handguns. Even moderate Republicans on the Judiciary Committee were prepared to go along with legislation curbing their availability. Over the months the subcommittee staff worked diligently—and in my view brilliantly—to craft a bill that would accomplish something significant, but that would not be so controversial as to be doomed to defeat. Their draft legislation was limited carefully to Saturday night specials. Indeed, they had kept the lobbyists for the National Rifle Association closely informed, and the latter had signaled that, while the NRA, with its die-hard pro-gun membership, would have to oppose the bill publicly, they would not mount a real campaign to defeat it.

Conyers called a press conference a few days before the scheduled subcommittee markup on the bill to announce his introduction of gun-control legislation. To everyone's surprise and horror, instead of the carefully crafted staff bill, Conyers introduced as his chair-sponsored bill a proposed total ban on the private possession of all handguns. This was, of course, a bombshell, and it completely undid the staff's months of careful and painstaking consensus building. Conyers had not confided in his subcommittee staff, so the bill caught them completely by surprise.

Chairman Rodino was exasperated, and he assigned me to try to work with the subcommittee staff and the subcommittee's moderate Republicans, led by Congressman Tom Railsback of Illinois, to bring some order to the chaos Conyers had created. Despite our best efforts, however, it was impossible, without Conyers' support as subcommittee chair, to put the initial staff bill back on track. Thus was a golden opportunity lost. And the experience with the gun-control effort, more than any other, convinced me that legislation was not really the field I wanted to put my energy into over the long haul.

❖ ❖ ❖

I had come to like and admire Peter Rodino immensely. He was a very intelligent man, a good lawyer, and someone who valued and made excellent use of good staff work. He read our memoranda for him on issues pending before the committee with care, and he asked penetrating questions. He was open to suggestion and consulted me and others on the staff about what he should do on important issues. And he was personally a pleasure to work with. With his wife and family remaining behind in New Jersey, the Congress and the Judiciary Committee were his daily life, and we often worked together late into the evening. But with my personal life in some disarray—Louise and I were separated for the second time while I was working for the committee—I was concerned about my reduced salary there, and I was not happy with the legislative process. So early in 1977 I began to contemplate a return to private law practice.

CHAPTER TWELVE

Return to Private Law Practice
1977–1989

As I mulled my options in early 1977, a number of my friends at Williams & Connolly said that it was a propitious time to try to return to the firm. The new partnership order was in place, several of them would be willing to lead the charge, and there was no reason to think that Ed and Paul would be unreceptive. And Joe Califano had, to the relief of virtually everyone, departed for the Carter cabinet. I also had discussions with a former Williams & Connolly lawyer, Sam Seymour, who had left the firm not long after I did. Sam and another lawyer from the firm, Tom Patton, had set up their own firm. They had recently come to a parting of the ways, and Sam was looking for a new partner. I had worked with Sam, whose practice in those days consisted largely of plaintiffs' antitrust work, and we were good friends.

I had reservations about both options. The money would be better at Williams & Connolly, and I would not have to worry about bringing in business at first, though that would doubtless be a factor in long-range compensation. But while Ed Williams said he would be happy to have me back, he made it clear that, despite the facts that my contemporaries were all partners under the new arrangement, that I had played a significant role in bringing the change about, and that I was coming off a public job that had some visibility in the legal community, I would have to serve at least a year as an associate. That made the prospect of returning to the firm psychologically less attractive. Sam Seymour was talking about ambitions to build an institution such as Williams & Connolly had become, and the firm would be called Seymour & Dudley. But the nature of Sam's practice meant that paydays, while usually quite handsome, were few and far between. Antitrust cases tend to be large matters that take years to litigate, and plaintiffs' lawyers operate mostly on contingent fees. The hope was that I could generate enough short-term paying business to carry the firm's expenses and hopefully show something of a profit while we waited for the antitrust cases to pay off. Then there was the matter of personal style. I knew Sam well, he was a first-rate lawyer, and we worked together. But Sam had something of an imperious way about him, and he enjoyed an expensive, not quite to say flamboyant, lifestyle. I wasn't sure how we would mesh together over the long haul.

About this same time Louise and I began to spend a lot of time with each other again. I came to my senses and eventually proposed getting back together. To my immense joy and relief, she agreed, despite the unhappiness I had put her through. From that day forward, my marriage has been very happy and the anchor of my life.

Louise and I talked a lot about which professional choice I should make. She was never a big fan of Sam Seymour's style, but she refrained from pushing me in either direction. After much agonizing, I decided that the prospect of trying to build a firm from the ground up with Sam was the more exciting of the two options, and I joined Sam in the late spring or early summer of 1977.

In retrospect, I think this was a mistake, but it is one that I do not really regret. The firm lasted four years, and I enjoyed the challenge of being a partner in a fledgling enterprise. Much of the work I did was interesting, and I liked the young lawyers in the firm and my increasing role in mentoring them. One of them, and my right-hand person for several years, was the famous Sally Regal of Rodino-for-Veep fame. We hired her when she graduated from Georgetown Law School. Sally was the best instinctive legal strategist I have ever known and an organizer par excellence. I tried to encourage her to take a courtroom role in litigation, but she never liked it and preferred to remain in the background.

Ultimately, it was the difference in personal styles that did in my venture with Sam Seymour. It is not important to chronicle our disagreements, but after about three and a half years I came to the conclusion that I no longer wanted to work with him. Our parting was bitter in the short term, and it entailed litigation, which was settled out of court. I have never really had anything to do with Sam since, but I am no longer upset with him. We were simply different to the point of incompatibility.

❖ ❖ ❖

The Church of Scientology

A great deal of my time at Seymour & Dudley was spent representing the Church of Scientology. Although I always was and remain skeptical of Scientology's claims as a method of psychotherapy and of its assertion that it is a religion, there is no question that the Church was persecuted on a rather large scale by the federal government for years, and the fallout from this persecution gave rise to some fascinating legal work.

My relationship with the Church went back to my time at Williams & Connolly. A psychiatrist named Peter Breggin, whom I had met when I used him as an expert witness in a psychiatric malpractice case, and who became both a good friend and my own therapist, referred the Church to me for some relatively minor legal problem. When I left for the Hill, Sam Seymour took over the account, and when he set out on his own, he took it with him. Before I joined him, Sam and others at his firm had filed a series of lawsuits against a number of government agencies under the then relatively new federal Freedom of Information Act. Part of my new portfolio was to take over supervision of these cases. Officers of the Church were convinced that these agencies were spying on them and making their lives as difficult as possible, and they were using the new federal statute to find out as much as they could about it. Perhaps their biggest battle was with the Internal Revenue Service. Each year, the IRS would deny the Scientologists' claim to be a tax-exempt religious organization and would assess very significant taxes and penalties on the amounts the Church collected from its members for the therapeutic services it provided to them. The IRS would force the Church to file a suit annually to obtain recognition of its status as a religion. Each such suit would involve years of hotly contested litigation, and each time, just before the case proceeded to trial, the IRS would back off, conceding a tax exemption for that year alone, without prejudice to its position regarding other years. It forced the Church, like Sisyphus of Greek mythology, to roll an enormous stone up a steep hill every year without end. I am agnostic as to whether the Church or the IRS had the better of the argument as a matter of tax law, but the IRS's tactic amounted to unconscionable harassment.

The government reacted with ferocious paranoia to the Church's barrage of FOIA suits. At every turn it would either deny the existence of documents sought by the lawsuits, and/or argue that any documents it did have fell under the FOIA's series of complicated exemptions, or else provide so few documents, and those in such heavily redacted form, that they were utterly useless. All the lawsuits were filed in the federal district court in Washington and were defended by the United States Attorney's Office for the District of Columbia. They were all assigned to an Assistant U.S. Attorney named Nathan Dodell, whose pompous manner and habitual verbal wrapping of himself in the American flag had earned him the derisive nickname of "Uncle Sam" Dodell throughout the courthouse. With Dodell every FOIA case was trench warfare, which of course was designed to and did, among other things, run up the Church's litigation costs enormously.

As time went on, Church officials, when met with another government stonewall, would suggest more specific ways to ask for documents in the government's possession, and these refined requests struck home with surprising frequency, as even Dodell would have to admit that documents within the increasingly narrowly described categories existed. Thus we would get some more documents, but also more arguments as to why the documents fell within an exemption from the requirement of production. And in circular fashion, the additionally produced documents were more elaborately redacted, resulting in yet another round of litigation. We at the law firm assumed that the Church officials' ability to predict what sorts of documents the government agencies would have was a byproduct of their dealings with those agencies. Knowing something about how the government was horsing them around, we thought, gave them insight into what kinds of information should be there. We were wrong.

Beginning sometime in the early- to mid-1970s the Church of Scientology had undertaken a major effort to infiltrate the federal government. One of its operatives was a young man in his late twenties named Mitchell Herman, who later became a personal client of mine. Mitch was quite simply a born spy and something of a genius at it. In a series of adventures that would be pure comedy if it were not for the serious consequences that ensued, Mitch and his minions penetrated the government with startling ease. Posing as workmen repairing the air conditioning, Mitch and another Scientologist planted a bug in the very conference room at the IRS where meetings were held to discuss strategy *vis-a-vis* the Church. They also obtained fake IRS credentials, which gave them no-questions-asked entry to all sorts of government buildings.

One of Mitch's greatest triumphs was a covert action against a former professional football player who was mayor of Clearwater, Florida. One of the Church's major operations, known informally as "Flag," was located in Clearwater. The mayor didn't like it and gave the Church a very hard time locally. When the mayor visited Washington, DC, for a conference, he made the mistake of picking up a young lady in some DC watering hole whom he took to be a prostitute. The "prostitute" was a Scientologist, who made sure that the mayor was arrested by the DC police for soliciting, a fact which, of course, was hot news in Clearwater, whose media were alerted anonymously by the Church.

Among the buildings to which Mitch's fake IRS credentials got him and others access was the federal courthouse on Constitution Avenue, where the U.S. Attorney's Office was located. This was the venue of some of the Scientologists' best spy work, but this work was also the undoing of Mitch and his operatives. A Scientologist managed to get herself hired in some capacity in the courthouse and at lunchtime one day purloined the key to Nate Dodell's office long enough to make a copy of it. Two of Mitch's operatives named Gerry Wolfe and Michael Meisner spent a number of evenings copying Dodell's files containing all the documents that he was withholding in the FOIA cases. To add insult to injury, they made the copies rather openly on the U.S. Attorney's Office's own Xerox machine. Thus did the Church officials gain their rather precise knowledge of what documents Uncle Sam Dodell was hoarding.

Flushed with success, Wolfe and Meisner went to the well once too often. They were caught manning the copy machine, and either their credentials were disbelieved or they were not deemed to be sufficient authorization to be where they were. Fortunately for them, the building guards did not arrest them, but simply escorted them out of the building with a warning not to return. Unhappily, they ignored the warning and returned to the scene of the crime a few nights later. This time credentials were seized and names were taken. Meisner panicked and was prepared to tell all he knew. Higher-ups in the Church were having none of that, and they kidnaped Meisner and held him incommunicado for several months, somewhere in a remote location out West. Ultimately Meisner managed to escape and tell his story to the FBI. Ugly stuff was about to hit the fan.

Armed with an affidavit that ran upwards of 125 pages detailing Mitch's depradations and Meisner's ill-treatment, federal prosecutors sought a search warrant. On July 8, 1977, several hundred FBI agents hit three Church offices in Los Angeles and Washington, in what was then, at least, the largest raid in the Bureau's history. They seized more than a million pieces of paper in a single day. While the raid was ongoing in Washington, Rick Moxon, the "legal officer" of the DC Church, though he had no legal training, came to my office and asked if there was anything we could do to stop the raid. I did a little quick reading, drafted a motion for an injunction against the raid, and sought an immediate hearing before the chief judge of the DC district court, who was then William Bryant, who had presided over the Mine Workers election case.

I thought then, and think today, despite an appellate ruling to the contrary, that the Scientology raids violated the Fourth Amendment's prohibition of "unreasonable searches and seizures." To understand why requires a little background in Fourth Amendment history. In the middle of the 18th century the British government, in an effort to suppress rising dissent, much of it concerning the government's policy toward the American colonies, resorted to a device called the "general warrant," also called the "writ of assistance." This was a document that authorized the King's agents to search a person's papers for, and to seize, any evidence of seditious activity they might find. The general warrant was rejected as a violation of English law in a famous case called *Entick v. Carrington*,[1] decided in 1762, which was by general agreement the major historical underpinning of the Fourth Amendment's Warrant Clause.[2] Indeed, the American revolutionary patriot James Otis famously declared that the writ of assistance was "the worst instrument of arbitrary power, the most destructive of English liberty ... that ever was found in an English law book."[3] Thus the Warrant Clause requires that all search warrants must "particularly describ[e] the place to be searched and the persons or things to be seized." The idea behind the Warrant Clause was that government agents should not be able to read all the papers in a person's possession or search his house or office and decide at their leisure whether what they found contained any evidence of potential criminal activity. The power to do that is the essence of tyranny. By requiring the government to specify in advance what it has good cause to believe will be found, the Warrant Clause seeks to limit the power of government agents to intrude upon individual privacy and liberty.

The Scientology warrant was cleverly drafted. It contained a list of 164 individual documents and categories of documents that the FBI agents were authorized to seize. The first items on the list were quite specific and clearly tied to the evidence set forth in the affidavit used to justify the issuance of the warrant. But near the end of the list, the categories became increasingly broad and vague, and item 164 permitted seizure of "any other evidence of criminal activity." This was, I argued to Judge Bryant, the essence of a prohibited general warrant. In an argument that lasted the better part of two hours, the judge said he agreed that this looked like a general warrant and came within an ace of putting a stop to the search of the Church's Washington office. But he was concerned whether an injunction to halt the search was the proper remedy, and at the last minute he pulled back and said that, assuming the search was illegal, the Church's remedy lay in a motion under the Federal Rules of Criminal Procedure to return any property improperly seized.

Such a motion was promptly filed, but before it could be heard, the U.S.

Attorney's Office, which now had every internal Church document relevant to its ongoing battle with the federal government, obtained from a DC grand jury a massive, multi-count indictment of eleven Church of Scientology officials, ranging from Mary Sue Hubbard, the wife of Scientology founder L. Ron Hubbard, down to several of Mitch's assistants. The battleground over the constitutional propriety of the search would be a motion by the defendants in the criminal case to suppress its evidentiary fruits.

Initially, I was not involved in the criminal case. The Church wanted to press its FOIA cases and a broader lawsuit that we in the firm had drafted accusing a variety of government agencies of conspiring illegally to destroy the Church, so I was assigned to continue the fight on the civil litigation front. But while a team of talented criminal defense lawyers was assembled to represent the individual defendants, none of them had any background in the structure and operations of the Church or its long-running fight with the federal government. So I was sucked, bit by bit, into the criminal case.

My first involvement on the criminal side involved opposition to the government's effort to extradite two of the eleven defendants from England to stand trial in Washington. The Church's international headquarters were in East Grinstead, Sussex, and the documents seized in the raid suggested that two very high Church officials from England were involved in the planning of what was claimed to be a long series of crimes. The Justice Department filed a formal request with the British government to hand over the two defendants.

The defendants opposed extradition on two principal grounds. First, an accepted doctrine in the law of extradition is the principle of "dual criminality." Under this doctrine extradition is not available from one country to another unless the crime charged is recognized as a crime under the laws of both countries. This doctrine often poses problems to the federal government because of the peculiarities of our federal system. Most ordinary criminal misconduct in this country is defined by, and punished under, the laws of the respective states. Until the last half century or so, federal criminal statutes were relatively few in number and highly specialized. However, as criminal activity took on an increasingly interstate, indeed often international, character; as the fear of crime became a political issue on the national level; and as it became clear that the federal government's law enforcement resources vastly outstripped those of any state, the scope of federal criminal law expanded dramatically. But because the federal government is, under the Constitution, one of limited, enumerated powers, Congress can make an act a federal crime only if in doing so, it is acting within one of its powers listed in Article I of the Constitution. The most frequently invoked power in federal criminal law is Congress's power to regulate interstate and foreign commerce. Thus federal criminal statutes often include a requirement that the prohibited activity occur in, or have some defined effect upon, interstate or foreign commerce. To take perhaps the simplest example, prostitution and running houses of prostitution are crimes in every state except Nevada. It is a federal crime, however, to transport a person across state lines for purposes of prostitution. Because most other countries are not federations like ours, it is often open to those whose extradition is sought by federal prosecutors to argue that there is no analogous crime in the other country to, say, transporting a kidnaped person across state lines. The English Scientology officials made this argument with respect to several counts in the indictment, hoping at least to limit their criminal exposure, if not actually defeat extradition entirely, since they could not be tried on charges for which they could not be extradited.

Second, and perhaps more important, the English defendants invoked the so-called "political defense." In international law, extradition and political asylum are closely linked; indeed, they are essentially opposite sides of the same coin. If a person can show that his or her extradition is sought, not for the legitimate purpose of enforcing the criminal laws of the extraditing nation, but rather for the purpose of pursuing a political vendetta, then extradition will be denied.

It was in connection with the political defense that my assistance was needed. The English defendants were represented by prominent barristers, who were perfectly competent to handle the dual criminality issue, but they needed help in trying to establish that the federal government was engaged in a campaign to exterminate the Church of Scientology. To do so they needed both expertise in such civil rights issues as freedom of speech and religion under the First Amendment to the Constitution and the Freedom of Information Act, and also evidence of what the government had been up to. The latter I could credibly provide in the form of documents in the American Church's possession and an affidavit concerning the federal government's legal harassment of the Church. In addition, I began to search for respected academic and other experts on the speech and religion clauses of the First Amendment. Here I ran into some trouble. The Church had not been in particularly good odor in this country to begin with, and the FBI raid, which received extensive publicity, together with the extremely serious allegations of the indictment, had put the Church in a very bad light. Most respected experts, I found, were unwilling to lend their names to the

Church, even if they agreed that it had been very badly treated.

I reported my difficulty to the barristers in London, whose reaction surprised me greatly. "You can be the expert witness," they said. I pointed out first, that while I had considerably more acquaintance with constitutional and civil rights issues than most American lawyers, I would hardly be accepted as an expert on these questions in an American court, and second, that I hardly fit the mold of an impartial expert witness, as I was representing the Church in the litigation that I would be describing. "Nonsense," they said, "you are our man." So, working with a young woman barrister named Hannah Leader, who spent most of the period of the criminal proceedings in Washington, I drafted a lengthy affidavit about, not only the federal government's mistreatment of the Church, but a whole range of legal and constitutional issues in addition. Hannah and I vetted the affidavit with the lead barristers in London, and they filed it in the extradition proceedings.

So I was off to London to appear as an expert witness in the extradition proceedings, which were held in the Bow Street Magistrate's Court, not far from Covent Garden. I was particularly delighted to appear in that court, for it was located around the corner from the Fielding Hotel where Louise and I had stayed a couple of times, and it had a fascinating history. In the late 18th century the novelist Henry Fielding was the magistrate there, and he was famous as an excellent judge and as a supervisor of criminal investigations. He developed a group of proto-detectives, known as the "Bow Street Runners," who were the precursors of Scotland Yard.

Sadly, the proceedings, which lasted more than ten days, were not quite up to Fielding's standards. The magistrate seemed competent and pleasant, but the court was not prepared for taking lengthy evidence. The recorder was an older woman with a shrill voice, who seemed perpetually out of sorts, though I could hardly blame her. Her job was not to produce a transcript of the proceedings, which would have been difficult enough, as she had no mechanical or electronic means of recording the testimony, and I don't think she took shorthand. Instead, she had to reduce the give and take of the lawyers' questions and the witnesses' answers to the form of a first-person narrative supposedly delivered by each witness. It was an impossible task. She did fairly well on direct examination, where the questions tended to be short and the answers contained much first-person narrative. But on cross-examination, where the lawyer leads the witness and engages in a battle of wits, trying to get the witness to admit certain propositions that may undermine his direct testimony, it was pure chaos. After every question or two, the poor woman would shout, "You'll have to slow down. I can't possibly write so fast!" I recall in particular my own testimony, which ranged on direct examination, as I have indicated, over a veritable smorgasbord of legal and factual topics. The poor government barrister trying to cross-examine me threw up his hands after about ten minutes, not because I was such a powerful witness, but because the poor recorder was interrupting him all the time. Giving me a sly grin, he sat down.

After a decent interval, the magistrate rejected the defendants' arguments and granted the U.S. government's petition to extradite them. The defendants then took what was in effect an appeal, though in form it was a petition for a writ of *habeas corpus* to the High Court of Queen's Bench. The barristers wanted me to return to London for the argument on the *habeas* petition, though I could not see what good I could possibly do them. So I spent another pleasant week in London and learned even more first-hand about the English legal system.

In this country, we long ago abandoned the tradition of extensive oral advocacy in the appellate process. The heavy lifting is done in written briefs, which are a better format for intricate legal analysis and citation of precedent, and oral arguments are usually quite short. Indeed, in today's world of federal appeals, far fewer than half the cases even receive oral argument at all. The English courts in the late 1970s had not yet discovered written advocacy. The Scientology defendants' *habeas* petition was heard for a solid week before the Lord Chief Justice of England and another colleague. The argument consisted of lengthy oral readings from the evidence—my own affidavit, it seemed at least, was read aloud in its interminable entirety— and from the opinions in precedents cited by the two sides. In this country, granting that it raised novel and difficult issues, the case would have received a maximum of an hour of oral argument time.

The Lord Chief Justice made short work of the defendants' political defense and affirmed the magistrate's extradition order. After an unsuccessful petition for an appeal to the House of Lords, still England's highest court (though the work is delegated to a committee of the House composed of distinguished judges, so it really does function as a supreme court), the two English defendants were shipped off to this country in federal custody.

Meanwhile, back in the States, the criminal case had been assigned to Judge Charles Richey of the Washington district court. I don't know what to say about Judge Richey except that he was hands down the worst judge I have ever appeared before. He was by turns imperious and fawning, and he was always smarmy. In my first appearance before him he implied that I had lied to him and threatened me with contempt of court. Later we encountered each other at some function on Capitol Hill and he learned that I was at the time general counsel to the House Judiciary Committee. Whenever I appeared before him after that he would slobber all over me and say I was one of the best lawyers in the city. Richey was reputed to be the only federal judge who got his job through Spiro Agnew, Nixon's corrupt vice-president, who resigned in disgrace as part of a plea bargain with federal prosecutors in October 1973, less than a year before Nixon himself resigned. My observation was that Judge Richey had a hidden personal agenda in every case and that one could never trust him simply to decide things on the merits. His law clerks were so miserable once they found what sort of man he was that years later, when writing clerkship recommendations was a major part of my job as a law professor, I refused to send letters of recommendation to Judge Richey.

The defense team knew that the case was hopeless with Richey on the bench and that a favorable ruling on appeal was their only hope, but they could not have predicted how bad it would become. Two days before the hearing on the motion to suppress the evidence seized in the FBI raids was scheduled to begin, Richey convened the lawyers on a conference call and announced that he was moving the hearing to Los Angeles. This was extremely disruptive to all the lawyers—on both sides—who had been gathering their enormous files and preparing for a hearing in Washington. The hearing was anticipated to take more than a month. On virtually no notice, hundreds of thousands of pages of evidence and other documents, together with a small army of lawyers and paralegals, had to be shipped three thousand miles across the country, and accommodations had to be found for all the material and the personnel.

Though I was still not formally a member of the criminal defense team, I was in Los Angeles the day the hearing began. As we entered the federal courthouse, we noticed a significant number of men stationed on the roof with what looked like submachine guns. Inside the building there was a metal detector placed outside Judge Richey's courtroom through which everyone entering the room had to pass under the eye of a federal marshal. This made it appear as if the extraordinary security measures were related to our case, but we did not understand why that should be. True, Michael Meisner had been held against his will by Church officials, but he was not physically mistreated, and the case involved no allegations of other violent behavior. At the instance of the entire team, Leonard Boudin, the venerable dean of the team and the lawyer for Mary Sue Hubbard, rose to inquire about the security. Leonard had a long and distinguished career as an advocate for labor and civil rights causes and as a criminal defense lawyer, and he had argued a number of landmark cases before the Supreme Court. He became a good friend. In response to Leonard's inquiry about the reasons for the tight security, Judge Richey simply lied. He said it was the result of some threats to judges on the district court in Washington that were unrelated to the Scientology case. This made little sense, as most of the defense team were Washington lawyers, who appeared in district court there on a regular basis, and there had been no visible extraordinary security measures there. It later emerged that Richey had requested the security when he moved the hearing to Los Angeles because of his intense fear of the Scientologists.

After the first day of the hearing, I returned to Washington to man the civil cases and work on the extradition proceedings. Thus I was not present for the month-long battle. It should be noted, however, that our analysis showed, and the government did not really dispute, that more than 99 percent of the documents seized in the three raids on Church offices had been seized under item 164 of the warrant, which strongly bolstered our argument that it was a general warrant.

As expected, not long after the hearing on the motion to suppress concluded, Judge Richey denied the motion, thus handing the government the entire treasure trove of documents for use as evidence against the defendants. This effectively precluded any defense predicated on contesting the allegations in the indictment. It was all laid out in excruciating detail in the seized documents, plus the government had a number of disgruntled former Scientologists, including Michael Meisner, who were prepared to testify to various acts of skullduggery. The only potential defense was justification, a form of organizational self-defense. The Church undertook its campaign against the federal government, the argument went, only after suffering years of intense and unjustified discrimination and harassment in violation of basic principles of constitutional law. Because I had the most significant background in the issues related to this defense, I was at this point invited to become a member of the defense team in the criminal case.

The defense team was an able and distinguished group. In addition to Leonard Boudin, it included Phil Hirschkop, a prominent civil rights and criminal defense lawyer from Alexandria, Virginia; Michael Nussbaum of the firm of Nussbaum & Owen in Washington; Roger Zuckerman, a former Assistant United States Attorney in Washington, who had recently formed his own firm, Zuckerman & Spaeder; and John Zwerling, an able and endearing criminal defense lawyer, also from Alexandria. Each lawyer or firm had one or at the most two individual defendants as clients, grouped generally by their place in the Church hierarchy. I was assigned to work with Michael Nussbaum on the defense of Mitch Herman and Cindy Raymond, who were mid-level operatives. Mitch was the spy who had infiltrated the government on behalf of the Church, and Cindy, a former airline stewardess and a real sweetheart, worked with Mitch, though more in an administrative capacity. I had known Michael Nussbaum for years, I had the highest respect for his abilities, and we had a large circle of mutual friends. Thus I was delighted to work with him. Though I entered an appearance for Mitch and Cindy and did a great deal of work on their behalf in connection with the ultimate sentencing, my principal role at first was as a consultant to the entire team on the justification defense.

As the case moved on toward trial, we were before Judge Richey a lot on status calls, chambers conferences, and a wide variety of motions. Close acquaintance did not improve our opinion of the judge, and Phil Hirschkop, who never met the legal fight he didn't like, began urging us to file a motion to recuse him. Phil had a leak in the Marshal's Office, a supervisor who was, I think, angry over the great expense to that office because of the judge's quixotic movement of the suppression hearing to Los Angeles and over what he saw as the judge's abuse of Marshal's Office personnel. He told Phil, and proved ultimately willing to sign an affidavit to the effect, that the extreme security measures we observed at the courthouse in Los Angeles were put in place at Judge Richey's personal request, based on his expressed fear of violence from the Scientologists. Phil argued, with some force, that such a level of fear based on no cause whatever meant that Richey had prejudged the case, that he was irretrievably biased against the defendants. The rest of us saw Phil's point, but we were very leery of filing a recusal motion because we were not convinced that it was a sure winner and because we recalled the old adage, "If you strike at the king, make absolutely sure you kill him."

Phil's source was also providing him with far more explosive material about what he claimed were sexual escapades on the judge's part and his abuse of Marshal's Office personnel. He claimed that the reason Richey moved the hearing was because he wanted to play in the fleshpots of Los Angeles and that he consorted with prostitutes while he was there. He said the judge moved from one hotel to another repeatedly because he was afraid of being discovered in his dalliances and that in the process he treated U.S. Marshals as his personal body servants. None of us but Phil was prepared even to contemplate filing a motion to recuse the judge on these grounds, as we had no knowledge to support the Marshals' supervisor's statements.

We took to calling this ground for recusal "megaton," and Phil would, in a tone that swayed between humor and dead seriousness, threaten to file "megaton" if we did not at least go along with the less sensational of the recusal motions.

Ultimately, Richey's bias against the defendants was so evident that all of us agreed to move to recuse him on the grounds of his security request and his lie about the reason for it. Later Phil filed "megaton" on his own. Judge Richey, predictably I thought, indignantly declined to recuse himself.

As the trial date loomed in the immediate future, Judge Richey made it perfectly clear that he was in no mood to try the case and put enormous pressure on both sides to reach a plea bargain. There was certainly plenty of incentive for the defendants to do so. Each was named in several felony counts in the indictment, so that if convicted on all counts, which was a virtual certainty, he or she faced the possibility of a very substantial jail sentence. If we could get the government to agree to a plea to a single five-year felony count, that would limit each defendant's maximum exposure and insulate them all to some degree from the judge's wrath. In this time before the Federal Sentencing Guidelines, some judges at least unabashedly laid the wood to defendants who "wasted" their time in long trials that resulted in guilty verdicts. The justification defense, good as it felt to talk about, was a certain loser in light of the mountain of evidence in the government's possession. Only the Church as an institution stood to gain from having the justification defense aired in court. Most of the individuals were not eager to sacrifice years of their lives to give the Church an opportunity to make its case in the court of public opinion. And the Church had to weigh the perceived benefits of airing the defense against the enormous expense of the anticipated trial. I have no real data on what the criminal case had cost the Church in legal fees, but I am certain it was well into the millions of dollars, and the trial was going to cost even more. Interestingly, cost was not a factor for the individuals, as it often is in the plea bargaining context, because the Church was paying the bills of the defense team.

On the government's side, the balance of incentives was less obvious. It was going to cost a lot in direct outlays to try the case and even more in the resources rendered unavailable for other work. There also might not be much of a payoff in enhanced sentences after a lengthy and contentious trial. On the other hand, the U.S. Attorney's Office felt violated by Mitch's invasion of their territory, and emotions ran high on their side as well. Indeed, we had moved, unsuccessfully of course, to recuse the U.S. Attorney's Office from prosecuting the case on the ground that it was the victim of the crime.

There was some precedent for such a motion, but Judge Richey denied it.

Emotions ran so high among the lawyers on both sides that as we got closer and closer to the trial date, relations between the U.S. Attorney's Office and the defense team reached a very low point. Only Roger Zuckerman and I were still on speaking terms with the prosecutors. Late in the week before the trial was scheduled to begin, Roger and I met with the prosecutors, who made what they said was a single, firm, non-negotiable offer. Each defendant could enter a contingent plea of guilty to the first count of the indictment, which charged a conspiracy to commit a variety of federal crimes and which carried a maximum sentence of five years in prison. The pleas would be contingent upon an appellate ruling on the constitutionality of the search. We had insisted very hard on this latter term, as we believed that a fair appellate court could not possibly uphold what we saw as the egregiously unconstitutional search, and without the documents seized in the raids, the government's case was pretty thin. Our meeting with the prosecutors was on Thursday or Friday, and they gave the entire defense team until 5 p.m. Sunday to respond with a yes or no answer. They made it clear that all defendants had to accept the deal for it to go into effect.

The defense lawyers spent the next day or so meeting individually with their clients to discuss the government's proposal. Mitch and Cindy were eager to accept it. So, it turned out, were all the other defendants, with the sole exception of Mary Sue Hubbard. Leonard reported that she was adamant that she wanted to go to trial and run the justification defense, and that she was unconcerned about her increased sentencing exposure. Everyone else on the team expressed their clients' displeasure to Leonard and urged him to make sure she understood the consequences of her position, not just to herself, but to the young people whose own exposure she would be increasing. On Saturday Leonard called me and asked me to go to Mary Sue's apartment with him to make one last push for her to accept the deal. At first she was in a state of rigid denial, but gradually we convinced her that the Church was not going to benefit greatly from the trial, that her refusing the deal would be a disaster for the other defendants, and that because of her status as the founder's wife and her high position in the Church, she might have the most to lose in terms of an enhanced sentence. Late in the afternoon, she agreed to accept the deal.

At about midday on Sunday all the lawyers and all the clients except Mary Sue Hubbard met at the offices of Nussbaum & Owen, which had become the principal gathering place for the defense team. People were milling about, nervous, asking last-minute questions to be sure the deal was in everyone's interest. In the midst of this chaos, Cindy had a physical emergency that required medical attention. I called Louise, who contacted her doctor, and someone, I forget who, drove Cindy to the doctor's office. After considerable discussion among the lawyers and clients, we agreed that everyone was prepared to accept the prosecutors' offer, but we had one last procedural detail—now forgotten, by me at least—that we wanted to clarify. In what was almost certainly a mistake, we assigned Phil Hirschkop, whose relations with the prosecutors were the worst of all of us, to make the phone call. At 4:58 p.m. he called the U.S. Attorney's Office and said to Ray Banoun, their designee to receive our answer, "Ray, I have one question." Ray snapped. He yelled, "No questions. The deal is off the table," and hung up. When Phil tried to call back and accept without asking the question, Banoun refused to speak to him.

The judge was aware that we were deep in negotiations and that Sunday afternoon was critical. We called him to report what had happened, and he postponed the start of the trial and scheduled a status conference for the next morning to review the state of affairs. The prosecutors were adamant that we had failed to accept their offer in a timely fashion. We were equally adamant that they were the ones who had prevented us from accepting before 5 p.m. We told the judge that we were prepared to file a motion to enforce the plea agreement, that it was a simple question of contract law, and that the prosecutors had in bad faith refused our effort to accept. The judge set a schedule for the exchange of motions papers and the commencement of a hearing in very short order.

That evening, Roger Zuckerman and I asked for one last meeting with the prosecutors in an attempt to put the agreement back on track. We were prepared, we said, to "grovel" before the government lawyers. We begged them not to inflict on the individual defendants, all of whom wanted the deal, the consequences of whatever breach of the time limit they perceived the lawyers to have committed. Our groveling was in vain. They steadfastly refused to reconsider.

As we prepared for the hearing on the motion to enforce the plea agreement, it occurred to us that we needed representation. We were lawyers in the case representing the defendants, but we were also now witnesses to what had transpired in the negotiations, and we could not ethically be in the position of arguing our own credibility to the court. So we retained one of Washington's most experienced, intelligent, and laid-back trial lawyers, Jacob Stein, to represent us in the hearing.

The same point had evidently not occurred to the prosecutors. When the hearing began, the Acting U.S. Attorney, Carl Rauh—son of my old friend Joe Rauh—stood up to make the government's opening statement. Carl had not been the point man in the negotiations, but he had been involved, he was almost certainly calling the shots, and he was a witness to numerous events. Gently, Jake Stein rose to his feet and inquired if Mr. Rauh could be both witness and lawyer in this setting. Rauh tried to brush Jake aside, but the judge made it clear that he too had a problem with Carl conducting the hearing. Rauh turned his back on the judge and stormed out of the courtroom, not to be seen again. It thus fell to the most junior member of the prosecution's team, Judy Hetherton, who had not been involved in the case before, and who as a result knew very little about the details of the negotiations,, to cross-examine a pretty tough and experienced crew of defense lawyers, who were loaded for bear. The hearing lasted for three days, and all the lawyers who were players in the negotiations on both sides took the stand. I recall it as an amusing and enjoyable, if still somewhat tense, experience.

A few days later, in the late morning, we received a phone call from Judge Richey's chambers announcing that he had just filed an opinion ruling on—and granting—the defense motion to enforce the plea agreement. The judge found that we had made a timely, good-faith effort to accept the government's offer, that the government had been unreasonable in rejecting that effort, and that the agreement was enforceable under basic principles of contract law. Roger Zuckerman was designated to go to the courthouse (no fax machines, let alone e-mails yet) to get a copy of the opinion. The rest of us repaired to Joe & Mo's, a restaurant and watering hole we all frequented, to wait for him. I shall never forget Roger racing into the restaurant and over to our table, holding a copy of the opinion aloft, and yelling, "Hooray, we lost!" As more of the defense team and the clients arrived, we proceeded to indulge in a long, liquid, and quite loopy celebration of winning the right for our clients to go to jail. In reality, we were celebrating the end of what had become a serious ordeal for all of us, clients and lawyers alike, and the avoidance of several more weeks in hell.

Pursuant to the plea agreement that Judge Richey enforced, we took an appeal of the denial of the defendants' motion to suppress the evidence seized in the FBI raids. We also appealed Judge Richey's denial of our motion to recuse him because of his fear of the Scientologists and his lie about that fear. Though I played a significant role in the drafting of our briefs, I was not a candidate to argue the Fourth Amendment issue in the court of appeals, as I had not participated in the extended hearing on the motion to suppress. Phil Hirschkop undertook that portion of the oral argument. I was assigned the unhappy task of arguing the recusal appeal. We drew an appellate panel that was led by Judges George MacKinnon and Roger Robb. Both were very conservative politically and were known for their pro-government approach in criminal cases. I think that they shared the U.S. Attorney's Office's sense of outrage at the violation of the sacred space of the courthouse by Mitch and his assistants. In what was in my view an opinion that ignored the commands of the Fourth Amendment, the court upheld the FBI search.[4] It also brushed aside our concerns about the objectivity of Judge Richey, despite his order of massive security in a case marked by no violence at all.[5] The entire appeal was pervaded by a sense that the Scientologists had, in the view of the court, forfeited any claims of constitutional protection by invading the space of the courthouse itself. The court, in sum, circled the wagons. It was not, perhaps, a surprising result, but it was certainly a disappointing one.

❖ ❖ ❖

The clients had a bit of a respite because of the appeal, but they still had to face the sentencing by Judge Richey. We worked closely with them in their interaction with the Probation Office, which compiled pre-sentence reports on each one and made recommendations, which were not binding on the judge, in each case. None of the defendants had a prior criminal record, and except for their battle with the federal government over its treatment of the Church, they were pretty much model citizens, so we hoped the Probation Office might weigh in on their side, to some extent at least. Mitch and Cindy lived in California, so they reported to the Probation Office in Los Angeles. Michael, Sally, and I went out West for their meetings with probation officers and helped them to develop as much positive information as possible and to prepare for the interviews.

It was a pretty dark time for these young people, but one incident served to create a little black humor that I believe helped sustain them as they faced the prospect of prison. The evening following Mitch's interview with his probation officer, a group of us, including Mitch, Cindy, Michael, Sally, and I, together with some others, gathered for dinner in the dining room of the hotel where Michael, Sally, and I were staying. After dinner we moved to the bar, where we talked and drank a fairly long time. I have a memory of looking up at one point as an attractive young woman wearing a long, slinky sheath dress brushed by me on her way past our table to resume her solo seat at the bar. I made some crack under my breath, intended for Mitch's ears only. Later, as I got in the elevator to head to my room for a night's sleep, I noticed Mitch and Cindy tiptoeing in a tipsy state through the lobby and looking very pleased with themselves. Earlier in the evening Mitch had been regaling us with the story of another covert action involving prostitutes that he had undertaken in New Orleans against a doctor from Boston who had been a big public enemy of the Church. The doctor and his wife were in New Orleans for an AMA convention. Mitch had hired two hookers to show up at the doctor's hotel room at midnight loudly proclaiming themselves ready to party. They found only the doctor and his very shocked wife, both of them in bed. Just as I had put on my pajamas and was getting into bed, I heard a knock on my door. I opened it to find the young lady in the slinky sheath dress standing there. "Dr. Dudley?" she asked, "Mitch sent me." To her evident chagrin—I don't know if Mitch had paid her anything in advance—I explained to her that I was not interested in her services. I now knew why Mitch and Cindy were looking so pleased.

On the plane back to Washington the next morning I plotted my revenge. I had some stationery made up purporting to be that of a Boston law firm, with all the lawyers' last names closely associated with the Scientology criminal case. On this stationery I wrote Mitch a letter stating that it was from a lawyer representing the wife of the doctor he had diddled in New Orleans, asserting a claim for damages arising from the ruin of her marriage and threatening to file a lawsuit unless Mitch paid a very large sum of money within thirty days. Mitch later told me it gave him five very bad minutes until he read all the names on the letterhead and realized it was a hoax. He had little trouble figuring out who the perpetrator was. As the group gathered in Washington for the day of reckoning in court, there was much laughter about the fact that someone had finally put one over on Mitch, and everyone winked at me and called me "Dr. Dudley."

The sentencing proceeding was tense and exhausting. The prosecution lawyers hammered at the defendants, urging harsh sentences for the outrages they said had been perpetrated against our government. Judge Richey was at his smarmy worst, posturing and lecturing and handing out serious time. It had been agreed among the defendants and the defense team that I would deliver a little speech outlining the essence of the defense that we had thought of running—not, I said, by way of justification, but rather by way of offering some insight into the mindset and motivation behind the collective actions of these otherwise upstanding citizens. The strategy backfired, and directly upon poor Cindy. I made the speech in the context of her sentencing, though I was as careful as I could be to separate it from direct consideration of her. The speech annoyed the judge, who gave Cindy a very stiff sentence, remarking, "I think she wants to be a martyr." Cindy let out a yelp of pain, and I assured the judge that she had no such intention, but the damage was done, and he refused to change his mind.

❖ ❖ ❖

Not long after the end of the Scientology criminal case, I concluded that the personal breach between Sam Seymour and me was irreparable. I told him I planned to leave the firm, and I began looking around. From the beginning my search was focused on Michael Nussbaum's firm, Nussbaum & Owen. As I said earlier, Michael and I had known each other for years, and we had worked very well together in the Scientology litigation. The defense team's use of the firm's offices as a meeting place had given me the opportunity to get to know the other lawyers in the firm, whom I liked quite a bit.

I knew Michael's principal partner, Marguerite Owen, in a different capacity. In the late 1970s she had become David Webster's second wife. David and his first wife Joan were both Irish Catholics from Rhode Island. They had five children together, and Louise and I saw a fair amount of them while I was at Williams & Connolly. But during the 1970s David and Joan encountered increasingly severe marital difficulties, which resulted ultimately in separation and divorce. After a while David began to date Marguerite Owen, herself a divorcee. After his divorce became final, David and Marguerite were married in a lovely ceremony at her aunt's home in Oxford, Maryland. To David's dismay, the ceremony could not be performed in a Catholic church (not only because he and Marguerite were both divorced, but because she was not a Catholic). Still, they were married by a priest, a close friend of David's named Father Paul Norton, who later became one of my all-time favorite clients.

I invited Michael Nussbaum out for a drink one evening shortly after I had told Sam Seymour I was leaving. I told Michael in general terms that Sam and I had come to a parting of the ways, and I expressed an interest in exploring whether he might have a place for me in his firm. I hadn't gotten very far when Michael broke in excitedly. "I have something to tell you in strict confidence," he said. "I had exactly this same conversation with Webster less than a week ago." Knowing that Michael and David were longtime friends and drinking companions and that Webster often chafed under the dominance of Ed Williams, I replied, "But Michael, you've had that conversation with Webster fifty times before." "I know," he said, "but this time it was 9 o'clock in the morning and he was completely sober."

The prospect of being reunited in practice with David made Michael's firm even more attractive to me. After a few weeks of talking, thinking, and checking client conflicts (there were none), David and I joined the firm in the spring of 1981, and it was renamed Nussbaum, Owen & Webster. Sally Regal joined the new firm with me. Not only had she and I worked closely together, but she and Sam never got along. Indeed, while I had been contemplating leaving Seymour & Dudley for a while, it was an event involving Sally that put my resolve over the top. Concerned about her long-range future, Sally had asked Sam whether he would ever consider making her a partner. I was deeply disturbed when, without even talking the matter through with me, he told her no. So I was committed to seeking a place for her wherever I went, assuming it was something that was attractive to her. For the first couple of years at the new firm, Sally continued to work principally with me. Then we decided it would be healthier for her if she worked with some others. She did a case with David, and from that time forward became even closer to him than she had been to me.

From the beginning I thoroughly enjoyed my new practice setting. I liked my new partners and associates, and we began to attract interesting, and sometimes lucrative, cases. Our growing clientele helped us attract top-flight entry-level associates. We were all committed to a healthy dose of *pro bono* work, a fair amount of which came from the Washington Lawyers' Committee for Civil Rights.

❖ ❖ ❖

Especially in my early years at Nussbaum, Owen & Webster, I did a lot of work with Michael Nussbaum. We worked on massive litigation involving insurance coverage disputes for Lloyd's of London; we traveled a lot together, especially to London; and came to know each other very well. For most of his career, Michael was a truly brilliant lawyer. He was also one of the most interesting, complex, and in most respects, lovable human beings I have ever known.

Michael Nussbaum was born into a well-to-do and highly educated Jewish family in Berlin in 1933, the year that Adolf Hitler and the Nazi party came to power in Germany. His father was a physician, and his mother, I was told, was one of the first women ever to earn a Ph. D. degree in Germany, though I have forgotten what her field was. Michael was born with a significant, though not debilitating, congenital deformity. Where his right arm should have been, a single thumb-like appendage hung several inches from his shoulder. Like many physically handicapped people, including me, Michael worked very hard to perfect the rest of his body and his physical skills, becoming a pretty good high school and college soccer player.

In the mid-1930s, as the Nazi grip on Germany tightened and as the virulent antisemitism of Hitler's policies became increasingly evident, Michael's parents escaped from Berlin to London, taking with them Michael's older brother Bernard, known as "Bud," and leaving Michael behind in the care of an aunt. In 1939, in an apparently daring escapade, the aunt managed to get herself and Michael out of Germany and safely to England. During one of our numerous trips to London, Michael learned that this aunt, who had moved to Florida, I believe, and to whom he had understandably remained very close, had died. The two of us spent a long, teary night telling each other stories of how the horrors of World War II had shaped and disrupted our childhoods.

❖   ❖   ❖

I practiced at Nussbaum, Owen & Webster for eight years, and I had many interesting cases there. In the interest of space, I will recount only two.

❖   ❖   ❖

Priests and Privileges

I mentioned representing David Webster's priest friend, Father Paul Norton. Sometime in the mid-1980s the parents of two small boys in the Maryland suburbs of Washington filed what I am sure was not the first, but was certainly one of the first, in what became a tragic flood of cases charging sexual abuse of children by Roman Catholic priests. Father Norton, I hasten to say, was not a defendant in the case.

Feelings in the case ran especially high, because the two young boys the defendant priest was accused of molesting were his own nephews. Because of the novelty of the claim and of this intense intra-family aspect, the case was the subject of considerable publicity, and the *Washington Post* in particular was covering it closely, with the full cooperation of the plaintiffs' lawyers.

Recognizing that a money judgment against an impecunious priest is economically worthless, the plaintiffs' lawyers had named the Archdiocese of Washington, DC, as an additional defendant. They thus undertook the burden to prove that some responsible official or officials in the hierarchy of the archdiocese knew, or with the exercise of reasonable care should have known, of the defendant priest's pederasty and nonetheless continued to sponsor him as a parish priest. This is where Father Norton came in.

The Archbishop of Washington had years earlier established the Archdiocesan Counseling Center, which was staffed by priests who were also licensed psychologists. Each member of a religious order subject to the jurisdiction of the archdiocese was required to undergo periodic counseling at the center, and those who were deemed in need of therapy were required to undergo that. During the relevant period of time Father Norton had been the director of the center. The defendant priest had been among those identified as in need of therapy, and Father Norton had been the one who provided psychotherapy to him. As soon as they learned all of this, the plaintiffs' lawyers served Father Norton with a deposition subpoena, figuring that they might be able to establish that he, at least, was aware of the defendant's proclivities and failed to take steps to insulate him from contact with young parishioners.

As soon as he received the subpoena, Father Norton turned to David for legal assistance. David was involved in another case that was going to keep him out of town during the period when Father Norton needed help, so he asked me to undertake the representation. I met with my new client and took an instant liking to him. He was then in his mid-seventies. He was a smallish man with a full shock of snow-white hair that sat atop a cherubic Irish grin. He was also one of the kindest, gentlest, most decent human beings I have ever known. He told me that he was not willing to testify about what the defendant had told him in their therapy sessions. He said he had taken two oaths, one when he became a priest and the other when he became a psychologist, and that on both occasions he had sworn to protect the confidentiality of whatever anyone said to him in either capacity.

The case was pending in the Circuit Court of Montgomery County, Maryland, and my research showed that the Maryland legislature had created two pertinent evidentiary privileges. An evidentiary privilege is a rule excusing a witness from testifying about certain matters. Most, though not all, such privileges protect the confidentiality of statements made within the confines of certain special relationships: husband–wife, attorney–client, etc. By statute Maryland protected statements made to members of bona fide religious orders for the purpose of obtaining religious or spiritual guidance, and those made to licensed psychotherapists for the purpose of obtaining counseling or therapy. After finding these statutes, I asked Father Norton whether his communications with the defendant priest fell into these categories, and he said that he was both providing religious guidance and psychotherapy. So I filed a motion to quash the deposition subpoena, feeling pretty good about my legal position.

Enter the human element in the person of the judge, an intelligent, experienced, thoroughly decent and humane man named Stanley Frosh, who had been an excellent trial lawyer before going on the bench. Judge Frosh had a very sophisticated understanding of how litigation works. He was sympathetic to the plaintiffs—who wouldn't be?—and he was determined to give their lawyers every opportunity to make a case against the archdiocese, if there was one to be made. He denied my motion on what I thought then—and still think—were flimsy, indeed insupportable, grounds.

The judge held that the privilege for statements to members of the clergy was limited to statements made under the seal of a confession in Catholic practice, and Father Norton had never been the defendant's confessor. It was true that the first judicial decisions in this country recognizing such a privilege—175 years earlier—had involved confessions to Catholic priests. But since then every state in the Union had enacted a statute recognizing such a privilege. While some statutes were susceptible of a narrow construction limiting them to confessions, the Maryland statute was among the most broadly worded in the country and made no reference to Catholicism or the practices of any particular religion, let alone to confessions. Moreover, there was no Maryland precedent limiting the scope of the privilege in this way.

As for the privilege for statements to psychotherapists, Judge Frosh held that the defendant had waived it by the very act of defending the lawsuit, which he said inevitably put the defendant's mental state in issue. Again, it is true that a party to litigation will in many instances not be permitted to take a position in a case and then block access to information relevant to an assessment of that position by invoking a privilege. Thus a defendant in a criminal case who pleads insanity will be held to have waived his privilege for any relevant statements to psychotherapists. But the defendant priest had not admitted molesting the boys and claimed that he did so because of some mental disease or defect, but had instead simply denied the acts of molestation, a defense that in no way implicated his mental state.

I was pretty confident that an appellate court would disagree with at least one, and very likely both, prongs of the judge's ruling—and we only needed to win on one—but the judge knew exactly what he was doing. His order denying my motion to quash the subpoena was not appealable because it did not finally dispose of the case. The only way that Father Norton could obtain an appellate ruling on the question of privilege was to refuse to testify and be held in contempt of court. If that happened, the judge would impose a "coercive" contempt sanction—a fine of X dollars a day or a jail sentence until he agreed to testify—which would then be appealable because it would be deemed a separate, final judgment with respect to Father Norton. The judge could stay the effect of such a sanction pending an appeal, but he had the authority to deny a stay, in which event Father Norton could wind up sitting in jail while I pursued his appeal, which might take weeks. The judge was playing a game of judicial "chicken" with my client.

I explained all this to Father Norton, and added that it was clear under the law that he had now exhausted his obligation to the defendant priest. One who is in the possession of information that is arguably subject to a privilege belonging to someone else (a privilege generally is held by the maker of a confidential communication) is required to raise the matter with the court and obtain a ruling, but has no obligation even to take an appeal if one is available, let alone to suffer contempt sanctions. I told Father Norton that my sole concern was his welfare and that therefore it was my advice that he testify about what had transpired in his sessions with the defendant priest.

It was at this moment that I learned that Father Norton was not only kind, sweet-tempered, and gentle, but also tough as nails. Without hesitating a second, he said, "I couldn't live with myself if I did that, Earl. I am old and retired now, but the two most important things I have done in my life were to become a priest and to become a psychologist, and on each occasion I took a solemn oath of confidentiality. I could not look myself in the mirror if my last professional act was to violate those oaths to save myself a little inconvenience. I am prepared to go to jail if I have to."

On the day of Father Norton's deposition, the lawyers for all the parties, the court reporter, Father Norton, and I gathered in the conference room at Nussbaum, Owen & Webster. The court reporter put Father Norton under oath. He answered general background questions and admitted that he had been the therapist for the defendant priest. The plaintiffs' lawyer then asked him to relate what had transpired in the therapy sessions. Father Norton took a deep breath and said, "I respectfully decline to answer your question." The plaintiffs' lawyer, being a lawyer and being sure that he was closing in on the key to the archbishop's pocketbook, began yelling at Father Norton, telling him that he had an obligation under the law to testify. I leaned forward and said, "Wait a minute. It is my job to advise Father Norton on his legal rights and obligations, and believe it or not, I have done so. Would you mind if I asked a couple of questions?"

The plaintiffs' lawyer had no objection, so I asked Father Norton to explain why he was refusing to testify. He spoke eloquently of his conscience and his oaths of confidentiality. I then asked him to whom this duty of confidentiality ran, and he said that it ran to the defendant priest. And I said, "If the defendant were to release you from your obligation of confidentiality, would you be willing to testify?" He said he would.

The plaintiffs' lawyer then adjourned the deposition and placed a call to the judge's chambers. We all got on the speakerphone, and the lawyer explained to the judge what had happened so far and made an oral motion for an order directing Father Norton to testify. Judge Frosh addressed my client directly, ordering him to testify about what had transpired in the defendant's therapy sessions. Expressing great respect for the court, Father Norton explained that he could not do so consistent with what he saw as the obligations of his conscience.

The plaintiffs' lawyer then made an oral motion to hold Father Norton in contempt and apply a coercive sanction. At this point I spoke up and requested the opportunity to brief and argue the contempt motion formally. The judge was a cautious man, and he recognized that contempt is a very tricky area of the law. He said he would take briefs and hear argument. He set a very fast schedule, however. He said that he was going into the hospital for back surgery a week from the following Monday, but that he was scheduled to return home on Tuesday. He said he would hear the motion at his house the following day, Wednesday, at 2 p.m.

Things, I thought, could hardly be worse. We had a judge who was hell-bent on getting the information in Father Norton's possession to the plaintiffs' lawyers. He had ruled against the claims of privilege, not once, but twice. Despite my request for briefing and argument, I did not have a defense to the contempt motion. The judge was going to hear us in the privacy of his own home, where he would feel psychologically strongest. And he was going to be a wounded bear, barely two days away from what had to be painful surgery. Only half in jest I said to Father Norton, "Bring your toothbrush to the hearing." I didn't think the judge would do so, but we had to be ready for the fact that he had the power to order Father Norton to report directly to jail.

On the appointed Wednesday I took Father Norton out to lunch and tried to distract him with conversation about other things. But by the time we arrived at the judge's house a little before 2 o'clock, we were in a pretty glum mood. When we got there, a little surprise was waiting for us. Literally camped on the judge's doorstep was a *Washington Post* reporter seeking admission to cover the hearing. My mood began to brighten, as I thought the plaintiffs' lawyers had made a big tactical blunder. I thought Judge Frosh was going to have little stomach for sending my very attractive septuagenarian client to jail for following the sincere dictates of his conscience, but that he would probably do so in order to get the information to the plaintiffs. I thought his stomach for the dirty job was going to be made a great deal queasier by the prospect that a big story on his order was probably going to appear above the fold on the front page of the Metro section of the next day's *Post*, very likely accompanied by a picture of my frail- and cherubic-looking client.

As I predicted, the judge was very annoyed by the presence of the reporter. Leaving the reporter outside, we all convened in the judge's dining room to decide whether to admit him. The judge looked to me for help. "Don't you have an objection, Mr. Dudley?" he asked. I assured him that I was as surprised as he and that we had had nothing to do with procuring the presence of the reporter. I said I would prefer that the matter proceed without publicity and agreed that the judge had the right to control who entered his home, but I noted that were it not for the judge's recent surgery, the hearing would be held in the courthouse, where it would be open to the press and the public. Thus, I said, "I don't see how I can object." I had tried to contain my glee at the reporter's presence, but the judge knew perfectly well what I was thinking, gave me a wry smile, and said, "Okay, let him in."

The judge convened the hearing around his dining room table, and the plaintiffs' lawyer made a perfectly straightforward presentation of the pertinent facts and argument on the contempt motion. The judge turned to me. I said, "Your honor, I submit that the plaintiffs' real quarrel is not with Father Norton, but with the defendant priest. At the deposition I asked Father Norton to whom his obligation of confidentiality ran and if he would testify if the defendant released him from that obligation. He said he would. The defendant has been represented by counsel at all these proceedings, yet he has made no move to release Father Norton. Father Norton is a mere stakeholder here, acting in accordance with his professional obligations and the dictates of his conscience. The privileges, if privileges there are, belong to the defendant. They are his to waive, not Father Norton's. So I would urge that if coercive sanctions are to be applied to anyone, it should be to the defendant and not my client."

This argument was legal nonsense. It was Father Norton who was in deliberate defiance of the judge's order to testify. But it was all I could think of, and as I made the argument, I could see a smile of great relief spread across Judge Frosh's face. I had given him a way out. He could still get the information to the plaintiffs, but by squeezing the putative bad guy, the defendant priest, and not my sincerely conscience-bound client. The judge said, "I agree with Mr. Dudley. I am going to deny the contempt motion, but I will entertain a motion for an order to the defendant to release Father Norton, subject to coercive sanctions."

The plaintiffs' lawyers promptly filed the motion that the judge had invited, and the latter granted it, ordering the defendant to release Father Norton on pain of having his entire defense in the case stricken. He gave the defendant two weeks to comply. This was because communication between the defendant and his lawyer was a bit difficult. The Church had then—and I believe still has—a facility in the New Mexico desert where it houses "troublesome" priests (to paraphrase King Henry II) while it figures out what to do with them. The defendant was there, and he was not really free to leave.

While the two-week period was running, I received a call from Kevin Bain, a partner at Williams & Connolly who, while he was not appearing in the case, was the archbishop's principal lawyer. He said, "I have been told that I should have a conversation about this case with you." We talked for half an hour or so, and I told him that while Father Norton had not revealed to me what the defendant had said in their therapy sessions, I was pretty certain that it was not in anyone's interest for him to testify. I added that if he was asking my advice, I thought the archbishop should write a big enough check to get rid of the case. Kevin said, "I hear you." A few days later the *Post* ran a story saying that the case had been settled on undisclosed terms.

The case raised serious legal issues that resounded through the decades of painful litigation of this sort. The plaintiffs' objective was always to find a way to establish liability on the part of some Church institution that had the resources to pay a large judgment. Often the best way to do that was to go after information confided by the defendant priest in some confidential capacity to some official in the Church hierarchy. But the effort to obtain that information engaged a complex tangle of interests. Assuming that the defendant priest had made some damaging admission to someone like Father Norton or some other Church official, he had a very strong personal interest in suppressing it. But of course, the Church had an equally strong interest in suppressing the information in its possession, since it might lead to a finding of liability on the part of the institution. From an economic standpoint, of course, the Church's interest was the stronger of the two, as the priest would typically have no money to lose. The priest might, however, face criminal prosecution. Nor were the motives of the possessor of the information entirely clear of potential suspicion. Father Norton, I am convinced, was motivated by the highest sense of professional loyalty and responsibility. But a Church official who deliberately failed to warn potential victims of sexual abuse that they were dealing with a predator could face public ruin and, in an extreme case, possible prosecution himself.

All these issues were at best dimly perceived at the time of Father Norton's case. They were not questions that the Church could afford to litigate and lose for all time in the unattractive setting of that case.

❖ ❖ ❖

Of Independent Counsel and the Supreme Court

In 1986 I was asked by my friend Alexia Morrison, a former assistant United States attorney in Washington and later head of enforcement litigation at the Securities & Exchange Commission, to serve as her deputy in the investigation of whether former Assistant Attorney General Theodore Olson had lied in testimony to the House Judiciary Committee or otherwise obstructed its investigation of the Reagan administration's invocation of executive privilege in a heated dispute with Congress. It would be my first and only exercise on the prosecution side of a criminal case.

Lex had been appointed to investigate Olson's conduct under the provisions of the Ethics in Government Act, which had first been enacted by Congress in 1976 in response to the Watergate scandal that brought down the Nixon administration. Congress was concerned that a series of Executive Branch scandals dating back to the Grant administration following the Civil War demonstrated, not only that the Executive Branch was hopelessly conflicted in the effort to investigate possible wrongdoing by its own members, but also that its monopoly of the investigative and prosecutorial processes created the temptation, which lay at the heart of Watergate, to cover up any wrongdoing of which it might become aware.

To address this problem, Congress sought to create an investigative and prosecutorial mechanism outside the Executive Branch to be invoked in cases of serious allegations of wrongdoing at the highest levels of the federal government. Under the statute the gatekeeper to the process was a special three-judge court to be appointed by the chief justice from among sitting judges of the United States courts of appeals. Whenever, after a preliminary investigation, the attorney general found reasonable grounds to believe that further investigation of such allegations was warranted, he or she was directed to apply to the special court to appoint an independent counsel, with specifically defined jurisdiction, to conduct the necessary investigation and, if he or she deemed it appropriate, to prosecute the high government official(s) involved. The independent counsel was given all the investigative and prosecutorial authority of the Department of Justice within the confines of his or her jurisdiction. Under the statute as it existed in 1986—it had been reenacted in amended form in 1982—only the attorney general could remove an independent counsel, and then only for serious malfeasance in office, with authority to review any such removal lodged in the special court.

From the beginning there were those who expressed doubt whether Congress could vest this segment of prosecutorial authority in an officer not subject to the control of the president, whose duties under Article II of the Constitution included "tak[ing] Care that the Laws be faithfully executed." But in the decade since its enactment there had been no occasion for any court, let alone the Supreme Court, to consider the statute's constitutionality. Our case would change that.

I had known Lex Morrison for several years, though up to that point not terribly well. We had met teaching advocacy skills to lawyers in Washington and had had lunch together several times. When she called me, I had some qualms about accepting the assignment. For one thing, I knew Ted Olson, the target of the investigation, though again not well. I had met him twenty years earlier during my summer at Gibson, Dunn & Crutcher in Los Angeles, when he was one of the very conservative young Reaganauts supporting the former actor's first bid to be governor of California. Olson had come East in 1981 with then-President Reagan and his attorney general, Gibson, Dunn partner William French Smith. Olson had served as assistant attorney general for the Office of Legal Counsel. In that capacity he was the president's principal legal advisor.

Another possible impediment to my service, I thought, was my stint as general counsel to the House Judiciary Committee, the very body to which Olson was accused of giving false testimony. At the behest of my old boss, Chairman Rodino, the staff of the Judiciary Committee, led by Alan Parker, my successor as general counsel, whom I had recommended to Rodino, had conducted its own investigation and prepared an extensive report. The possibility that the chairman and staffers who had worked under me at the committee might turn up as witnesses against Olson might lead some, I feared, to question my ability to be objective.

I raised these concerns with Lex, and after careful deliberation, she said she was satisfied that there was no ethical reason why I could not serve, so I signed on to her staff, which included two other lawyers, Hank Schuelke and Rick Otto, both experienced prosecutors, and two FBI agents. Lex, Hank, and I served part-time, continuing our own law practices, while Rick and the agents were full-time.

From the beginning, controversy swirled around our investigation. In 1982 two committees of the House of Representatives had subpoenaed documents and other information in the possession of the Environmental Protection Agency dealing with that body's enforcement of the so-called Superfund environmental cleanup program. The Democrats in control of Congress suspected that Superfund cleanup awards and the timing of the announcement of those awards had been manipulated to benefit Republican candidates in the electoral process. With the attorney general out of the country when the subpoenas were returnable, Olson advised EPA Director Anne Gorsuch Burford, already a controversial figure whose commitment to serious environmental reform was doubted by many, to invoke executive privilege, a doctrine designed to protect the confidentiality—and hence the candor—of the process by which the leaders of the Executive Branch receive their advice. Acting on Olson's advice, Burford refused to comply with the subpoenas. The two congressional committees voted to seek contempt citations on the floor of the House, which voted to hold Burford in contempt. By law, the officer charged with prosecuting contempts of Congress was the U.S. attorney for the District of Columbia, himself a member of the Department of Justice. Not only did the U.S. attorney take no steps to prosecute the contempts, but the Department of Justice sued the House of Representatives in the name of "the United States" to void the contempt citations. This did not lower the political temperature. Ultimately the administration granted the House Committees limited access to the documents, and the contempts were never prosecuted.

Meanwhile, it emerged that Ted Olson had not actually reviewed the documents that the EPA was withholding before advising the invocation of executive privilege, which severely undercut the claim that their continued secrecy was essential to the functioning of the agency. And it further turned out that the documents did arguably provide evidence of the consideration of partisan political issues in the administration of some aspects of the Superfund program. Burford and one of her principal aides were forced to resign.

The House committees that had subpoenaed the documents and the speaker of the House, frustrated by the Executive's refusal to prosecute the contempts, asked Chairman Rodino and the Judiciary Committee, which exercised oversight of the Department of Justice, to investigate the whole affair. The committee called Olson before it and questioned him at some length about his role in the controversy, and Olson went into what the boxing fraternity calls a "bob and weave." He tried to give as little accurate information as possible without actually lying.

The Judiciary Committee staff then sought access to internal Justice Department documents involving the whole EPA affair. Top officials in the department were not, according to the staff, forthright or cooperative in response to their document requests.

After a lot of pulling and hauling, the committee staff wrote a lengthy report accusing three top Justice officials of illegally obstructing the committee's inquiry. The three were Deputy Attorney General Ed Schmults, Assistant Attorney General for the Lands Division Carol Dinkins (herself later deputy attorney general), and Ted Olson. The chairman forwarded the report to Attorney General Edwin Meese under the Ethics in Government Act, with a formal request that he seek the appointment of an independent counsel by the special court to investigate the conduct of all three officials.

Meese asked the Public Integrity Section of the department to do a preliminary investigation. The section found that there was credible evidence of misconduct by all three, and it recommended that an independent counsel be appointed in line with the committee's request. Such preliminary investigations were typically reviewed by the assistant attorney general in charge of the Criminal Division, but most of the leadership of that division had recused themselves because of their knowledge of the situation or their close working relationships with Schmults, Dinkins, and Olson. So Meese asked for a review of the work of the Public Integrity Section by the U.S. Attorney for the District of Massachusetts, William Weld, later governor of Massachusetts. Weld agreed with Public Integrity that an investigation of all three was warranted.

Meese then took the matter personally under advisement. Bucking the recommendations of all the professionals in the department who had looked at the matter, he declined to refer the conduct of either Schmults or Dinkins to an independent counsel. He sought an appointment limited to the question whether Olson had lied or obstructed justice. The special court appointed Lex to serve as independent counsel.

Once Lex's operation was up and running, our first task was to review the reports of the Judiciary Committee staff, the Public Integrity Section, and U.S. Attorney Weld. That review convinced us that there was at least as much reason for further investigation of Schmults's and Dinkins' conduct as of Olson's. Lex approached the attorney general seeking the further referral, but was brusquely rebuffed. She then applied to the special court for an expansion of her jurisdiction. In an opinion that was, ironically, of considerable help later in refuting the claim that the independent counsel statute was unconstitutional, the special court concluded that it had no authority to confer jurisdiction beyond that requested by the attorney general.[6]

The question of the constitutionality of the Ethics in Government Act pervaded the air in Washington in the spring of 1987. Conservatives within and without the government argued that the statute encroached on powers reserved by the Constitution to the president. Whether coincidentally or not, the conduct of numerous high officials in the Reagan administration, including Attorney General Meese himself on two separate occasions, had come under scrutiny by independent counsels. More importantly, all previous and ongoing independent counsel investigations were overshadowed by the Iran-Contra affair, which broke publicly in November 1986. In that burgeoning scandal, it was alleged that high-ranking members of the administration, possibly including President Reagan himself, had secretly agreed to sell arms to the Iranian government for use in its war against Iraq in return for the release of American hostages held by Iran—an action the president had pledged never to undertake and later said he had not undertaken—and had then transferred the money, in direct violation of congressional limitations, to the anticommunist rebel "Contras" in Nicaragua. Former federal judge Lawrence Walsh had been appointed as independent counsel to conduct this very complex and extremely important investigation, which had the potential to result in impeachment proceedings against the president. Lt. Col. Oliver North, a deputy on the White House National Security Council staff, refused to comply with subpoenas issued by a special grand jury at Walsh's behest, arguing that Walsh's appointment to conduct the investigation under the statute violated the Constitution. North was represented by

Brendan Sullivan, the next lawyer hired after me by Williams & Connolly in 1969.[7]

The Reagan administration was in a very difficult position regarding the constitutional issue. President Reagan had signed the re-enactment of the Ethics in Government Act, though he expressed some constitutional doubts in doing so. Many members of the administration had a vested interest in a successful attack on the statute. But politically the administration could not be perceived as trying to save its own skin by derailing the Iran-Contra investigation, which involved by far the biggest potential scandal since Watergate. The solution adopted by the administration was to offer Judge Walsh a so-called "parallel appointment" to continue his investigation. This consisted of an appointment pursuant to a regulation issued by the attorney general that was identical in language to the statute and to the jurisdictional definition contained in Walsh's appointment by the special court. Acceptance of this appointment by Walsh would blunt the constitutional issue, since he would then be acting under the control of the president through his agent, the attorney general. Technically the attorney general could fire Walsh, or revoke the regulation, at any time, but politically that would be suicidal, as Nixon's firing of Watergate Special Prosecutor Archibald Cox in 1973 had made excruciatingly clear.

The pressure on Walsh to accept this arrangement was very heavy. He could not afford to risk losing the fruits of his extremely visible and important investigation by insisting on litigating a fine point of constitutional law. Insulated from reprisal as he was by the political dynamic, Walsh accepted the parallel appointment. The Court of Appeals for the District of Columbia Circuit upheld the appointment by the attorney general and Walsh's exercise of powers under it.[8]

To the disappointment of conservatives, the Justice Department had little desire to litigate the constitutional question. Meese and his high-ranking appointees in the Justice Department, who were all true-believing movement conservatives, almost certainly agreed that the statute was unconstitutional, but it was hard for them to sustain the notion that they were acting in the public interest in attacking it when so many of them were or had been under investigation pursuant to its provisions. Moreover, though there was nothing in our legal and constitutional structure that required the attorney general to support the constitutionality of federal legislation in court, that was seen as a traditional part of his duties, and refusal to do so would constitute a rare and historic breach with the Congress. Finally, there was the risk that the Supreme Court would uphold the statute and render an opinion that set the conservative legal agenda back significantly. So Meese offered every sitting independent counsel, including Lex Morrison, a similar parallel appointment in an effort to avoid the whole constitutional issue, at least while Iran-Contra was pending. With the exception of Lex, I believe that all accepted the offer.

Lex's situation was quite different. Her investigation was aimed at the heart of the Meese Justice Department. She believed that Meese had already narrowed the permissible scope of the investigation improperly for the purpose of protecting individuals at the top of the department. As a result of the skirmish over the scope of the investigation, Lex's relations with the political appointees in the department were already quite touchy. She had no reason to trust Meese's offer of investigative powers that he had the unchecked authority to retract, and she lacked the protection of public opinion that insulated Walsh from any efforts by Meese to undermine his investigation. It was her inclination to refuse the offer of a parallel appointment and to rest her authority solely on the statute. After lengthy discussion, all the lawyers on the staff agreed that she was right. Thus Lex declined the parallel appointment, and a clash in court over the constitutionality of the statute became inevitable.

At Lex's request, a federal grand jury issued subpoenas for documents to Olson, Schmults, and Dinkins. (The fact that the latter two were beyond her prosecutorial jurisdiction did not mean that she could not seek evidence from them relating to Olson's conduct.) All three refused to comply, and we filed a motion to compel their compliance, subject to contempt-of-court sanctions. They opposed the motion, arguing that she had no authority to investigate under the statute, as it was unconstitutional. We were off to the wars. The briefing and initial argument of the constitutional issues fell to me.

There were essentially three distinct, though related, lines of constitutional attack on the statutory scheme. They all rested on the doctrine of separation of powers, an essential component of our constitutional structure. The basic concept is that the three branches of the federal government—the Congress, the Executive, and the Judiciary—exercise distinct, if sometimes overlapping, powers, and that they act as natural checks on each other and thus as bulwarks against potential tyranny.

The first, simplest, and most powerful, though also the riskiest, attack on the statute rested on the so-called "Vesting Clause" of Article II of the Constitution. That clause provides that "[t]he executive Power shall be vested in a President of the United States of America." Thus, the argument ran, any governmental power that was "executive" in nature belonged exclusively to the president. There is no definition of "executive Power" in the Constitution or elsewhere in federal law, but two things supported this argument. First, Article II, section 3 lists certain duties and prerogatives of the president, among them that "he shall take Care that the Laws be faithfully executed." And second, everyone agreed that as a matter of history and structure, criminal prosecution was an "executive," as opposed to a "legislative" or "judicial" function. Thus, the statute's opponents argued, no arrangement that deprived the president of control over federal criminal prosecution was permissible.

For all of its simple power, this argument was risky because it flew in the face of history. Over two centuries, Congress had enacted, and presidents had tolerated, many incursions on "executive Power," at least as conceived in this sweeping definition, and the Supreme Court had upheld several of them. Indeed, as a practical matter presidents had little real control over criminal prosecutions until the creation of the Department of Justice in 1875. Most participants in the debate agreed that, while it was not necessarily binding, the gloss of longstanding practice was strong evidence of the meaning of the Constitution.

The other two lines of constitutional attack on the Ethics in Government Act focused on the role of the special court created by the statute.

Article II, section 2 empowers the president to appoint principal government officers "with the Advice and Consent of the Senate." It goes on to provide that "the Congress may by law vest the Appointment of such inferior Officers, as they think proper, in the President alone, in the Courts of Law, or in the Heads of Departments." The Appointments Clause argument had two parts. First, an officer with the authority to investigate and prosecute the very highest officials in the government was not an "inferior Officer" whose appointment could be vested by Congress in anyone other than the president. And in any event, the power to appoint an officer wielding what everyone agreed was "executive Power" could not be vested in a court of law. By implication, it was asserted, the appointing power of the courts should be limited to officials, such as court clerks and marshals, whose duties involved direct service to the Judicial Branch.

The third line of attack on the statute rested on Article III of the Constitution, which creates the federal courts and defines their powers. Section 2 of the Article contains a definition of "judicial Power" that is limited to deciding "cases" and "controversies" brought before the courts for adjudication, and there was considerable Supreme Court precedent to the effect that Congress could not give federal judges duties that were not "judicial" in nature. Opponents of the statute argued that it went far beyond empowering the special court to appoint an independent counsel; it gave the court considerable supervisory authority over the activities of its appointees, thus entangling the judiciary improperly in the investigative and prosecutorial processes.

Our responses to these arguments were, we thought, powerful. The independent counsel was inherently an "inferior Officer." She had no general governmental authority—she had no department or agency under her command—but was limited to a narrow slice of investigative and prosecutorial power that history showed could not, as a matter of ethics or practical politics, be lodged in an appointee of the president. The Constitution should not be read rigidly to prevent the creation of a mechanism to investigate alleged wrongdoing in the Executive Branch. By the same token, the power to appoint a prosecutor was not something alien to the duties of courts. They had sometimes been empowered to fill prosecutorial vacancies, and by virtue of their control over grand juries and over the conduct of prosecutors who practiced before them, they were familiar with, and well suited to police, the ethical duties of prosecutors. Finally, we argued, a proper reading of the statute gave the special court no real supervisory authority over the actions of an independent counsel beyond the traditional power of a court to ensure the accountability and ethical behavior of prosecutors.

Initial argument of the constitutional issues was before the chief judge of the federal district court in Washington, Aubrey Robinson, a tough, no-nonsense former prosecutor. He made short work of the respondents' attack on the statute, ordered them to comply with the subpoenas, and held them in contempt of court when they refused to do so.[9] He stayed the effect of his contempt order pending an expedited appeal.

In the D.C. Circuit Court of Appeals, we drew a three-judge panel that did not bode well for us. The presiding judge was Ruth Bader Ginsburg, a Democratic appointee to the bench who had not always been as liberal in her decisions as her background in practice suggested she might. She had been a powerful advocate of women's rights as a lawyer, blazing many new trails, but sometimes seemed a bit plodding and literal on the bench. Of course, she was later elevated to the Supreme Court by President Clinton. The second member of the panel was Laurence Silberman, a very intelligent but staunchly conservative judge with extensive Executive Branch experience. Indeed, I had first met Judge Silberman when he was deputy attorney general in the Ford administration and I was general counsel to the House

Judiciary Committee. The third judge was Stephen Williams, a relatively new Reagan appointee from the West with a background in administrative law and a reputation as ideologically very conservative.

We briefed and argued the appeal on an expedited basis, and the argument took place almost to the day on the 200th anniversary of the report of the Constitutional Convention of 1787. The courtroom was packed, and the atmosphere was very tense. The argument was supposed to take an hour, but the judges had different ideas. I had barely opened my mouth before Judge Silberman began peppering me with questions. My allotted half-hour stretched to an hour and twenty minutes, most of it taken up with dialogue between Silberman and me. Early on he posed a tricky hypothetical question designed to get me to admit an important premise of the opposing argument. I saw where he was going and refused to bite, much to his evident annoyance. A few minutes later he came at the same issue from a slightly different angle. I said, "Judge Silberman, a few minutes ago I think you were unhappy with my refusal to grant the premise of a hypothetical that you posed. It was because I knew this was where you were headed that I refused to do so." The whole courtroom laughed, Judge Silberman included, and after that the tone of the argument was more serious and searching, and less adversarial. At another point, he said, "I realize I have monopolized your time and not given you a chance to make your argument as you would like. Why don't you do that now?" I started to, but thirty seconds later he could not restrain himself and began firing questions again. It was the most enjoyable oral argument I ever made.

In January 1988, the court of appeals issued a lengthy opinion by Judge Silberman holding that the Ethics in Government Act was unconstitutional.[10] Judge Ginsburg wrote a much shorter, but in our view, of course, more persuasive, dissent.[11] Interestingly, Judge Silberman shied away from the Vesting Clause argument, focusing instead on the Appointments Clause and on the supposed supervisory authority of the special court.

We filed an expedited petition for review in the Supreme Court, which was granted in time to squeeze our case into the Court's last argument session in April before its traditional summer recess. We had an interesting time trying to figure out what to call the case, which had up to that point been styled simply *In re Sealed Case* because it involved proceedings before a federal grand jury, which were by law secret. By now, of course, the cat was out of the bag, and Supreme Court rules require that cases have named parties. There was some sentiment for styling it *United States v. Olson, et al.*, since if we brought a prosecution against Olson, we would do so in the name of the United States. On the other hand, we knew that the Justice Department, which always styled itself "the United States," was on the other side, and we were aware of how angry representatives on both sides of the aisle had been when the department sued the House of Representatives over the contempt-of-Congress citations in the name of "the United States." Ultimately we agreed that we would call the case *Morrison v. Olson, et al.*

I proceeded to begin drafting our brief in the Supreme Court, but Lex and I agreed that we needed all the help we could get. She decided to seek the assistance of Louis Claiborne, who had served on two separate occasions as the chief deputy in the Office of the Solicitor General, who is charged with representing the government's interests in the Supreme Court. He had a wealth of experience in major cases and in Supreme Court practice generally that would be invaluable. Louis was from an old and well-to-do New Orleans family (his sister was Liz Claiborne of designer clothes fame). He was retired and living mostly in London; Lex literally tracked him down on a beach in Spain. He agreed to come back to the States and help out as a consultant. I finished the first draft of the brief about the same time that Louis arrived in Washington. He read over the draft and made many suggestions that improved it greatly. Getting to work with him was one of the real pleasures of my career.

The next question was who would do the argument in the Supreme Court. I had argued the case before Judge Robinson and the court of appeals, and Lex and the others were happy with my performances. But we decided that, since the attack on the statute attempted to depict the very idea of an independent counsel as part of a runaway, out-of-control machine, Lex herself was in some ways the main exhibit in our case. It would help our case a great deal from a psychological perspective if she could demonstrate that she was a superb lawyer and a person of great judgment and caution. Since she was all of those things, we were confident that she could pull it off. As the date of the argument in the Supreme Court approached, we did several "moots" in which Lex was questioned in detail by lawyers, including Louis and me, who were familiar with the issues in the case.

Lex's argument in the Supreme Court was as good as it gets. It was one of those rare occasions when not a single unanticipated question was asked by the Court and every answer given was the best we had. The only hostile questioning came from Justice Antonin Scalia. We were not surprised. We figured that his rigid conservatism would lead him to oppose our position.

One feature of the argument was curious and striking. The Justice Department took the extraordinary step of opposing the constitutionality of the statute, and the solicitor general had asked for oral argument time as *amicus curiae*. This term means "friend of the court," and individuals and organizations who are not formal parties to a case often file "*amicus* briefs" arguing their point of view. It is rare for an *amicus* to be granted oral argument time, but the Supreme Court is often interested in the expressed views of the Department of Justice, so the Solicitor General's Office is sometimes allowed to appear and argue orally in cases where the government is not actually a party. Since the dispute in the case was between Lex as independent counsel and the subpoena respondents as private individuals, the department was not directly involved. But it definitely wanted to be heard, having now mobilized behind the conservative position. The Court granted the solicitor general fifteen minutes of argument time, and to be balanced, agreed to allow the counsel to the Senate fifteen minutes as *amicus* in support of our position.

Until the solicitor general rose near the end of the hour-and-a-half argument session, the Court had shown a lively interest in the case and asked many questions of all counsel. The solicitor general, a former Harvard Law School professor named Charles Fried, had decided to make the oral argument himself. It was well known in Supreme Court circles that the justices were not happy with Fried, who had brought a sharp ideological approach to the office that many considered inconsistent with its traditions. The federal government has far, far more cases before the Supreme Court than any other entity, and the justices are dependent upon the solicitor general, not only for sound advocacy of the government's position, but for advice about which cases to take and how various positions on issues may serve the long-range institutional issues of the government in general and the Court in particular. The SG is sometimes referred to as "the tenth justice." Fried was perceived, rightly or wrongly, as an unrelenting advocate, not for the long-range interests of the Court or the Executive Branch, but for the conservative political agenda, and he was thought not to be careful with truth or precedent.[12] When he stood up to speak, the justices engaged in a display that took my breath away. Several of them turned their chairs away from him. None of them looked at him. And not one of them asked him a question through his entire fifteen minutes.

As Lex, Louis, and I left the courtroom, Louis and I gave each other a look of immense satisfaction with her performance. One of us—I no longer recall which—said, "Seven to one, Rehnquist writing," meaning that we would lose only Justice Scalia (Justice Anthony Kennedy had recused himself), and that Chief Justice William Rehnquist would reserve the opinion to himself in a case of this magnitude. Our prediction was spot-on.

The Court's opinion in *Morrison v. Olson*[13] was all that we could have hoped for. Chief Justice Rehnquist marshaled a coalition of all the Court's liberals and all but one of its conservatives behind a very workmanlike opinion that tried very hard to establish little or no new constitutional law. It focused on the Appointments Clause and Article III issues, agreeing with us that under a proper reading of the statute, the special court had no real supervisory authority over an independent counsel (relying here on the refusal of the special court to expand Lex's jurisdiction when the attorney general refused to do so). It also agreed that solid precedent supported our reading of the Appointments Clause. Remarkably, the chief justice did not even bother to engage Justice Scalia's fiery dissent, which was based on the notion that only the president could exercise a power that was "executive" in nature.[14]

Once Lex's authority to proceed was established, we returned to the business of conducting a criminal investigation. In some ways, the investigation itself was an anticlimax. The constitutional issue, in everyone's view, overshadowed the much less significant question whether Ted Olson had diddled the Judiciary Committee. This was especially the case since our ultimate conclusion was that, while Olson had been less than candid and had indeed sought to mislead the committee about the events surrounding Burford's invocation of executive privilege, he had not actually lied within the meaning of the perjury statute or criminally obstructed a congressional investigation. Thus Lex never sought an indictment of Olson, and he was considered "clean" enough to serve as solicitor general later in the administration of President George W. Bush.

Out of this experience I garnered many benefits, first among them a lifelong friendship with Lex Morrison, with whom I have spent a lot of time teaching advocacy and other matters to students at the University of Virginia School of Law. Another was a series of very interesting and pleasant exchanges with Judge Silberman, of all people. The day after we filed our brief in the Supreme Court, he called me on the phone. He had sent his law clerk to the Court to obtain a copy of the brief, and he had read it carefully. He began by saying that, since the case was out of his court, he thought there was no reason we could not discuss it. He complimented my performance in the oral argument and said that our brief in the Supreme Court was a first-rate piece of advocacy, though of course he disagreed with it. We talked for probably half an hour, debating the issues in a friendly way. After the decision in the Supreme Court, I was asked to write a piece on the case as an introduction to a symposium on its significance in the *American University Law Review*[15], and I sent Judge Silberman a copy of the article. This provoked further friendly exchanges with the judge. I admired his ability and willingness to engage this way with someone on the other side of an issue about which we both felt strongly.

❖ ❖ ❖

Interestingly, despite our solidarity on the constitutional issue, Lex and I later came to disagree on the continuing value of the independent counsel statute. We both still believed that some mechanism to permit independent investigation and prosecution of Executive Branch misconduct is necessary. But I came to feel that the statute itself had become over time a pawn in a political game that served mainly to keep partisan tensions at a boil. Whichever party was in power, its opponents in Congress would, at the faintest hint of allegations of misconduct in the administration, begin calling for the appointment of an independent counsel. If the attorney general, after reviewing the evidence, declined to seek an appointment, it would be said that the decision was part of a coverup. If an independent counsel was appointed, congressional opponents of the administration would trumpet it as confirmation that misconduct had occurred. What both Lex and I agreed was the grave abuse of the office of independent counsel by Kenneth Starr in the investigation of President William Clinton led me to conclude that Congress was correct to let the statute lapse. The press's vigilance and the nature of the partisan process, together with the history of Executive Branch scandals, will, I think, effectively force future presidents and attorneys general to appoint truly independent investigators in matters of real serious concern.

❖ ❖ ❖

Another result of the Olson investigation for me was a significant boost in what was already a growing interest in a major career change. Teaching at the university level had always appealed to me. After all, I had begun my post-college career in academic graduate school. During my third year in law school, I was approached by the academic associate dean, who asked if I might have any interest in teaching there. I said that I might some day, but that I really wanted to give law practice a try first. For the next decade or so I would receive periodic feelers from the dean's office about my interest in teaching, but I was always having too much fun practicing law. Eventually the approaches ceased.

A number of factors made 1988 a propitious time for me to think about moving to academia. First, I was not really having as much fun practicing law any more. While I still enjoyed my colleagues at Nussbaum, Owen & Webster a great deal, the firm's practice was increasingly grounded in commercial litigation. I did a lot of work for Lloyd's of London. Lloyd's is a fascinating institution, and I found some of the work challenging intellectually. But money has never interested me a great deal, and there were in the late 1980s an increasing number of days when I found it hard to care about which large economic entity got the huge dollop of cash that was at stake in whatever case I was working on at the moment. Everyone has ho-hum days in his or her career, but as an advocate I felt I could not afford many of them, or my clients would not receive the quality of representation they were entitled to. The Olson case reminded me of the things that really moved me in the world of the law.

In addition, like many others in the profession, I was saddened and turned off by what I saw as a progressive diminution in standards of civility, cooperation, and candor among many lawyers, for whom winning and making money seemed to be their only lodestars.

At the same time, life in the law firm was deteriorating in ways that had little to do with me. I still got along well with everyone, but there were increasing tensions between David and Michael, and Marguerite was ground down trying to mediate between them. Indeed, within six months of my departure in the summer of 1989, though certainly not because of it, the firm broke up. David, Sally, and a couple of the younger lawyers joined the firm of Caplin & Drysdale, while Michael and most of the others continued in the old suite of offices. Marguerite left private law practice entirely. Moreover, I was actually engaged in a good deal of teaching, and I found that it was the part of my job I was coming to enjoy the most. In the early 1970s I had taught Federal Courts for three years as an adjunct member of the faculty at Georgetown University Law Center. Throughout the late 1970s and 1980s I spent several days a year—sometimes more—teaching in programs run by the National Institute for Trial Advocacy in Washington and other places. Beginning in 1982 I taught a seminar in Trial Advocacy at the University of Virginia Law School, commuting down to Charlottesville on alternate weekends one semester a year. Within the firm itself I was increasingly involved in teaching and mentoring the young lawyers, and I thoroughly enjoyed this process and the young people I was working with.

My experience in the Olson investigation reminded me of another important thing. I really did enjoy legal research and writing. During my early years in practice I spent a lot of time in the library, and I wrote many briefs. I enjoyed the process of crafting legal arguments and building detailed support for them through intensive research. But in the kind of practice that I did throughout my career—moderately complex cases that, if and when they went to trial, usually took somewhere between a week and a month to try—one is inevitably priced out of the library as time goes by. As one's experience increases and one's billing rate goes up, one is paid for strategy, judgment, and forensic skill in the trial or appellate courtroom. The time-intensive initial research and writing are left to the younger lawyers with lower billing rates. In the decade or so before the Olson investigation I had rarely drafted a brief myself. I would read, critique, and edit the work of the younger lawyers. There was no body of younger lawyers on Lex Morrison's staff. I was the most experienced constitutional lawyer in the group, and it fell to me to do the research and draft the briefs on one of the burning and interesting constitutional issues of the day. I remembered how much fun it was to spend time in the library and at the typewriter. I felt I was now ready to enjoy the scholarly side of legal academia.

It was also from an economic standpoint a good moment in my life to contemplate a change. Will would graduate from Williams College in 1989, and Susan was two years behind him, studying at Duke University. Thus we would soon be finished paying big tuition bills, and we could stare at a reduced income with some equanimity.

Louise and I talked over my interest in a change at great length. As always, she was entirely supportive. She said that if my professional happiness was at issue, we could make anything work economically. She was also enthusiastic about the prospect of a return to Charlottesville—my strong first preference was to teach at Virginia—where we had enjoyed our three years during law school immensely. She liked living in Arlington, as did I, and she had a three-quarter-time job as the editorial director of Heldref Publications, a non-profit organization that published some forty-five scholarly journals. While she enjoyed the job for the most part, there were enough aggravations that she would not be broken up about leaving it. And since the children were almost completely out of the nest, we would not be disturbing their personal and family lives greatly by moving.

Finally, I had a last opportunity to test the degree to which my psyche was invested in advocating in a courtroom. In the fall of 1988 I defended a client on a criminal contempt charge in the Southern District of New York.

Actually, the very setting of the date of the trial brought into stark relief one of my discontents with litigation. Will was a senior at Williams, and he was both the captain of the water polo team and a member of the All-East team in that sport. For more than a year Louise and I had been planning to attend the eastern regional water polo tournament at Williams, on which occasion the school was going to inaugurate its new natatorium. When we discussed scheduling the trial with the judge, I mentioned these plans and asked him to try to avoid conflicting with them. Nonetheless, the court set the trial to begin the Monday morning after that weekend. There was no way I could attend the tournament and prepare properly for the trial, so I missed out on an important family event. This had happened too often. I was tired of judges and opposing counsel running my schedule.

The trial lasted for a week, and I was consciously endeavoring the entire time to look over my shoulder to determine whether this kind of advocacy was so deeply in my blood that I would miss it too much if I made the change I was contemplating. Though I think I did a good job in the trial, my conclusion was that I was indeed ready to move on to something else.

Thus during one of my teaching weekends in Charlottesville in the fall of 1988, I stayed over to play golf and have dinner with my old teacher and friend Peter Low and his wife Carol. I told Peter of my growing interest in becoming a full-time teacher, gave him a copy of my resume, and discussed the prospects for possibly joining the faculty at Virginia. Peter seemed enthusiastic and said he thought my chances of getting a job offer were fairly strong. The law school had a new dean, Tom Jackson, whom I had met once at a fund-raising dinner. Tom was the first dean for some time who had come from outside the Virginia faculty, and Peter said that the first step was to get to know Tom and explore the issue with him. Peter ran interference for me with the new dean, and shortly thereafter Tom Jackson had business in Washington, and Louise and I invited him to our house for dinner. We hit it off very well, and Tom was of immense help in presenting my case to the faculty. I also enlisted the help of Walter Wadlington, my old friend who had chosen my law school class as acting dean of admissions, and of John Jeffries, later dean himself, who was then a younger member of the faculty whom I had recruited for Williams & Connolly when he graduated from the law school. With the backing of these folks, I was invited by the Appointments Committee to Charlottesville for a day of interviewing. In the spring of 1989 Tom Jackson called and offered me a job. I took about a nanosecond to accept.

Notes

1 19 Howell's State Trials 1029 (1762).
2 See Boyd v. United States, 116 U.S. 616, 624-30 (1886).
3 *Quoted in Boyd*, 116 U.S. at 625.
4 United States v. Heldt, 215 U.S. App. D.C. 608, 668 F.2d 1238, 1253-69 (1981).
5 *Id*. at 1269-74.
6 In re Olson, 260 U.S. App. D.C. 168, 818 F.2d 34 (1987)
7 Lex and I both had prominent clients in the Iran-Contra affair, though they were both in the private sector and not government officials. Because it was possible that we might find ourselves defending the constitutionality of the Ethics in Government Act in the Olson investigation, while our clients in Iran-Contra might deem it in their interest to attack the law, we told the latter up front that we could not make that argument for them, but that we would refer them to other lawyers for advice on that subject. Our clients accepted this limitation, and we arranged separately for them to consult other experienced constitutional lawyers on the constitutionality of the statute.
8 In re Sealed Case, 264 U.S. App. D.C. 265, 829 F.2d 50 (1987).
9 In re Sealed Case, 665 F. Supp. 56 (D.D.C. 1987).
10 In re Sealed Case, 267 U.S. App. D.C. 178, 838 F.2d 476 (1988).
11 *Id*. at 238, 838 F.2d, at 536.
12 For a description of the solicitor general's dual responsibilities to the Supreme Court and the Executive Branch and the office's traditional special relationship to the Court, see Lincoln Caplan, *The Tenth Justice: The Solicitor General and the Rule of Law* 1-50 (1987). For an account of the breakdown of this relationship and the erosion of the Court's trust in the office under Fried, see *id*. at 235-67.
13 487 U.S. 654 (1988).
14 See *id*. at 697 (Scalia, J., dissenting).
15 Earl C. Dudley, Jr., *Morrison v. Olson: A Modest Assessment*, 38 Am. U.L. Rev. 255 (1989).

CHAPTER THIRTEEN

Academia
1989–2008

I resigned from Nussbaum, Owen & Webster at the end of May 1989 and spent the summer preparing to teach Civil Procedure to first-year law students and helping to organize the move to Charlottesville.

From the very beginning Louise and I both loved our new life in Charlottesville. Teaching was everything I had hoped it would be. I was pleased and honored to join a number of my own teachers who were still on the faculty in 1989. The students were bright, engaged, eager, and fun to be with. The classroom, as I often said, was a lot like the courtroom, except that there was no opposing counsel to object to what you said and no judge to tell you that you were wrong. On the way to my first class in Civil Procedure, I stopped off at the office of my own Civil Procedure teacher and good friend, John McCoid. I said, "John, I feel like a Christian being thrown to the lions." John looked at me quizzically and replied, "You've got it all wrong. *They* are the Christians."

I taught a wide variety of courses over the years, most of them related in some way to litigation. My first year I taught Civil Procedure, Evidence, and Constitutional Law. In later years I also taught Criminal Investigation, Trial Advocacy, Professional Responsibility, the American Jury System (to undergraduates), and a course called the Prosecution Function, which I co-taught with Lex Morrison. For the last ten years or so, I have taught a series of seminars in Ethical Values with my close friend on the faculty, George Rutherglen. (I am still teaching one this year to keep my hand in.) These seminars were essentially glorified book groups, and George and I covered a variety of themes, including biographies of great lawyers, the history of the civil rights movement, great trials through the centuries, detective novels, religion and morality, and the lawyer in fiction. I also enjoyed writing a number of law review articles, several in collaboration with George,[1] and played a lot of catch-up in the reading department.

Louise soon found an exciting new job as well. When I was in law school she had worked for the University News Office. For her last year in that office, the director was a young former reporter for the *Richmond*

Times-Dispatch named Bill Fishback, with whom Louise had worked very well. In 1989 Bill was still there and was still the principal spokesperson for the university, though the scope of his operation had expanded dramatically and he had moved several rungs up the bureaucratic ladder. Louise called Bill when we moved to Charlottesville, and they met for lunch. His position in the university, Louise thought, would permit him to watch for job openings that might be suitable for her. It wasn't long before the man who held the title of news

Louise and I in about 2001.

director, essentially Bill's job in the 1960s, left to take a position in the president's office. Bill invited Louise to apply for the job, and she was hired.

Within a year or two of our arrival, Bill Fishback moved to a different position in the president's office, and Louise replaced him as director of university relations. Unhappily, the university, which was dealing with major state budget cuts, did not hire a replacement for her old position for three years, so she was doing two demanding jobs at once. Her position gave her a unique window into what was going on all over the university. As the principal spokesperson for the entire institution, she had to be informed on all crises and controversies, and her boss, Leonard Sandridge, the university's chief financial and operating officer, trusted her and brought her into the strategic planning operations as well. She was quoted in the newspapers and appeared on radio and television with some frequency, so she became something of a minor celebrity in town. She presided over crises ranging from the seizure of three fraternity houses in a drug raid by the federal government, to the collapse of a portion of one of Thomas Jefferson's pavilions on The Lawn during graduation in which one person was killed and a number injured, to the treatment of nationally famous actor Christopher Reeve at the university's medical center after his neck was broken in a horseback accident. She did a difficult job with aplomb and integrity, and she was respected by all within the university and the journalistic community.

Before long I found myself also engaged in university administration. It all began in 1991, when the athletics director, Jim Copeland, learned that the university's sports booster organization, known then as the Virginia

Student Aid Foundation, had for years been making small loans to student athletes, almost certainly a violation of the rules of the National Collegiate Athletics Association, the governing body of collegiate sports. Jim immediately reported what he had learned to the president of the university, John Casteen, and they self-reported the matter to the NCAA. Casteen appointed a committee of three to make a full investigation of the situation. The chair of the committee was Peter Low, and Peter asked me to work on the matter with him and in particular to help him with the interrogation of the many witnesses the committee would interview. We conducted an extensive investigation, in which we interviewed well over 100 witnesses, more than 50 of them on the record with a court reporter making a transcript. We also gathered and analyzed records from the Student Aid Foundation and the Athletics Department.

The good news was that the loans were small and generally designed to cover immediate personal needs—eyeglasses, for example. There was no spreading around of cash designed to let the star players live well. The bad news was that the loans were made only to student-athletes; thus they plainly constituted an extra benefit for those athletes above and beyond their athletic scholarships, and hence a violation of NCAA rules. Worse, the fact that no one appeared to have recognized that the loans were a problem exposed a major failure in the university's education of its boosters and its oversight of what they were doing.

There was even worse news, of different kinds. First, the University of Virginia had adopted something of a holier-than-thou posture within the NCAA. Our faculty representative was on the NCAA Infractions Committee and apparently was quite fond of saying, "Well, at Virginia, we …" when scolding errant schools. Thus not many tears were shed by NCAA staffers when Virginia took its lumps. Second, the loans—and hence the lack of any serious oversight—went back to the athletics directorship of Dick Schultz at Virginia, who had gone on to become executive director of the NCAA. We interviewed Schultz on the record, and he made seriously inconsistent statements about his role in the process and wound up being fired by the NCAA, after a separate investigation, for his lack of candor with our investigation. But worst of all was a terrible rift in the Virginia athletics community. Despite Virginia's rather ostentatious pride in its honor system, some boosters, including members of the university's Board of Visitors, never forgave Jim Copeland, an entirely honorable man and an alumnus of the university, for reporting the violations in the first place. They argued that he should have swept the situation under the rug and simply told the

VSAF to stop making the loans. After a year or two, these people essentially succeeded in running Jim Copeland out of town. He left to become athletics director at Southern Methodist University in Texas.

My role in the NCAA loans investigation led to a long-term working relationship with the Athletics Department. Whenever there was a potential NCAA issue of any seriousness (the NCAA rule book is large, complicated, and often unintuitive in its prescriptions, and schools routinely self-report minor infractions with no real consequences), the department would ask me, often in combination with others, to conduct an investigation. I also served on two search committees to recommend new athletics directors. I chaired the second such committee, which, I am delighted to say, recommended that the university hire the first African-American athletics director in Atlantic Coast Conference history, Craig Littlepage, who has done an outstanding job.

I served in other administrative capacities in the university over the years. For six years I was a part-time associate general counsel to the university, in which capacity I defended several lawsuits brought against the university and helped advise the president and the Board of Visitors on a wide range of topics. As part of that assignment I served for almost the entire time as the legal advisor to the university's Honor Committee, which administers the entirely student-run honor code. Partly because the only sanction for a violation of the honor code is permanent expulsion from the school, the Honor Committee found itself embroiled in numerous internal disputes and became a target for lawsuits brought by students who had been expelled. I also conducted some internal investigations of alleged misconduct unrelated to the Athletics Department and served on several university-wide committees. In 2006 I chaired the committee that conducted half of the university's decennial reaccreditation process with the Southern Association of Colleges and Schools. Within the law school, I served for eighteen years as a member of the Admissions Committee, an assignment that I truly enjoyed. During my last several years on the faculty, I chaired the university's Judicial Review Board, which hears appeals in all student disciplinary matters not involving the honor code.

All of this administrative activity, especially taken in combination with living with the university's public relations manager, taught me a great deal about how a major university is run and brought me into close contact with many of the very talented and dedicated members of the administration and of faculties outside the law school. I very much enjoyed the entire process.

❖ ❖ ❖

While Louise enjoyed her job, she decided to retire in December 2002. In large part this was because she felt increasingly torn between the demands of a sometimes all-consuming job and her desire to do other things, including spending more time with our grandchildren and taking on volunteer activities in Charlottesville. The time also seemed right because the university was beginning to gear up for a new capital campaign, and it would be better to have a new public relations leader in place from the beginning.

I followed Louise into retirement in May 2008, after more than five years of envying her new freedom. I still loved my job, but I decided that there were so many other things I wanted to do before I died, that I needed to get going.

Note
[1] The following is a list of my law journal articles since I joined the faculty in 1989: Earl C. Dudley, Jr., *Discovery Abuse Revisited: Some Specific Proposals to Amend the Federal Rules of Civil Procedure*, 26 U.S.F.L. Rev. 189 (1992); Earl C. Dudley, Jr., *Getting Beyond the Civil/Criminal Distinction: A New Approach to the Regulation of Indirect Contempts*, 79 Va. L. Rev. 1025 (1993); Earl C. Dudley, Jr., *Federalism and Federal Rule of Evidence 501: Privilege and Vertical Choice of Law*, 82 Geo. L.J. 1781 (1994); Earl C. Dudley, Jr., *Terry v. Ohio, the Warren Court, and the Fourth Amendment: A Law Clerk's Perspective*, 72 St. John's L. Rev. 891 (1998); Earl C. Dudley, Jr. & George Rutherglen, *Ironies, Inconsistencies, and Intercollegiate Athletics: Title IX, Title VII, and Statistical Evidence of Discrimination*, 1 Va. J. Sports & Law 178 (1999); Earl C. Dudley, Jr., & George Rutherglen, *A Comment on the Report of the Commission to Review Title IX Enforcement in Athletics*, in Rita J. Simon ed., Sporting Equality: Title IX Thirty Years Later 103 (2005); Earl C. Dudley, Jr. & George Rutherglen, *Deforming the Federal Rules: An Essay on What's Wrong with the Recent Erie Decisions*, 92 Va. L. Rev. 707 (2006).

CHAPTER FOURTEEN

Personal Life

1977–2008

As I have already said, my reconciliation with Louise in the summer of 1977 marked the beginning of a new and very happy phase of my personal life. In the last thirty years we have had our disagreements, as all married people do, but there has been an underlying love and stability that has never wavered. I am blessed to be married to someone whom I love and who is also the finest human being I have ever known.

The years from 1977 to 1989 were exciting times in our family. Will and Susan were growing up, and life with them was never dull. They were both excellent students and good young citizens. Much of their time outside of school was devoted to sports, principally soccer and swimming. Louise and I spent a great deal of enjoyable time at soccer games and swimming meets, she always involved in providing organizational support and snacks, and I taking pictures of the action with my camera. As they got older, both Will and Susan dedicated themselves more intensely to swimming. Susan had a spectacular sophomore year in high school,

Susan, 13, wearing one of her many All-star medals.

in which she was named a high-school All-American and her times came within a couple of hundredths of a second of qualifying her for the national meet in the breaststroke. When she was unable to duplicate those times the following year, she made a difficult but sober-sided decision to lower her level of commitment to the sport. She still swam on our summer-pool team and for her high-school team, but she cut back on her year-round practice. This did not end her involvement with swimming, however; she coached in the Northern Virginia Swim League for several summers after graduating from high school. Will continued beyond high school and competed on the swim team for two years at Williams College, but then turned his attention to water polo, at which he excelled.

❖ ❖ ❖

Our close friendship with Rick and Gail Lowery continued and blossomed throughout the 1970s and 1980s. Rick and I rode to and from work together virtually every day for twenty-two years. In the early 70s we began the tradition of vacationing together, mostly at the little town of Long Beach (later renamed Oak Island), North Carolina. In the early years we would get a medium-sized house and put the children on one side and the adults on the other. These early cottages lacked such amenities as air conditioning, phones, and television sets. Rick and I would often repair for hours at a time to outdoor phone booths in the steamy August weather to edit legal documents and confer with our law-firm colleagues.

As an outgrowth of our close friendship with Rick and Gail, their children and ours grew up doing virtually everything together. They became like brothers and sisters, and those relationships have continued over the years. Susan still complains of the time she visited Clay for a party at his fraternity at the University of Virginia. Clay was so protective of her, just as a big brother would have been, that none of his friends dared come near her.

One of the saddest days of my life was my birthday in 1989, January 8. We were planning to spend the day taking Susan and her roommate back to college for the spring semester of her sophomore year. While we were getting dressed in the morning, Rick called to say that Gail had died during the night. She had been having some difficulties with menopause, and Rick and the two of us had urged her strongly to see a doctor. However, none of us thought her condition was life-threatening. The doctor said that her electrolytes had become imbalanced, which triggered heart stoppage. We both miss her to this day.

Gail's death preceded our move to Charlottesville by only a few months, but despite the greater distance between us, Rick has remained essentially a part of our extended family. He and Clay, and for a while Rick's mother, have shared Thanksgiving dinner with us virtually every year since we moved to Charlottesville. We always get together over the Christmas holidays. We still go to Oak Island together every year. And Rick has been like a second father to Will and Susan, taking them in whenever they have needed a place to stay and helping them in a wide variety of ways. Will's son Cole observed a few years ago, "Mr. Lowery is like having an extra grandpa."

❖ ❖ ❖

I have mentioned that I played golf as a teenager and until after my clerkship. I gave up the game, however, when the children were small. Between parenthood and law practice, there simply wasn't time to spend several hours on a weekend wandering the course. When Will was about ten or eleven, he came to me one day and said that he would like to learn to play the game and asked if I would take it up again, pointing out that it was something we could do together. I couldn't refuse this wonderful invitation, so I dusted off my old clubs and became a hacker again. I had never taken any golf lessons, and I was pretty horrendous. I determined that Will should learn the right way, so I got him lessons with a local pro. Within a couple of years he was beating me like a drum. So in self-defense I took some lessons myself and became a real nut about the game. At one point, I had my handicap down to a 10, but that lasted only a brief time. The game has given me enormous pleasure, much happy time with Will, and many friendships over a long period of time.

For a number of years, I would play golf almost every day of our beach vacation with Will and Kirk and Clay Lowery. That is still my favorite

My favorite foursome—Kirk and Clay Lowery, Will and I—at the Old Course, 2001.

foursome. When I turned 60, at Kirk's urging, I organized a group of eight fellows—four old guys and four "flat-bellies," as we called them—to play golf for a week in Scotland. The younger group was composed of Will, Kirk, and Clay and one of my former students at the law school, John Herrmann. The old guys were my Criminal Law teacher Peter Low, my Amherst friend Marty Lowy, and David Wilson, the husband of Louise's cousin Judy. It was the trip of a lifetime, and I made sure that I played the Old Course at St. Andrew's with Will, Kirk, and Clay.

Will and Clay have gone on to become very impressive golfers, both with single-digit handicaps and occasional scores in the low 70s.

I can't resist a small tad of bragging (what else is golf about?). In August 1986, playing with Will and Kirk in North Carolina, I had the first of my (to date) four holes-in-one. Louise says it is a sure sign that I have played too much golf.

Golf continues to be very important to me, and Louise has taken it up in her retirement years, but since early 2006 my back has limited my play very severely. I hope that physical therapy and exercise will permit me to play at least a fraction of the golf I have always intended to play in my retirement.

❖   ❖   ❖

Another source of family pleasure over the years has been our collective devotion to the Washington Redskins. Baseball was my first love, but when the major leagues took the Washington Senators away the second time in 1971 (the old Senators moved to Minnesota in 1961, where they became the Twins, while the new expansion team went on to be the Texas Rangers), I pretty much swore off of the game. At this time I was a junior lawyer at Williams & Connolly. I have mentioned that Ed Williams was then president of the Redskins and that he gave out tickets to the lawyers in the firm for most home games. As the Redskins became a better team in the early 1970s, the demands on Williams's tickets increased. So he let each lawyer in the firm buy two season tickets, jumping a very long queue of waiting applicants. Of course I bought the tickets, overcoming my not very heavy guilt about queue-jumping.

The dividing-up of the tickets among the family became an annual ritual of great delight. Susan always wanted to go to the New York Giants' game because Steve Umin, one of my close friends in the firm and a great admirer of hers, sat directly in front of us and rooted for the Giants. She love to rub his balding head when the 'Skins were winning.

The Redskins game was a fixture of Sunday afternoon in the fall for many years. The time between 1971 and 1992 were glory years for the franchise, and we soaked them up with great joy. Gail Lowery was an even bigger Redskins' fan than we were, if possible, and she would ride with us to the home games every Sunday and buy a ticket from one of the scalpers outside the stadium.

Between 1982 and 1991 the Redskins under head coach Joe Gibbs played in the Super Bowl four times. The first time, in January 1983, I put my name in the lottery of season-ticket holders for two Super Bowl tickets. I won and gave one of the tickets to Gail. At the last minute, the Thursday before the game, I was dragged (no one believes it, but it was true) to Los Angeles, the site of the game, to cover a deposition on Friday in a case I was doing. So Gail and I went to the game together and rooted the Redskins to a great victory over the Miami Dolphins.

❖ ❖ ❖

In the 1970s and 1980, Louise and I took three vacation trips to the British Isles, where I indulged my longstanding interest in British history and my relatively newfound passion for photography.

In 1974 we went to England with Rick and Gail. Rick was stuck part of the time in Washington working on a case, so Louise, Gail, and I spent the first week in London, and then met Rick out in the countryside.

I shall never forget my first experience driving on the left side of the road. We rented a car, which was delivered to our hotel in the heart of London the day we left the city. I was terrified and had a difficult time locating where the left front tire (tyre?) was, but with gritted teeth I somehow managed to get us out of the city without calamity. Once in the country, things were more relaxed. We made quite a circuit, going from Canterbury to Brighton to Exeter, on to Cornwall, and then up to York. It was a splendid trip, full of castles and cathedrals, and I made a point to visit as many places associated with Richard III as possible. I have always believed that he was a good king who was grievously slandered by the Tudor propagandists, principally Thomas More and William Shakespeare.

Louise, who has always been able to eat considerable quantities of food, including desserts, without gaining weight, earned a nickname on the trip. At most of the restaurants the waiters would bring dessert around on a little cart they called the "sweet trolley." Louise took such delight in making her selections that we started calling her "Sweet Trolley Lou." Rick even made a miniature sweet trolley that Christmas and gave it to Louise.

In 1979 Louise and I spent seventeen days in Scotland, where we sampled a different single-malt whisky each night. After four nights in Edinburgh, we moved to a small hotel in the south-central Highlands, near the village of Kinloch Rannoch. The hotel was owned and run by a retired British army officer and his wife. It had been built as a hunting lodge for the Duke of Atholl, and it was located directly on Loch Tummel, a beautiful lake. The view from the bar was spectacular. The first night we were there we noticed an older couple, in their late seventies, who were being made much of by the owner and others in the bar. As he took our order, the owner asked me, "Do you know who that is?" I said no, and he told me it was Sir Gerald Templar. I said that wasn't much help, so he went on to say that Sir Gerald had finished World War II as the second-in-command to General Eisenhower at Supreme Allied Headquarters in Europe and had later run the only successful campaign against a communist insurgency in the 1950s in Malaya. He was, the owner said, in Scotland to "take the salute" at the Military Tattoo at Edinburgh Castle, and he and his wife were staying at the hotel because the owner had been in Sir Gerald's regiment during the war. The hotel had assigned tables, and by chance our table was next to that of Sir Gerald and his wife. We struck up a conversation the first evening, and that night and the next three we joined them for post-dinner coffee in the hotel's sitting room. Both of us recall those evenings quite fondly. We listened to Sir Gerald's stories of the war, and we talked about American politics. ("It's all been downhill for you Yanks since Ike and Harry, hasn't it?") His wife, who was a beautiful woman even at her age, told us about her privileged childhood in Edwardian England. Sir Gerald pretended to believe that I must be a senator.

We later moved on to Culloden Moor for another four nights and to the Isle of Skye for two. It was a fabulous trip. One memorable moment occurred on the day we drove around Loch Ness, without, I should report, spying Nessie. We had had a very substantial breakfast at our hotel, and we ate a large and delicious lunch in the middle of the day. That evening we went to a beautiful restaurant out in the countryside, where we put down another large and tasty meal. When time for dessert came, Louise's eyes literally bulged out and glazed over. For the first and only time since I have known her, Sweet Trolley Lou had OD'd on food!

In 1980 we took Will and Susan to England. They were thirteen and eleven respectively. We found as many things that would interest them as we could, but I think they were less than happy with my penchant for touring historical sites. As the four of us drove into the quaint little seaside town of Mousehole (pronounced Mouzel) in Cornwall and reached our hotel atop a cliff overlooking the harbor, we could see quite a bit of activity below. The proprietor explained that it was Mousehole Harbor Sports Day, and that there were all sorts of contests going on—sailing and swimming and the like. We asked on a lark if entry was open. He said it was. So we headed for the harbor with Will having put his swimsuit on under his clothes. We got there in time for the boys' under-fourteen 100-yard breaststroke race. The breaststroke being Will's best event, he decided to enter. What he hadn't thought about was that there was no swimming pool: the race took place in what was essentially a small harbor directly off the English Channel. Even though it was the middle of August, I believe the water temperature was around 60 degrees. Will later said that diving in was such a shock to his system that it gave him an instant headache. The only thing he could think of to do was to swim as fast as possible so as to end his torture. The boys raced out to a log fifty yards from the start, turned around, and came back. We were standing by chance near a group of local swimming mothers. As Will, shivering all the way, was lengthening his lead on the second leg, they were all clucking and asking, "Do you know that lad?" He won easily. There was a fairly sizable trophy, and ordinarily the winner's name was engraved on it and he got to keep it for a year, until the next Harbor Sports Day. Will had to be content with the engraving, as they weren't willing to entrust the trophy to a Yank kid. But it was great fun.

❖   ❖   ❖

In 1984 there occurred an event that saddened our whole family greatly. My dear friend and law school classmate Lee Davis, who had introduced me to his father-in-law, Army Boothe, committed suicide. We had stayed in close touch with Lee and his wife Misty, who lived in Richmond. Roughly once a year we would get our families together, often with mutual friends. Their children and ours got along extremely well, especially Will and their son Evan, who was three weeks younger than Will. Whenever the two boys saw each other, it seemed that they were engaged in the same things. They were both swimmers, and both excelled in the breaststroke; they were both outstanding students; they read and liked the same books; and they played and enjoyed the same games. Whenever we saw the Davises, Lee seemed to be a proud and happy husband and father and a capable and prosperous lawyer who enjoyed his practice. His suicide came as a bolt from the blue. To this day I have no idea what drove Lee to kill himself, though we did learn that he had been treated for depression. I recall feeling both sad and angry, angry that Lee had killed my dear friend.

At Lee's funeral Misty told me that Evan, who was then a junior in high school, was very interested in small New England liberal arts schools. So were Will and Clay Lowery. I told Misty that I was planning to take Will and Clay on a New England college tour and that I would be happy to have Evan join us. So at the appointed time, Misty drove Evan up to Arlington, and we set off on a jaunt that took us to Wesleyan, Trinity, Amherst, and Williams. Will and Evan both fell in love with Williams, and they both eventually went there. In college their friendship blossomed. They swam together, they roomed together one year, they bicycled across Europe for nine weeks together one summer, and for a time they even became passionately interested in the same girl. She preferred Evan, but Will and Evan remained friends, and Evan's relationship with the young lady did not last very long. Evan and Will continue to enjoy a close friendship to this day.

❖ ❖ ❖

Before entering college Will had shown considerable aptitude in math, and he charted a course initially to major in the subject. But he took some philosophy courses along the way and became seriously interested in 18th- and 19th-century German philosophers. So he did a double major in math and philosophy. He graduated near the top of his class at Williams and won a two-year fellowship to Emmanuel College, Cambridge. He enjoyed his first year there and became one of the stars of the Cambridge water polo team, which crushed Oxford in their 100th anniversary match, with Will scoring three goals and making a splash on British national television. He was somewhat frustrated academically, however, as he was unable to get into a graduate program in philosophy and wound up doing fairly uninteresting undergraduate tutorials. He came home to work for the summer at a company called Applied Energy Services (AES), which designed, built, bought, rehabbed, and ran coal- burning power plants with advanced scrubber technology around the world. One of the principals in the firm was a swim-team and golfing friend, Roger Naill, who became a mentor to Will. When AES during the course of the summer offered Will a permanent job, he decided to forego the second year of his Cambridge fellowship. It was a decision that turned out to have important consequences.

After a year or so at AES, Will was shipped off on short notice to London to help in the acquisition of four power plants in Northern Ireland, which was privatizing its electric utility system. The firm had been the low bidder on the project, but that only began a year or so of negotiations with the government of Northern Ireland, the relevant labor unions, and the banks that provided the $400 million in financing for the purchase. His immediate boss on the project was a young woman with an MBA degree from Wharton named Janette Kessler. By the time the project was over, Will and Janette had become a serious item. After he entered graduate school in philosophy at Northwestern University in 1992, Janette moved to Evanston and opened the Chicago office of AES, a very flexible company that valued her services a great deal.

In 1994, Will and Janette were married near Los Angeles, where she had grown up. In 1998 he accepted a one-semester appointment to teach philosophy at Williams. After two more single-year contracts, Will was given a tenure-track position at the college, where he has been teaching ever since.

On September 23, 1998, Janette gave birth to our first grandchild, Nicholas Kessler ("Cole") Dudley. I was teaching a class in Trial Advocacy when the news arrived, and my secretary burst into the classroom with an enormous grin on her face and handed me a note announcing Cole's arrival.

A little more than two years later, on November 6, 2000, Cole was joined by his sister, Elizabeth Kessler ("Ella") Dudley.

Seeing as much of Cole and Ella as possible and watching them grow (they are ten and eight, respectively, as I write this) has been one of the great pleasures of recent years for Louise and me.

Cole and Louise at the beach in Rhode Island, 2008.

Ella and J.J. at the beach in Rhode Island, 2008.

❖ ❖ ❖

Susan, who has never liked cold weather, decided to reject the family propaganda favoring New England liberal arts colleges. She chose Duke University, where she did very well, majoring in history and obtaining a teaching certificate along the way. She began her career as a fourth-grade teacher in the Arlington County, Virginia, schools. She left after a couple of years and spent the next several working in marketing, mostly for private companies that provided educational services at the elementary and high-school levels.

In 2000 Susan expressed, to our complete surprise, an interest in attending law school. She entered Georgetown University Law Center in the fall of 2001 and finished first in her class in the spring of 2004. She clerked for a year for Judge Leonie Brinkema of the United States District Court for the Eastern District of Virginia in Alexandria. She and Judge Brinkema formed a close personal relationship that continues to this day.

After her clerkship, Susan entered law practice in Washington with the firm of Zuckerman Spaeder, founded by my old friend Roger Zuckerman from the Scientology case. It is an excellent firm that does mostly litigation, and Susan is very much enjoying her experience there.

In October 2005 Susan married Tom Klaff, whom she met through mutual friends, with Judge Brinkema performing the ceremony. They decided to adopt a child, and on August 14, 2007, Justin Joseph ("J.J.") Klaff was born in Gulfport, Mississippi. They brought him from the hospital to their hotel when he was three days old. Though, sadly, Susan and Tom have come to a parting of the ways, J.J. has been and continues to be a source of great joy to all of us.

❖   ❖   ❖

I thought it would be worthwhile to spend some time discussing the economic aspects of our move from Arlington to Charlottesville and our changes of careers in 1989. It offers some insight into changing values of money over time. We had purchased our house in Arlington—a nice but modest three-bedroom house in a pleasant but not really upscale neighborhood—in 1970 for what seemed then like the enormous sum of $47,000. (My parents had built a larger house in Fairfax County in the mid-1950s for only $18,000.) We had put a small addition on the house in 1981, which essentially enlarged the master bedroom and bath by a few feet and added a small room on the ground floor in back to support the larger bedroom. The addition cost considerably more than the house had only eleven years earlier—$81,000. When we sold it eight years later, the house fetched $400,000. With what seemed like a lot of money in our jeans, we purchased a larger new house on one of the most desirable streets in downtown Charlottesville for $300,000, and finished the basement for another $45,000. As I write this in the fall of 2008, our house and lot are assessed for tax purposes at a startling one million dollars.

We took less of a hit in income by moving to academia than I had feared we might. Salaries for lawyers in complex big-city practices had skyrocketed in the little more than twenty years I spent in practice. During my first year at Wilmer, Cutler & Pickering, 1968-69, I had been paid at an annual rate of $14,500—and this after the legal world had been shocked in 1968 by the New York firms' unheard-of increase from less than $10,000 to $15,000 in entry-level lawyers' salaries. Though Nussbaum, Owen & Webster's income had fluctuated with the vicissitudes of business and though smaller firms definitely made less per lawyer than big ones, I had been averaging somewhere around $150,000 annually there in the 1980s. Big-city firms, especially those in New York, continually found it difficult to attract top law-school graduates without paying them quite handsomely. The steady increases in entry-level firm salaries had in turn put pressure on salaries in all corners of the legal profession, including the law schools. Top law-school graduates who were interested in teaching were willing to take significantly less money in return for the prestige and the more stimulating and less demanding lifestyle in academia, but there was a limit to the differential in salary that would allow the law schools to continue to compete for the best and brightest. The law schools' effort to keep entry-level law firm salaries within shouting distance benefitted more senior faculty members as well. I remember being pleasantly surprised when Tom Jackson offered me a salary of $80,000 in the spring of 1989. With smaller mortgage payments and what we thought would be a less expensive lifestyle in Charlottesville, and with tuition bills about to come to an end, Louise and I were confident we could make it on this amount of money. Of course, the law firms' upward pressure on legal academic salaries did not stop in 1989, and my salary considerably more than doubled in my nineteen years on the faculty.

Louise was soon adding more to the family pot than she had in Arlington. From the beginning hers was a very responsible full-time job, and it paid much better than Heldref Publications had.

❖ ❖ ❖

In recent years, after a significant hiatus, Louise and I have resumed traveling abroad. I mentioned earlier my golfing trip to Scotland in 2001, to celebrate my 60th birthday.

In 2003 Louise and I spent three weeks or so in Germany, France, Belgium, and the Netherlands. The impetus for the trip was to visit Will, Janette, and the children while Will was on sabbatical at the University of Muenster in Germany. Because the Virginia Law School has an exchange relationship with the law school at Muenster, I paid for part of the trip by teaching all of American Constitutional Law to forty German law students in five three-hour sessions!

In 2005, as I mentioned earlier, we visited the Philippine Islands to celebrate the 60th anniversary of the liberation of the Islands near the end of World War II. In 2006 we spent a week each in Rome and Paris, visiting many beautiful and significant historic sites. In 2007 we went to China for a little over three weeks with a small group of Amherst friends. The tour was planned and led by the cousin of one of our friends, who teaches Chinese history in Sweden and who has led many tours of China. In 2008, we visited

Ireland for the first time and were struck by the wild beauty of the country and the warmth of the people. The economy and our health permitting, we hope to continue our wandering ways.

I am finishing this in the fall of 2008, only a few months after retiring from the law school faculty. My life up to now has been exciting and interesting. If I perceive a major flaw in my account of that life, it is that I have given too little attention to the things that have, at the end of the day, given me the greatest pleasure—my family, my many friends, and my non-professional interests that have helped to sustain me over the years, including photography, travel, British history, and sports. In less than three years, Louise and I will celebrate our 50th wedding anniversary. Will and Susan, and now their growing families, have been a constant source of pride and joy. There is no pleasure in life that matches playing with grandchildren and watching them grow.

Then there are the happy rituals of existence that have so enriched my appreciation of both family and friends. Every year since our marriage, with one hurricane-caused exception, we have gathered for Labor Day weekend in Avalon, New Jersey, with a varying group of family and friends, first at the house owned by Louise's Aunt Louise and Uncle George, but since their deaths in various rented cottages.

Since about 1970 Louise and I have celebrated Thanksgiving annually with my sister Liz, her husband Fred Wilbur and their family, which has, like our own, grown over the years to include children, their spouses, and grandchildren, and our traditional gathering has come to include numerous others near and dear to us.

The Christmas holidays have always been a source of great joy, ever since the sad little gathering in our apartment the day we buried my mother. We have celebrated Christmas almost every year with Louise's brother Jim, his wife Jan, and their children David and Lisa, and most years we have been joined by Louise's youngest sister Liz, known to our children as "tiny Aunt Liz" to distinguish her from my own sister of the same name, who is both older and taller.

For almost forty years, we have celebrated New Year's Eve quietly with a black-tie potluck gourmet dinner with a group of friends that has varied little over that time and that has included Rick and Gail Lowery and Bill and Kathe McDaniels from my days at Williams & Connolly.

For almost the same length of time we have vacationed annually at Oak Island, North Carolina, with Rick and his family.

We have remained in close touch with a number of our college friends, and especially with a small group of Amherst friends and their wives whom we see from time to time and in various places and groupings.

Amid all this, I feel surrounded by a great deal of love and joy. My life has not only held my interest but it has been very blessed.

❖ ❖ ❖

I recall realizing with a jolt at my Aunt Rosamae's funeral in 1999 that I was now the oldest member of my family. How did that ever happen? I didn't feel old, and I still don't, though my body certainly creaks a lot more than it used to. But I look at retirement from my profession as a new beginning, and I have plans to do many things. This book was first on my list, and I plan now to turn my attention to genealogy, with a view to writing at least one book about family history. Seeing more of my children and grandchildren, seeing more of my country and the rest of the world, becoming a better photographer, playing better golf, and reading some of the many books I have foregone over the years because of the demands of the law are all priorities. I look forward greatly to what my old friend and former physician, Tom Connally, calls the "third third" of my life.